Tastes of the Pyrenees, Classic and Modern

The **HIPPOCRENE COOKBOOK** library

AFRICA AND OCEANIA
The Best of Regional African Cooking
Good Food from Australia
Taste of Eritrea
Traditional South African Cookery

ASIA AND MIDDLE EAST
Afghan Food and Cookery
The Art of Persian Cooking
The Art of Turkish Cooking
The Art of Uzbek Cooking
The Best of Korean Cuisine
The Best of Regional Thai Cuisine
The Best of Taiwanese Cuisine
The Cuisine of the Caucasus Mountains
Egyptian Cooking
Flavors of Burma
Healthy South Indian Cooking
Imperial Mongolian Cooking
The Indian Spice Kitchen
Japanese Home Cooking
Sephardic Israeli Cuisine
A Taste of Syria
A Taste of Turkish Cuisine

MEDITERRANEAN
The Best of Greek Cuisine, Expanded
    Edition
A Spanish Family Cookbook
Taste of Malta
Tastes of North Africa
Tastes of the Pyrenees, Classic and
    Modern

WESTERN EUROPE
The Art of Dutch Cooking, Expanded
    Edition
The Art of Irish Cooking
A Belgian Cookbook
Cooking in the French Fashion (bilingual)
Cuisines of Portuguese Encounters
Feasting Galore Irish-Style
The Scottish-Irish Pub and Hearth
    Cookbook
The Swiss Cookbook
Traditional Food from Scotland
Traditional Food from Wales
A Treasury of Italian Cuisine (bilingual)

SCANDINAVIA
The Best of Scandinavian Cooking
The Best of Finnish Cooking
The Best of Smorgasbord Cooking
Icelandic Food & Cookery
Tastes & Tales of Norway

CENTRAL EUROPE
All Along the Rhine
All Along the Danube
The Art of Hungarian Cooking
Bavarian Cooking
The Best of Austrian Cuisine
The Best of Czech Cooking
The Best of Polish Cooking
The Best of Slovak Cooking
Hungarian Cookbook
Old Warsaw Cookbook
Old Polish Traditions
Poland's Gourmet Cuisine
The Polish Country Kitchen Cookbook
Polish Heritage Cookery
Treasury of Polish Cuisine (bilingual)

EASTERN EUROPE
The Art of Lithuanian Cooking
The Best of Albanian Cooking
The Best of Croatian Cooking
The Best of Russian Cooking
The Best of Ukrainian Cuisine
Taste of Romania
Taste of Latvia
Traditional Bulgarian Cooking

AMERICAS
Argentina Cooks!
The Art of Brazilian Cookery
The Art of South American Cookery
Cooking With Cajun Women
Cooking the Caribbean Way
French Caribbean Cuisine
Mayan Cooking
Old Havana Cookbook (bilingual)
A Taste of Haiti
A Taste of Quebec

REFERENCE
International Dictionary of Gastronomy

Tastes of the Pyrenees, Classic and Modern

Marina Chang

HIPPOCRENE BOOKS, INC.

NEW YORK

Grateful acknowledgment is made to Alfred A Knopf Inc. for permission to reprint from *Delicioso! The Regional Cooking of Spain* by Penelope Casas, copyright © 1996 Penelope Casas; and to *Wine Spectator* for permission to reprint from *Culinary Summit* by Thomas Matthews, an article published in the May 15, 1995 issue of the magazine, copyright © 1995 M. Shanken Communications Inc.

Interior art by A. Robida and Marina Chang

Book and jacket design by Acme Klong Design, Inc.

For more information, address:
HIPPOCRENE BOOKS, INC.
171 Madison Avenue
New York, NY 10016

ISBN 0-7818-0949-5
Cataloging-in-Publication Data available from the Library of Congress.
Printed in the United States of America.

*This book is dedicated
to the memory of my mother,
who had a great appreciation for good food.*

Table of Contents

Map of the Pyrenees Region

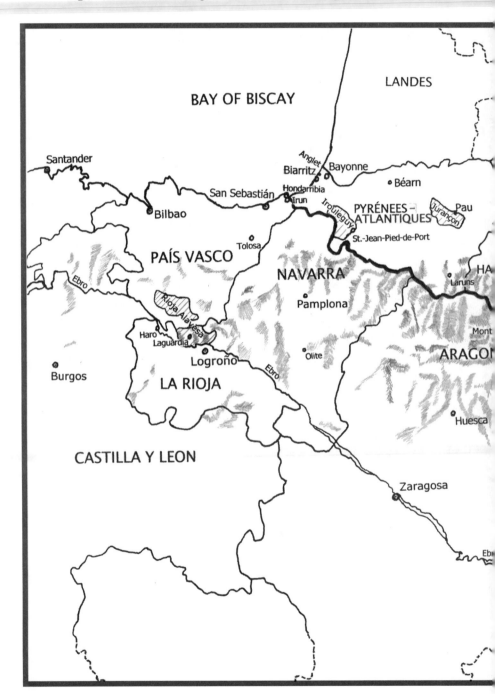

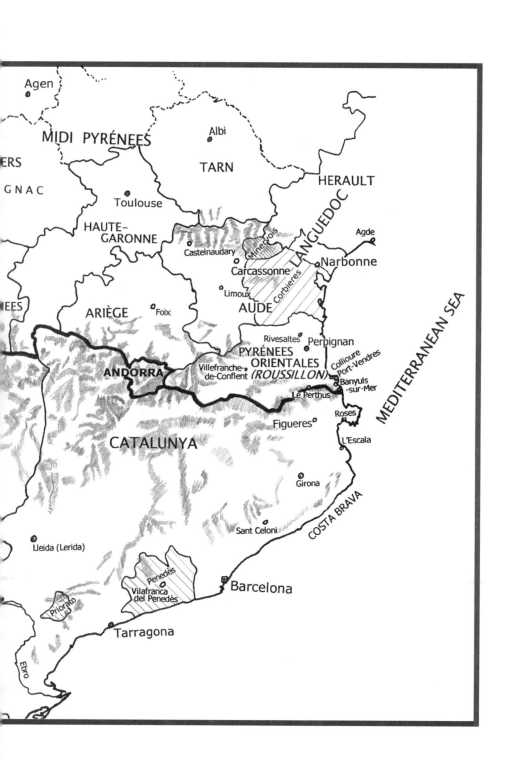

Acknowledgements

ALTHOUGH I AM FASCINATED by the complex history and cuisines of the regions bordering the Pyrenees mountain range, I am by no means an expert on this area. I wish to thank a number of people who have helped me through the research, cooking and writing of this book. First, I want to thank George and Ludmilla Blagowidow, whose enthusiasm for my cooking and faith in my ability to write a cookbook started me on this path. They opened my eyes to several wines from southwestern France and we enjoyed many a happy hour sharing new wine discoveries from regions surrounding the Pyrenees.

I am extremely grateful to the chefs, restaurateurs, and innkeepers who very graciously welcomed me into their kitchens and took the time to share recipes and cooking tips with me. Special thanks to: in Spain, Ferran Adrià of the cutting edge *El Bulli*, located in Roses, and Martin Berasategui of the Basque restaurant bearing his name in Lasarte-Oria; in France, Madame Nicole Galinier and her daughter Delphine of the inn, *La Maison sur la Colline*, located in Carcassonne; and in the United States, Oumar Sy and Frederic and Cecile Darricarrere, owners of *Petits Plats* of Washington, D.C., Daniel Olivella, chef and owner of *B44* in San Francisco, and Corey Basso, chef and owner of *Le Bistro* in Petaluma.

This book would never have been written without my friend Natalie Blagowidow, who, along with her husband Jim Murray, have always welcomed me as a part of their family, and who provided level headed, balanced advice in moments of panic and hair-pulling.

I also wish to express deep thanks to my editor, Anne McBride, who was unflappably patient and an extremely supportive coach. She translated old French passages for me and resolved publishing issues that were above and beyond the call of her editorial duties.

Closer to home, I wish to thank my father, William Y. Chang, for his unflagging support of my efforts to write this book, for his thoughtful editorial and journalistic contributions, and for his love of the written word. One hopes that a small bit of the bombardment on the finer points of writing, word usage, and spelling that we received as children, during mealtime, has stuck with me.

The ever wise, understanding, and happy soul who is my husband, Craig, receives my most heartfelt love and appreciation for all the support he provided me on so many fronts during the formulation and completion of this book. Thanks also to many of his co-workers at the Washington, D.C., office of Hunton & Williams for their taste-testing assistance.

M.C.

Arlington, Virginia
Santa Rosa, California

INTRODUCTION

WITH RELIEF, WE SPOTTED THE RESTAURANT El Bulli on a parched coastal bluff a few miles outside of the Costa Brava town of Rosas. We would not be late for our early afternoon repast. My husband and I had arrived in Barcelona airport—fortunately on time—a few hours after a flight over the Atlantic and a change of plane in Madrid. We sped up the motorway north toward the French border, with barely a thought to the area's history—the early Greek traders who settled nearby at Empúries and Hannibal, who, with his elephants traversed one of the nearby low passes of the Pyrenees in the third century B.C. before making camp in what is today Elne in Roussillon. We had scheduled our trip to ensure that we could enjoy El Bulli before it closed for the season at the end of September. When we were informed that reservations were impossible for any of the three days we were in the vicinity, Craig essentially begged by e-mail in Spanish for a reservation, explaining that this restaurant was an essential experience for my book on Pyrenean cuisine. Luis Garcia, who has assisted in the management of El Bulli for 10 years, greeted us like old friends. He explained that they had prepared a "special tasting menu" for us, but first ushered us into the kitchen where a swarm of white-coated cooks prepared a myriad of dishes. I immediately recognized a slight but distinguished man: Ferran Adrià, a gifted magician of a chef and the inspiration behind the wondrously unique cuisine of El Bulli. After a few words of greeting, we took our seats on a tree-shaded terrace overlooking the azure bay. Immediately gin fizzes appeared, concocted so that the top layer of lime foam was steaming hot and the refreshing liquid below was icy cold. This was the beginning of an unforgettable experience that lasted well over four hours.

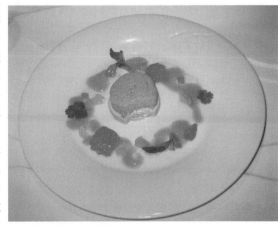

MONK FISH *FOIE GRAS*

For about an hour we tasted a series of 10 small appetizers on the terrace, including lacy sheets of caramel seaweed brittle; long sticks of crisp baked cheese dusted with tomato powder; savory

Parmesan "ice cream" sandwiches; fresh strawberries encased in Campari gelatin; and a shot glass of pea and mint soup that was hot on top and cold at the bottom. We then took our seats inside the main dining room of a centuries-old farm house, where we were served 13 small entrees. We sipped a fine cava or sparkling wine by Rovellats in Catalonia between courses. The dishes included a monk fish *foie gras* with tomato seeds; cuttlefish "raviolis" with coconut milk filling; tagliatelli noodles, cut from jellied consommé, in carbonara and truffle oil sauce; marinated fried sardines with herbs; black "rice" made with bean sprouts and squid ink; and rabbit with creamy *foie* sauce and cubes of jellied apple. Desserts began to arrive at the three-hour mark. We were served four in the main room, including raspberries with yogurt chips, accompanied by black beer ice cream; and a frozen chocolate powder that tasted like ice cream, served with jelly cubes of fresh lime and wasabi. We returned to the terrace, the sun significantly lower in the sky, for coffee. Eight additional sweet and savory tastes paraded by while

we enjoyed our coffee, including a raspberry ice-cream cone with candied ginger; mango marshmallows; discs of white chocolate with truffle oil; pineapple with mint and ginger foam; and saffron-orange jelly cubes. Afterwards, Mr. Adrià explained that he was already beginning to experiment for the next season, and that although El Bulli would be closed for six months he would be as busy as if it were open. Satisfied, but curi-

MARINATED FRIED SARDINES WITH HERBS

ously not stuffed, we departed knowing that this cutting edge restaurant, with a few new additions, creatively used the same ingredients that had been available in Catalonia for centuries if not millennia, was a fitting beginning to our culinary exploration of this region.

This book focuses on the polyglot of cuisines of the Pyrenees region, whose mountains stretch almost 300 miles from the balmy beaches of the Mediterranean to the turbulent Atlantic coast. For my purposes, this region includes the lowlands drained by the range, the dense forests and valleys of the foothills, and the wild, rugged peaks clad in ice. A few recipes are from Cantábria, reflecting the suggestion of the French geographer Élysée Reclus that the Cordillera Cantábrica (including the Picos de

Europa) should be considered the westernmost portion of the Pyrenees.

Today's border between Spain and France was mostly established by the Treaty of the Pyrenees in 1659, which ended centuries of conflict, although Andorra was created in 1278 as a "suzerainty" between the bishops of Foix (France) and Seo de Urgell (Spain). These political borders divided the Catalan and Basque peoples, but could not change the fact that the foods and culinary traditions of this region acknowledge no such boundaries and are derived from a cross-fertilization of many cultures whose men and women crisscrossed the region over dozens of centuries. The recipes in this book include ones from what today

SIGN IN VILLEFRANCHE-DE-CONFLENT

is Catalonia in both Spain and France (Roussillon), Languedoc, Andorra, the Midi Pyrenees, Aquitaine, the Basque country (*Euskal Herria*) in both France and Spain, Asturias, Navarra, and Aragón.

The Pyrenees is an exciting culinary region in part because it has been buffeted by the influences of so many cultures. The proud traditions of a Basque chef in his *txokos* or gastronomic society in San Sebastian (Donostia), a grandmother in her rural *masía* in the Catalonian foothills, or a chef in a Béarnais café in Pau each hearken back centuries if not millennia. Their dishes ultimately are a product of the natural foods that can be grown, gathered, or hunted in their immediate environs, and the experience and wisdom of their ancestors as to how to prepare these products. In addition, there has been an explosion of creativity in the kitchens of this region in recent years, which makes an exciting culinary journey for the traveler to this area. Chefs such as Ferran Adrià and Santi Santamaria in Catalonia, Juan Mari Arzak, Martin Berasategui, Pedro Subijana, and Hilario Arbelaitz in the Basque country are among the most creative and wonderful chefs in the world today. What follows is a brief summary of the natural and human history that provides a background for today's cuisines of the Pyrenees.

DEFINING THE PYRENEES:

Factors that shaped the region, its peoples and its food

The Formation of the Pyrenees
and Early Humans

SEVERAL EUROPEAN MOUNTAIN RANGES, including the Pyrenees, were formed by continental collisions during the Paleozoic. About 50 million years ago, the African continental plate approached the European plate, and thick sediments of limestone that had been accumulating for tens of millions of years were compressed into long belts of mountain ranges on both land masses. For almost 25 million years, the crusts of each plate buckled and tilted upward to form the central portion of the Pyrenees range. These plate tectonic movements simultaneously raised the Atlas Mountains of northwest Africa and the Carpathian Mountains in east-central Europe.

The Pyrenees, whose average altitude exceeds the Alps, are a great mass of limestone with a complex internal structure resulting from their formation by the folding and faulting of rock layers. Monte Perdido at the center of the Parque National de Ordesa y Monte Perdido is the highest limestone peak in Europe. The range has two axes, one running inland from each coast. They fail to meet in the central Pyrenees, which is one reason that the border between Spain and France takes an unexpected north-south turn just west of the Vall d'Aran. There has been a longstanding misconception that the Pyrenees consist of two separate mountain ranges that overlap for about 45 miles there. The French petroleum company Elf-Aquitaine concluded a definitive geo-morphological map of the Pyrenees in 1973 and debunked this view. On the northern side there are deep indentations caused by torrential rivers that rose in the watershed and cut chasms in the rock while rushing down to the plains of France to empty in the Atlantic or Mediterranean. From France the Pyrenees appear to be sharply serrated with a breath-taking majesty. South of the watershed there is a welter of minor ranges that generally run parallel to the axis so that the rivers often must run east or west for some time before draining into the great plain of the Ebro River en route to the Mediterranean. Thus the mountains descend more gradually and do not afford a view of the Pyrenees as dramatic as what can be seen most anywhere on the French side. Throughout the region, underground rivers have riddled the limestone mountains with caves.

Twenty thousand years ago, towards the end of the most recent ice age, the polar ice cap was spread like a mantle over northern Europe. When it began to retreat, it left many *cirques* in the Pyrenees—such as the *Cirque de Gavane*—which are essentially dead ends to major valleys that resemble huge rock amphitheaters. A few glaciers remain today, a testament to the last ice age and a reminder that the glaciers sculpted the mountains, leaving a backdrop of peaks, cliffs, and gorges.

The conditions of the last glaciation began to ameliorate around 18,000 years ago. At that time, there were no hardwood forests north of the Pyrenees—it was primarily wooded tundra—and the deciduous forest was restricted to a narrow coastal strip along the Mediterranean. As the Northern Hemisphere warmed, woodland vegetation gradually extended north to displace the tundra. Eleven thousand years ago, much of Spain's central plane became thick oak forests, and southwestern France grew forests of beech, oak, chestnut, yew, ash, and maples. Fir and black pine grew higher in the mountains, with moors above the tree line.

Humans have lived in the vicinity of the Pyrenees for a very long time. A cave at *Caune de l'Arago* in Roussillon near the Corbières Hills contains evidence of human habitation 700,000 years ago. The remains of "Tautavell Man" here represent one of the earliest settlements in Europe. Some 200,000 years ago an ancient race of people called Neanderthals (*Homo sapiens neanderthalensis*) inhabited Europe, roaming over the plains, forests, and mountains of northern and western Eurasia. Then during the middle of the last Ice Age, from roughly 40,000 to 30,000 years ago, a new type of human began to proliferate. Called "early modern humans" or Cro-Magnons because their skeletons were generally less robust than those of the Neanderthals and other early humans, their bodies were still more primitive than those of present-day humans (*Homo sapiens sapiens*).

Cro-Magnons and Neanderthals coexisted in Eurasia for several thousand years, and many scientists now believe that the early modern Eurasians were a new type of human that migrated into the realm of the Neanderthals and ultimately replaced them. Some believe that in certain regions, Neanderthals evolved into modern humans on their own, while elsewhere early modern Eurasians replaced them. Many anthropologists and writers including Mark Kurlansky in *The Basque History of the World* believe that the Basque people—whose agglutinating language is unrelated to any Indo-European language and whose blood has certain peculiarities—might be a remnant population of Cro-Magnons. The orphan Basque language *Euskara* seems to have its roots in the Stone Age, and has been spoken since about 6,000 B.C. For example, the Basque words for knife and ax, both include the root word for stone: *aitz*. Basque geographical names can be found far from what historically we consider their territory. For example, *Aran* in Vall d'Aran (northwest Catalonia) is Basque for "valley," and the town of Elne near the Mediterranean in Roussillon was once called Illiberis, a Basque name.

The earliest humans were hunters and gatherers, living in nomadic or semi-nomadic communities. They were successful predators of wild animals for meat—from hares, boars, partridges, waterfowl, and other small game to massive creatures such as bison or mammoths, brought down through cooperative hunting. Near oceans, lakes, or streams they fished with spears and primitive nets or gathered other aquatic creatures such as clams. They gathered various seeds, nuts, berries, tubers, and roots, which probably required humans to migrate during many seasons. Indeed, Spanish field naturalist and founder of *Transhumancia y Naturraleza* Jesus Garzón believes that the ancient *cañadas* or cattle passageways first developed millions of years ago when herbivores such as mammoths, bison, horses, and sheep migrated along these routes at the onset of the hot summer towards the mountains in the north and returned before winter to the valleys in the south. These movements generated a huge network of tracks that are really meadows thousands of miles long.

The first Pyreneans spent much of their time huddled by fires near cave entrances, protected from the cold, wild beasts, and other clans. As long ago as 35,000 years ago, they created wonderful paintings of wildlife in limestone caves throughout the region. The best public views of such cave art are to be found in the *Grotte de Niaux* (near Foix), now that the Altamira (Cantábria) and Lascaux (Dordogne) caves have been closed to all but official researchers.

The Neolithic Revolution began 10,000 years ago with the first farming in the Fertile Crescent on the eastern shore of the Mediterranean. The earliest crops were wheat and barley, followed over several thousand years by oats, rye, lentils, peas, apricots, figs, grapes, dates, pomegranates, pistachios, and olives. In addition, humans domesticated sheep, goats, cattle, and pigs and maintained the seasonal movements of herds. By 3,000 B.C. oxen plowed fields.

Gradually the ice retreated north of the Pyrenees as the climate became more temperate and deciduous forests spread north. Fire allowed human life on the fringes of ice. Around 5,000 years ago much of western Europe had been recolonized by forests and humans. Stone structures—dolmens—appeared in the Pyrenees region. Their function has spawned much speculation, ranging from burial chambers to seasonal shelters for shepherds tending their flocks. Moreover, agriculture was discovered in the region. Before the Bronze Age began around 2,000 B.C., Pyrenean people—as elsewhere in Europe—began to live together in fortified villages, prompted in part by changes in agricultural economics. The first settlements tended to spring up near the cattle ways, where markets and fairs were established. The ensuing increases in human population eventually resulted in great disruptions of native vegetation as large areas of native habitat were converted to croplands and pasture. The British ornithologist R.E. Moreau believes that these changes in the natural landscape had a great effect on the populations of woodland migrant birds, which pass over the Pyrenees each spring and fall from and to wintering areas in Iberia or Africa. He has estimated that the retreat of glaciation caused the number of western European migrant birds to increase by a factor of 10, followed by a decline of 75 percent today after millennia of human depredations. The oak forests of central Spain are now essentially gone, and the few remaining trees are mostly scrubby Encima oaks. On a more positive note, much of the avian richness of woodland Europe is a by-product of forest clearance and timber management.

Human Migrations
in the Pyrenees

THREE THOUSAND YEARS AGO the Pyrenees region began to experience a succession of invasions by various peoples that lasted until the thirteenth century A.D. when the Moors were effectively driven from the Iberian Peninsula. Apparently the Basques were already well-entrenched, and the Romans who first encountered the "Vascones" believed that they were an ancient people. Many of the invaders brought new plants or new means of harvesting from the land or sea, shaping the food habits of the entire region. From the North came Celtics and Teutonic peoples, and from the South came the Iberians of Northern Africa. The Celtics tended to settle in Catalonia and Galicia, providing some of the light-skinned and blue/hazel-eyed individuals found there today. These peoples mingled over time to create the Celtiberians, who populated the core of interior Spain with a culture of shepherds, subsisting largely on meat, milk, and cheese and trading wool and crafts. The Basques had already occupied South Aquitaine as far north as Bordeaux and south to the Ebro River basin.

The Iberian littoral off the Mediterranean became a necklace of foreign settlements—more commercial than political. The Phoenicians arrived from the eastern Mediterranean by the twelfth century B.C. In 550 B.C., the Greeks established their first colony (Empúries) in this region near Rosas on the Catalonian coast. By that time the Greeks had begun to export olives and Greece was considered the "Napa Valley" of its time until the great Italian vintages appeared four centuries later. No doubt the Greeks brought these admirable products to their trading post in Catalonia, either for their own use or for barter. A cuisine based largely on wine, olive oil, and seafood developed along the Mediterranean coast.

In the third century B.C. Carthage and Rome had each become powerful Mediterranean states. The Carthaginians arrived in Spain about 300 B.C., and called it Ispania or "spahn" after the innumerable rabbits. After occupying Catalonia, the Carthaginians used it as a base for Hannibal and his 40 elephants to cross the Pyrenees near the Col du Perthus in 214 B.C. en route to Italy. Rome was forced to realize the strategic importance of the Iberian Peninsula, which became a political football until the Romans expelled the Carthaginians after winning the Second Punic War a few years later. Rome then annexed the Pyrenean region, including Iberia to the South and Gaul to the North, as integral parts of its empire. Within a few generations, they brought language, law, public works, and philosophy to the defeated tribes of this area. The indomitable Basques remained largely independent in Vasconia—residing in rural areas outside the towns and trading in new towns such as Pamplona founded by the Romans. During their six centuries of domination over this region, the Romans endowed the Pyrenean foothills with a network of roads, bridges, and settlements. They also began the large-scale cultivation of olives, grapes, and wheat, making Spain the granary province and wealthiest of the empire. The Romans also introduced leavened bread, fava beans, lentils, chickpeas, and quite possibly taught the locals how to cure ham. They founded Narbonne as the capital of Gaul, and established wine making nearby in Minervois and Cahors, as well as Tarragon in Catalonia and Mérida in Extremadura. According to the British historian Edward Gibbon, the Romans greatly improved fishery techniques along the Mediterranean. For example, they developed aquaculture for oysters at Leucate in Roussillon, techniques that were lost after the fall of the Roman Empire. The sea-faring Basques probably needed no such assistance from the Romans and were already exploiting coastal fin fish and shellfish. They may have already begun whaling in the Bay of Biscay, although the first commercial records of the sale of whale meat or oil date from the seventh century. In would be another millennium before the Basques traversed the Atlantic to exploit the rich cod fisheries off Newfoundland to return with their invention of *bacalao*, cod preserved through salting and drying.

Germanic tribes from across the Rhine and Danube overran Rome in the fifth century A.D. Even before the fall, Roman order had declined when the Pyrenean region experienced a series of invasions by people from the north—Franks, Swabians, Alans, and Vandals—who in turn had been pressured by other peoples such as the Huns invading their former territories. The Visigoths, former allies of the Romans, generally took control of the Pyrenean region in the fifth century, although they never subjugated the Basques or the bellicose tribes who inhabited the Cantabrian Mountains. Emperor Constantine adopted Christianity as the Roman religion in 325 A.D., and Christianity took root in the midst of the chaotic Visigoth rule. The Visigoths established capitals in Barcelona and Toulouse, and bishops became the civil administrators in the void left by the loss of Roman bureaucrats. They left their name in Catalonia, which is derived from Gothalunia. While Christian in name, the Visigoths were barbaric in deed. Kings were usually elevated or deposed in blood baths, and the average length of a king's reign was only a few years. The Visigoths encouraged the ancient movements of animal herds whereby flocks of sheep moved from summer to winter pastures. This custom ultimately may have been a primary motivation for the *Reconquista*—a desire to reacquire winter pasturage in the South for northern Spaniards.

Invasions of the Moors
and the Medieval Era

THE MOORS CONQUERED SPAIN IN A VIRTUAL BLITZKRIEG. In 711, Tarik lead a Berber force of 7,000 across the Strait of Hercules (renamed Jebel-al-Tarik, or Gibraltar) and quickly dispatched the squabbling Visigoths. Within a decade the Moors controlled most of Iberia, as far north as the Pyrenean foothills. The Moors continued to press north into France, and controlled for half a century Roussillon and parts of Languedoc. Eventually the king of the Franks Charles Martel, grandfather of Charlemagne, stopped them at the battles of Poitiers and Tours and ensured that Europe did not become Muslim. Martel drove the Mohammedan invaders out of Aquitaine and south of the Pyrenees, expanding his empire to include both the northern and southern slopes of the Pyrenees. Within Spain, tradition says that the Moors were first stopped at Covadonga in Asturias. Thus the direct influence of the Moors in this region was largely eclipsed long before the Moors' fate on the Peninsula was decided against them in the battle of Navas de Tolosa in 1212 by the united armies of León, Castille, Aragón, and Navarra.

For the 800 or so years after Charlemagne, as boundaries waxed and waned over time, the Moors continued to control great parts of central and southern Spain. During the Dark Ages many of the civilized ways of the Romans were lost for a thousand years, including most of their cuisine. While feudalism was deeply rooted in most of Europe including southwest France, it was never widespread in Spain. For hundreds of years, Spaniards were constantly moving south into new areas liberated from the Moors, founding towns and receiving land grants. Individuals who fought bravely could move up, and the class structure was not as rigid as elsewhere.

Not only did the Moors establish a new religion in Iberia, they brought new irrigation techniques such as waterwheels and irrigation ditches. They also left an indelible mark on the cuisine. Among the new foods that the Moors introduced were oranges, lemons, black pepper, almonds, hazelnuts, eggplant, spinach, saffron, rice, sugar, and sweetmeats such as marzipan and nougat. They also established some of the local pastry styles, and left Catalonia with a taste for using honey or sweet fruits in sauces with savory meats or fish. Unfortunately, the Moors also introduced the barberry bush for its use both as a spice for mutton and as a curative potion. This plant is host to a rust that ravaged the wheat crops in Spain, causing massive famines in the early tenth century. According to food historian Reay Tannahill, hungry bands of thugs roved the countryside during this era, literally preying on travelers.

During the Middle Ages the great goal of European pilgrimage was the tomb of the Apostle St. James (Santiago) at Santiago de Compostela. The French Benedictine Order of Cluny provided much of the infrastructure—monasteries, roads, hospitals, even protection from bandits—for the pilgrims whose journeys brought them through France and over the Pyrenees on what was called the *Camino Francés*. The Crusades provided an opportunity for Christian knights to travel afar to the Middle East, although few Spaniards participated because they were busy at home fighting the Moors in the *Reconquista*. The sword and the cross were joined in this effort, and many monks became soldiers. The Crusaders returned home with new spices that greatly affected the cuisine in the Pyrenees—cinnamon, cardamom, cloves, and ginger.

In the twelfth century, mainstream Catholics began the Albegensian Crusade in Languedoc to "cleanse" the countryside of heretics known as Cathars who had practiced a variant form of Christianity for about four hundred years. Today's ruined castles clinging precariously to hilltops exemplify the religious and political strife of that era. The ancient region of *Langue d'Oc* was originally settled by peoples of various races who felt they had little in common with the French people who lived farther north. Their language—Occitan—is similar to Catalan, Gascon, and Provençal. Those activities brought commerce, culture, and new cuisines to the Pyrenees region. Before the Black Death struck the Pyrenees in the fourteenth century, the population in the mountains exceeded that of today as evidenced by the many mountain villages that were abandoned and now stand in ruins. Village life had much less of the rigid class distinctions found in Spanish or French cities, and minor aristocrats, clergy, and ordinary villagers socialized on relatively equal terms. Life was fairly confined, and many people passed their entire lives in their village, punctuated by occasional visits to a local market town.

The thirteenth through fifteenth centuries were an economic and political golden age in Catalonia. In 1324 one of Europe's earliest cooking manuals was written—*Libre de Sent Soví*—which was influential throughout Europe. Virtually nothing is known about its author or even the meaning of the manuscript's title. Some of its recipes were reproduced a century later in the Italian *Libro di Arte Coquinaria*, which described Catalan chefs as the world's best. Another Catalan classic from the late fifteenth century was *Libre del Coch* (Book of the Cook). The first French cook to leave his mark on the history of gastronomy was Taillevent, a man who served five French kings. Two years after the publication of the *Libre de Sent Soví* he compiled *Le Viandier de Taillevent*, which borrowed from two earlier anonymous manuscripts. One, *Petit Traité de 1306*, is the oldest known collection of recipes in the French language. The first cookbook in Spanish appeared in the sixteenth century, and was a translation from Catalan.

Voyages of Discovery and the Modern Era

THE DEFEAT AND EXPULSION OF THE MOORS from the Peninsula in January 1492 sparked the voyages of discovery to the New World later that year, opening new vistas of cuisine for all of Europe. Columbus had been entreating Ferdinand and Isabella for their patronage for years, and the culmination of the *Reconquista* allowed the monarchs to refocus their energies on his proposed explorations. Among the new foods that Columbus and other explorers brought to Europe were maize (corn), potatoes, sweet potatoes, squash, peanuts, tomatoes, capsicum peppers, chocolate, vanilla, green peppers, and turkeys. Potatoes, a staple of the region today, were originally consumed mostly by animals. They were banned at one time in Burgundy because some thought that potatoes caused leprosy, and were not accepted for human consumption in France until the mid-eighteenth century.

Despite the potential availability of so many new food products, most medieval fare tended to consist of the most readily available local foods. In addition, the church calendar determined days of meat eating and fasting (abstaining) from all products of land animals, including eggs and milk. The original stock pot (*pot-au-feu*) provided an ever-changing broth that was enriched daily by whatever vegetables happened to be in season or the luck of the hunt. In Roussillon such dishes were called *ouillade*. Even in the seventeenth and eighteenth centuries, Spanish cuisine had little upper class cooking and Catalonian cuisine had apparently declined with the region's economic and political fortunes. Except for the Spanish court (which ate varied and highly seasoned foods) most everyone was likely to eat a salad and a version of an *olla podrida*—a thick meat stew to which was added garbanzos, cabbage, carrots, or squash and cooked in a three-legged earthen pot. Even today a stew of the omnipresent rabbit is a mainstay in rural areas. On Friday, the main course was lentils; on Saturday boiled bones; and on Sunday pigeons. In coastal areas, seafood was abundant, common fare, and salted cod (*bacalao*) was available far from the coast.

Many believe that the arrival of Italian-born Catherine de Medici in France in 1533 was pivotal to the development of France's culinary arts. De Medici and her cooking staff introduced delicacies previously unknown to the French, as well as strict etiquette policies. French royal cuisine became much more refined in the mid-seventeenth century when it became known as the *grande cuisine*. Changes included vegetables (green peas, asparagus, carrots, artichokes) becoming food in their own right, the use of flour and butter roux as thickening agents, and the growing importance of soups. Indeed, the earliest collections of French recipes (which reflected the diets of aristocrats and nobles) were essentially devoid of vegetables because physicians believed they had little nutritional value. Nevertheless, vegetables in the south of France, including the Pyrenean region, have always had a more important role than they do in northern regions. These refinements were codified by the chef Pierre François de la Varenne in *Le Cuisinier François* (1651), in which he created sauces that later would become the basis of haute cuisine. During the ensuing century, improvements in cooking spread from the nobility to ordinary people. Cookery books such as *La Cuisinière Bourgeoise* by Menon (1746) became popular with housewives. The medieval menu consisting of meat and bread survived in many parts of Europe and North America through much of the eighteenth century. By the beginning of the nineteenth century, cooking in France had been elevated into food for philosophy as well as nutrition for the stomach. Frenchmen in their inimitable manner became convinced that in matters of taste, France was superior to all nations and cultures. Truffles became fashionable in France in the nineteenth century, although the hills and forests of the Pyrenees region have provided a wide variety of fungi that the locals have consumed with alacrity since time immemorial—ceps, yellow chanterelles, saffron milk caps, and morels.

By the early nineteenth century the French meal had evolved into three courses: appetizers and main dishes; "afters" or puddings and savories; and pastry. Marie Antoine Carême set the standards for classic French cooking with a five-volume publication, which was later modernized and perfected by Georges Auguste Escoffier. Catalonia experienced a renaissance, and its cuisine benefited from French and Italian merchants and the immigrant restaurateurs who fed them. The first relatively modern cookbook—the anonymous *La Cuynera Catalana*—appeared in Barcelona in 1835. Basic foods throughout Europe slowly improved with the development of scientific agriculture in the eighteenth century. Successive modernization of transportation has enabled cooks in recent times to employ a wider variety of fresh products that are produced far from her or his home. Developments in preservation technologies such as canning and freezing have improved cuisine, as well as the manufacture of stoves that provide even heat.

Hunting and the Effects of Humans on Wild Game

WILD GAME HAS ALWAYS BEEN AN IMPORTANT COMPONENT of the diet in the Pyrenees and continues today in part because considerable wildlands remain that provide habitat to support game. Wild boar (*javalí* or *sanglier*), venison from roe deer (*corzo* or *chevreuil*), rabbit, hare, red-legged partridge, woodcock, wood pigeon, quail, and pheasant can be locally common fare, often to be found on restaurant menus. Hunting is a favored pastime of rural men in the Pyrenees during autumn and early winter, which takes the form of either stalking individual animals or cooperative methods of driving game. Eating some creatures may seem peculiar to North American tastes or sensibilities. For example, the ortolan bunting, a small seed-eating songbird, is captured in wire traps called *matoles* baited with grain in southwest France. They are fattened in captivity and drowned, ironically, in *eau de vie* or Armagnac. The birds are then roasted and eaten essentially whole, although it is no longer legal to serve this dish commercially. Those consuming ortolans are easily identified, as it is traditional to cover one's head with a napkin large enough to extend tent-like over the plate while dining on these birds. This allows the diner to sequester all the exquisite vapors of the dish, while protecting others from exposure to the messy affair of ingesting the entire contents of the bird(s). Other species such as skylarks and thrushes can be table fare in such places as Catalonia, although hunting of songbirds is banned in North America for conservation reasons.

LARGE MAMMALS

UNFORTUNATELY DURING YEARS AND CENTURIES PAST some game—especially the larger mammals—were often harvested without concern for the sustainability of the hunt. The creatures that once provided much of the traditional food in this region are now either extinct or in jeopardy of extinction so that hunting is either banned or greatly curtailed. Game populations were especially stressed during the famine years associated with the Great Depression and the civil war in Spain. The establishment of parks and hunting reserves throughout the region, coupled with modern conservation and game management, has generally reversed this trend. During the lean years the best hunters in the Pyrenean villages were often hired as game keepers. In Spain, most of the Pyrenees today is protected by public *Reservas Nacionales de Caza* where strict quotas are enforced or by private *cotos privados de caza*.

Mouflon (*Ovis aries musimon*) are a medium-sized sheep with short, non-fleecy hair and large, curled horns. They became extinct in the Pyrenees during the prehistoric era (possibly from climate change rather than hunters), but have been reintroduced from Corsica and Sardinia in the Carlit Massif and on Pic Pibeste near Lourdes. Their natural habitat is forest in the high mountains, but they can adapt to open areas above the tree line. The last Pyrenean sub-species of the Spanish ibex (*Capra hircus pyrenaica*) was found dead in Ordesa National Park in 2000, although ibex can still be found in the Sierra de Gredos and the Sierra Nevada. Distinguished by a thick coat adapted to frigid mountain temperatures and weather, the *bucardo* or *bouquetin* became endangered from hunters seeking their heads and horns as trophies. Although protected as an endangered species since 1973, shrinking habitat and poachers eliminated the remainder of this mountain goat's population.

Pyrenean brown bears (*Ursus arctos*) are considered to be technically extinct in the Spanish Pyrenees by Dr. Juan Carlos Blanco of Spain's *Fundación Oso Pardo* because only one or two remain, who have not bred for years. There are still a few on the French side in the wildest areas such as the Aspe, Ossau, and Roncal valleys. The Pyrenean bear population has always been relatively small in size and timid, consuming mostly vegetarian fare. Bears have been declining steadily in the region for centuries because of hunting and a general decline in wild habitat between 3,000 and 5,500 feet in altitude. During the past 30 years they have been caught accidentally by snares set for wild boar or killed by poisoned bait set for wolves. The five remaining adults bears in France have been assigned names (Papillon, Chocolat, Cannelle, Pyrène, Camille), and the cub that was born in 1998 might be the last in the Pyrenees. Smaller creatures depend upon large game in the Pyrenean ecosystem to survive. For example, Lammergeyers (*Gypaetus barbatus*)—large and rare vultures—eat mostly large bones and flesh taken from dead animals. The birds drop bones on rocky slopes to break them into suitably-sized pieces for consumption.

Isards (*Rupicapra ruricapra*) are Pyrenean chamois with short chestnut-colored fur, contrasting head markings, and slender, slightly hooked horns. This nimble and graceful goat-antelope climbs very well, and stands three feet tall at the shoulder. Overhunted in the 1950s, they might have disappeared had it not been for the creation of parks and refuges as well as dedicated conservation policies. Since the 1960s, isard populations have steadily grown to about 50,000 animals divided more or less equally between Spain and France. A limited take is allowed each year for older animals that the game keepers select for the hunters. Their flesh is usually tough and strong-smelling, thus isard dishes are rarely to be found on restaurant menus. They are the only common wild herbivore in the mountains, thriving in such places as France's Parc des Pyrénées, Spain's La Cerdanya, and Spain's Cadí-Moixeró Park where a herd of 1,000 females and young can be found. Rarely active at night, isards feed at dawn and dusk in high mountain meadows during summer, descending in winter to the forest zone.

Three species of deer populate the Pyrenees. Red deer (*ciervo* or *cerf rouge*) are magnificent 400-pound creatures whose branched antlers can measure six feet along the beam. Stags are mostly sought for trophies, although their flesh has an exquisite gamy flavor that can inspire chefs. Young animals are usually deemed more worthy of culinary attention. Red deer had died out in the Pyrenees but have been successfully reintroduced. Known as elk or wapiti in North America and *Cervus elaphus* by scientists, they inhabit deciduous woodlands while avoiding coniferous forests. Generally nocturnal, small herds can be seen feeding on grasses, leaves, and other vegetation at the forest edges of meadows in early mornings and late afternoons. When threatened, red deer can gallop extremely fast and are capable of jumping long distances. Roe deer (*Capreolus capreolus*) live throughout Eurasia and have dark red, tender flesh that is discretely gamy and highly regarded. Considered the "ghost of the forest" because of their stealthy movements, they are the most numerous deer in Europe. Small and graceful, the red-brown males have small, branched antlers and stand just over two feet tall at the shoulder. They were reintroduced into Navarra and the Luz Valley of the Parc des Pyrénées in the 1980s and populations seem to be growing rapidly as evidenced by an expansion from their preferred habitat in sparsely wooded valleys into high mountain areas. Small family groups can most easily be seen grazing in open fields at the fringes of young woods at twilight where dense undergrowth provides good cover. Curiously, roe deer can bark like dogs when threatened. Male fallow deer (*Dama dama*) possess handsome palmate antlers, engendering more interest in them as trophies than venison. They are reddish-brown with white spots and can weigh up to 200 pounds. Fallow deer prefer deciduous woods with luxuriant undergrowth as well as parklands. Chiefly nocturnal and shy, their small herds are generally comprised of females and young.

Wild boars (*Sus scrofa*) are high on the culinary list. The tender meat of young boars up to sixteen months of age (called *marcassins* in France) are considered a delicacy. Older animals have a stronger, gamy flavor unless raised on a farm. Weighing up to 200 pounds in the Pyrenees, males possess razor-sharp tusks that are capable of inflicting mortal wounds. Widespread in this region, females and young live in packs comprised of related animals that are born in large litters. Wild boars can be found most anywhere except in the highest mountains or in open land without cover. They are especially numerous in the thick undergrowth of deciduous forests or in wild moorlands where they consume acorns, chestnuts, roots, and any small creatures that they encounter on the ground. Wild boar fare poorly in areas where foresters manage the land for tall conifers, because the forest floor lacks the varied and rich undergrowth of deciduous forests. Boars are the favorite quarry of many hunters, including farmers protecting their crops. One common method—called *la chasse aux chiens courants* in France and *la montería* in Spain—is to use dogs to drive the animals from cover into a clearing or strategic pass where marksmen wait in ambush for a clear shot.

SMALL MAMMALS AND BIRDS

HARE (*LIEBRE* OR *LIÈVRE*) AND RABBITS (*CONEJO* OR *LAPIN*) HAVE BEEN A FAVORITE of hunters for millennia and remain common table fare today in the Pyrenees. Hares (*Lepus capensis*) tend to be larger and have white, tough meat that elicits a slightly gamy taste. Rabbit (*Oryctolagus cuniculus*) flesh in contrast is very tender, near red in color and exceptionally gamy. The best hares are taken between eight and ten months of age (*lièvre de l'année*) when they retain a youthful tenderness but have not yet developed the strong flavors of adults. Both species live in colonies and are widespread in the region, with rabbits more common in valleys and hares better adapted to forests and high altitudes. Rabbit numbers began to decline during the first half of the twentieth century with the loss of pasture-scrub-woodland habitat when goat herding declined in favor of mechanized grain cultivation, fewer cattle migrated in the ancient *cañadas* and agricultural practices left fewer and fewer plots of unfarmed land. Rabbits and hares suffered accelerated population declines in the 1950s when they were decimated by the disease myxomatosis. Rabbits and hares are the main prey of the Iberian lynx (*Lynx lynx*), which was once widespread in Spain and Portugal, including the Pyrenees. Lynx populations have declined in tandem with rabbit populations. By the early 1970s, lynx were essentially limited to the southwestern corner of the Iberian Peninsula, in relatively inaccessible mountainous regions and controlled hunting reserves in the Guadalquivir River delta. The International Union for the Conservation of Nature considers the Spanish lynx population to be so fragmented that only two groups have sufficient numbers to engender long-term prospects of viability. In addition to the availability of prey, lynx have been pressured by illegal sport hunting for its coat, persecution due to damage to livestock, killing by snares set for rabbits, and poison baits set for predators such as foxes. On a more optimistic note, French biologists have recently found persuasive evidence that small lynx populations remain in the French Pyrenees although it is an open question whether they are of the endangered Iberian race.

Alpine marmots (*Marmota marmota*) are thick-set 20-pound rodents that disappeared from the Pyrenees at the end of the last glacial era about 10,000 years ago. They were reintroduced into France's Luz Valley in 1950, a restoration project that has been so successful that their colonies have spread throughout the Pyrenees at altitudes between

3,000 and 8,000 feet. Visitors can encounter them in broad daylight on flat ground or on rocky slopes, although during winter they hibernate in nest chambers within deep burrows. The marmot's return has encouraged the increase of the royal eagle (*Aquila heliaca*) population, and the shadow of a bird of prey's silhouette can elicit warning cries and high-pitched whistling yaps in the colony. Henri Toulouse-Lautrec published a simple recipe for stewed marmots in his 1866 *The Art of Cuisine* in which he advised the cook to "treat it like a stewed hare which has a perfume that is unique and wild."

Capercaillies (*Tetrao urogallus*) are large, non-migratory grouses that inhabit old beech and fir forests at similar altitudes as marmots in temperate regions of Europe and West Asia. Males can weigh up to 13 pounds, but hens are considerably smaller. Of about 10,000 breeding pairs in Europe, over one-third are found in the Pyrenees, especially in the wilder central portion of the range. Capercaillies are renowned for their spring courtship displays in which males strut and fan their tails and chase interlopers from their territories. Females nest on the ground adjacent to rocks or tree stumps, which leaves chicks vulnerable to lynx and other predators. Capercaille populations are decreasing throughout Europe from overhunting, the felling of old forests and disturbance by tourists.

One of today's great wildlife spectacles in the Pyrenees is the enormous southern migration of migratory birds such as honey buzzards (*Pernis apivorus*), kites, cranes (*Megalornis grus*), and white storks (*Cinconia cinconia*) that use the identical low passes each year. In particular, millions of *palombes* or *palomas*—wood pigeons (*columba palumbus*)—pass through Col d'Organbidexka (Basque Country) and Col d'Eyne (Catalonia) during mid-October en route to the south of Spain and North Africa. The most common and widespread European pigeon draws some 25,000 Basque hunters (mostly city dwellers) each autumn to harvest birds that breed in the British Isles, Russia, and Scandinavia. Over 600 years ago monks at Roncevaux Abbey observed that falcons and hawks ambushed wood pigeons in these passes. The monks noticed that pigeons would try to escape attack by diving and flying near ground level, and developed the now-traditional technique that can be seen today. From tall, camouflaged towers erected high among the trees hunters throw wooden disks whitened with chalk above pigeon flocks to imitate a bird of prey's attack. Others wave huge white flags, blow on horns, beat drums and shout, hoping to frighten the flocks into the center of the pass where nets have been set to entangle the birds. Other hunters hide in blinds where they try to bag this tasty delicacy with shotguns.

Inevitably the passes draw both hunters and birders, which engenders some conflict. Indeed, some hunters' errant shots kill or cripple birds of prey or other unintended species. The hunt is sufficiently controversial that wildlife officials monitor the take

fairly closely, and estimates in some breeding areas indicate that wood pigeon populations seem to be stable or increasing despite the netting or shooting of about 1.5 million *palombes* each year. As long as the magnitude of the hunt is managed rationally so
that it remains sustainable, this activity can continue as an important part of the culture, heritage, and cuisine of the Pyrenean people. A more difficult problem for many
creatures is the loss of habitat. The British ornithologist R. E. Moreau estimates that
the populations of European waterbirds have declined dramatically and continuously
since the Roman era as marshes and other wetlands have been drained and filled.

Perdices—red-legged partridges (*Alectoris rufa*)—have been served at feasts to kings,
princes, and bishops in Spain since the Middle Ages. A popular proverb implies that
eating the succulent yet lean meat from this common fowl symbolizes well being and
happiness:

> *Fueron felices y comieron perdices*
> (They were happy and ate partridges.)

This stout fowl has stubby wings and a short tail. In the field its red beak and legs
stand out, as does its long white brow line and white throat. Widespread and abundant in the Iberian Peninsula, these sedentary birds prefer cultivated fields, vineyards,
and hillsides where they feed on grains, grasses, and insects. Red-legged partridges are
considered to be one of the swiftest hunted birds in the world, and a challenge to bring
down. Hunters can employ dogs or domestically-reared "Judas birds" whose calls lure
unsuspecting wild birds into an ambush. A common method in Spain called an *ojeo*
uses large hunting parties in which a line of men beat an area to drive partridges to
hunters hidden behind a camouflaged blind where they are shot. Note that red-legged
partridges are now raised commercially, and birds served in restaurants may not be
truly wild.

•-•

WE HURRIED FROM AX-LES-THERMES down the valley created by the upper Ariège
River to the village of Niaux, nearby Tarascon. The road signs directed us to smaller
and smaller roadways, which eventually ended at a small parking lot adjacent to a
blocky modern building constructed mostly of glass at the base of a massive rock
overhang. The government bureaucrats acknowledged the reservation that we had made
a month before, and a band of 10 assembled for the afternoon tour of the *Grotte de
Niaux*. An archeologist issued each couple a flashlight, and lead us through a low claus-
trophobic natural opening in the cliff through a steel door. Moving slowly in the inky

blackness, our flashlights allowed us to maintain our footing as the narrow passage opened up to the cool expansive recesses in the bowels of the Pyrenean foothills. We walked and walked what seemed to be an interminable distance, but which the guidebooks say is only about one-half mile. Suddenly we stopped and were instructed to turn off our flashlights. Our guide used her light to direct our attention to a drawing of an ibex on the wall—now extinct in the Pyrenees thanks to trophy hunters—an artistic marvel that seems strikingly modern. As she explained that the artists or shamans of 12,000 B.C. used "crayons" of manganese oxide and bison fat to sketch their representations, we saw other wonderful sketches of bison, red deer, and wild horses. These creatures have each suffered local extinction, although the red deer has been successfully reintroduced. In other caves representations of wild boar and reindeer (which lived in these parts during the last Ice Age) can be found. While our primitive ancestors no doubt found an element of magic in the beasts with whom they shared their Pyrenean existence, they surely depended upon them for food, clothing, and perhaps tools. As I embarked on this journey to describe the contemporary cuisine of the Pyrenees, I often thought of the lives of the original people in this region at the dawn of mankind. In the thousands of years since the era of these cave painters, each succeeding generation has built on the foods of their parents, clan, and extended families to develop their own styles of cuisine. This past has surely been the prologue to today's cuisines.

REGIONAL WINES

The Wines of the Pyrenees Region

CLUSTERS OF HEAVY, PURPLE CARIGNAN GRAPES drooped from the vines in early October in the fields surrounding the medieval walls of Carcassonne, Languedoc. Next to La Maison sur la Colline, a country farm house that provides a bed and breakfast, workers in *ouvrier-bleu* overalls operated tractors on stilts, maneuvering above rows of vines to pluck the clusters. Signs of the autumn harvest or *vendange* are unmistakable along the wine roads of Minervois and Corbières. They are choked with conveyances overflowing with grapes, including tractors pulling decrepit carts, large modern trucks, and wagons that defy description. Near Gasparets, three generations of grape growers grinned and waved their purple forearms exuberantly when I photographed them stuffing *raisins* into their backpack containers. Ten days later in an ancient Navarran town, the harvest or *vendimia* elicited an aura of excitement from the residents gathered at a cooperative just outside the walls of Olite. An aging farmer raked Carignan grapes (locally called Mazuelo) from the back of his station wagon, the floor of which was covered by a blue tarp, into a large intake tank at ground level. He removed some branches, twigs, and leaves before a small auger bored into the grape pile, apparently measuring the sugar and acid content. After his afternoon's contribution was weighed, the crusher converted the *cosechero's* grapes into a small torrent that streamed down a drain into a stainless steel tank where it commingled with the juices of his neighbors. Inside the building, we tasted their products from a glass *porrón*, which is held like a *bota* bag while you attempt to stream the wine into your mouth instead of down your chin. The cooperative sold its honest and unpretentious plonk in cardboard containers for under two dollars per liter.

PORRÓN

The grapevine that is the source of most modern wines, *Vitus vinifera*, is a native of Eurasia. Apparently wine making began some 6,000 years ago in the southern Caucasus, in the mountainous region between the Black Sea and the Caspian Sea. Grapes can readily ferment into wine if a yeast (*Saccharomyces cerevisiae*) that naturally occurs on oak bark is present. Thus, the harvesting of both grapes and acorns as food may have transferred yeast to grape skins and fostered the discovery of wine making.

The evolution of wine making from an infrequent, haphazard event to a common cultural practice required the development of a settled lifestyle because a nomadic way of life is incompatible with the accumulation of grapes to produce significant quantities of wine. From its origins in the Caucasus, domestic grape growing and wine making probably first spread southward into Mesopotamia and later to Phoenicia and Egypt around 3,000 B.C. Egyptian tomb paintings and papyri indicate that wine was used for social and religious purposes from the earliest days of the Old Kingdom.

The modern age of wine began about 1,500 B.C. when the Greeks and Phoenicians colonized the western Mediterranean, planting the first vineyards there. Greek poets lavishly praised and documented their own wines, although it is impossible to know how such wines tasted. In the time of Homer (eighth century B.C.), wild grape vines grew in Sicily and probably Italy. According to the British historian Edward Gibbon, the "savage inhabitants" there did not have the skill to "afford a liquor grateful to the taste." Colonists from ancient Greece transported vinification and industrialized wine making into Sicily and southern Italy, describing Italy as the "land of the vines." The Greeks apparently were the first to establish vineyards in Provence (600 B.C.) and Agde, Languedoc (400 B.C.). These vineyards may have been planted by Etruscans who learned Greek methods in southern Italy and developed large-scale wine making in Tuscany. The Phoenicians or perhaps the Carthaginians brought vineyards to the Mediterranean side of the Iberian Peninsula from Andalucía to Catalonia.

The Romans expanded the wine-making traditions they inherited from the Greeks and Etruscans to establish immense operations at many new locations throughout the empire. They cultivated using festoons of vines on trees, as depicted on friezes of classical buildings or observed in vineyards today in southern Italy. During most of the imperial era, Italy's own wines were considered the best in the empire. According to Gibbon, Italy could boast that she made two-thirds of the 80 most celebrated wines in 200 A.D. Like today, Romans writers loved to write about wine and wine making, especially the great vintages. Virgil's instruction to grape growers that "vines love an open hill" is timeless excellent advice. Italy's great vintages were drunk for long periods of time, and essentially rendered Greek wines unfashionable. The famous Opimian from 121 B.C. was said to be enjoyed 125 years later.

Over the course of several centuries, the Romans expanded the viticulture that the Greeks, Phoenicians, and Carthaginians had begun in the Pyrenees. They encouraged the systematic planting and development of efficient vineyard estates, perhaps using a varietal similar to today's Syrah. In France, the Romans started in Provence, moved up the Rhone valley, and later concentrated vineyards around Narbonne and Beziers, Languedoc. Roman efforts south of the Pyrenees began near Tarragona (then Tarraco), the imperial capital of the Peninsula. During seven centuries of rule,

Romans planted vineyards in the Priorat, northern Catalonia, Navarra, Aragón, and Rioja Alavesa (north of the Ebro River). The wines of the Pyrenees region were initially consumed locally, but eventually Rome imported countless shiploads of wines that had become famous for their quality. Indeed, the wines from Narbonne were of such high quality that Italian growers persuaded Emperor Domitian in 92 A.D. to decree that some of the vines be uprooted because the Italians were losing too much business. The Romans transported wines in seven-gallon earthenware amphoras similar to those used by the Greeks, glass amphoras made using Syrian techniques, and wooden barrels. Specially designed ships could carry 10,000 amphoras. While the methods of sealing the amphoras is not known with absolute certainty, the Romans may have sealed them with corks—a technique that was subsequently lost for a thousand years.

Following the Roman Empire's collapse in the fifth century, the Pyrenean region had a long period of instability. The barbarian tribes from the north that engulfed the Romans were not wine drinkers, and Moors from North Africa raided as far north as Beziers in 714 to destroy its remaining vineyards. While the subsequent relatively tranquil reign of Charlemagne helped viticulture to survive in Languedoc, vines were not actively cultivated again in many areas south of the Pyrenees until after the *Reconquista* in the tenth century because Islam officially prohibits the consumption of alcohol. Beginning in Aragón and the foothills of Catalonia, vineyards were gradually reestablished in areas such as Penedès and the Priorat which are now Catalonia's premier wine regions. Wine there was both consumed locally and transported by mule in sewn goatskins lined with pitch.

In 1000, King Sancho el Mayor of Navarra realized the importance of El Camino Santiago (also called *Camino Francés*) as a great trans-European thoroughfare for pilgrims en route to Santiago de Compostela. He encouraged the creation of churches, hotels, hospitals, and monasteries along the route. Wine was normally safer than water to drink, and the pilgrims' drinking habits enabled the local wine industry to flourish. The *Codex Calixtus*, an early guide for pilgrims, extolled the virtues of the good bread, abundant meat and fish, and *"excelente vino"* at Estella, Navarra. Throughout the Pyrenean region the monastic orders of the Catholic Church, especially the Benedictines and the Cistercians from Burgundy, obtained land grants to found monasteries that included requirements to plant or reestablish vineyards. Wine making was not only important to Christians given their use of wine in the sacrament, but became a principal source of wealth. Madiran, Gascony, was a typical village on pilgrim route. Benedictine monks established an abbey there in the eleventh century, bringing wine-making skills to a region where vineyards had flourished eight centuries previously. The Cistercians founded a monastery in Fontfroide, Corbières, in 1145, and developed vineyards there that still exist. French monks from Fontfroide soon thereafter began a new monastery in Poblet, Penedès, and planted Tempranillo, a close relative of Pinot Noir. Today the Monasterio de Poblet is surrounded by vineyards whose grapes are used to make high-end Torres wines and sold in the monastery's gift shop. Carthusian monks from Grenoble founded the monastery of Scala Dei in 1163, reestablishing vineyards in the Priorat. Spain's warm climate assured a substantial grape harvest, and its medieval wines compared favorably to those in France. During this period of stability wine making techniques matured and evolved, slowly becoming varieties that are now familiar. Religious strictures notwithstanding, thirteenth-century Moors taught distillation techniques to make aguardiente from wine in Penedès and Beziers.

Pyrenean wines improved from technological advancements in storage and transportation. The Spanish agriculturist Alonso de Herrera had observed in the sixteenth century that "wine from barrels is more fragrant than wine from jars," reflecting the fact that Spanish wines were fermented and aged in huge earthenware or concrete vats called *tinajas*. For centuries French wines had spent all of their lives in wooden barrels, typically being brought to the consumer at the table in a pottery jug. Once a barrel was opened and exposed to air, the wine quickly oxidized and became undrinkable. The English rediscovered and improved glass-making technology by making glass bottles heavier, stronger, and cheaper. Moreover, monks in Catalonia apparently rediscovered the use of corks to seal wine bottles, perhaps after using them to stopper water bottles. Catalonia today is a major cork producer from oaks. It became evident that wine kept in tightly corked bottles lasted far longer than wine kept in barrels, and that such wine aged differently. It acquired a "bouquet," providing an opportunity to increase the price of wines capable of aging, as well as setting the stage for the development modern wine maturation techniques. The widespread use of barrels treated with sulfur greatly increased the likelihood of better quality wine production and a longer life for the end product.

In the sixteenth century, the slow fermentation of grapes in the French autumn would often be interrupted by winter's chill and fermentation would not resume until temperatures rose in the spring. This phenomenon, called secondary fermentation, creates sparkling wine if the tiny bubbles of carbon dioxide do not dissipate. The Benedictine abbots of St. Hilaire, Languedoc, mastered this process in 1531, and produced the world's first sparkling wine called Blanquette de Limoux. A century later Dom Perignon in Champagne traveled to St. Hilaire and learned the secret of containing the pressure of sparkling wine by using heavy, specially blown bottles, stopped with wire-wrapped cork. He may also have learned about the uses of cork during a sojourn at a monastery in Gerona, Catalonia. Both Blanquette de Limoux and "real"

Champagne are made by the same painstaking method of vinification in the bottle now called *"la méthode champenoise"* or *"méthode traditionelle."* The world owes the monks at the abbey of St. Hilaire most of the gratitude that is usually reserved for Dom Perignon.

Like vineyards throughout Europe, those on either side of the Pyrenees were obliterated by a series of biological catastrophes in the nineteenth century. Outbreaks of oidium (a powdery mildew) and plasmopara (a downy mildew) damaged the fruit in mid-century. Then phylloxera, an insect, arrived on vines brought from North America and killed the roots of European vines. Within a few decades after first being sighted in 1868 near Arles, phylloxera had destroyed the vineyards of Gascony, Languedoc, Roussillon, and Catalonia. Among the ancillary effects of this ecological and economic calamity was a depopulation of the countryside of southwest France. Growers responded by grafting European varieties onto American rootstock (which are resistant to the insect) and replanting. The Catalan vineyards continued to produce during the 10 to 15 years it took the French vineyards to recover, and Catalan wine was in such great demand that vineyards expanded. Unfortunately, most Catalan producers at that time increased production with a corresponding drop in the quality of the wine. *Viticulteurs* in Languedoc-Roussillon (collectively called the Midi) also focused on quantity over quality, and replanted their vineyards along the fertile coastal plain instead of on the poor hillside soils where better grapes are produced. They began to concentrate on a number of reliable *cépages d'abondance*—grapes such as Carignan, Aramon, and Alicanté which worked well in a variety of soils and provided heavy crops of ordinary red wine. The numerous *châteaux* dating from this period are an indication of the level of the region's prosperity, although it was short-lived. Navarran growers replanted Garnacha Tinta (a Spanish grape) instead of Tempranillo, focusing on bulk production in cooperative wineries. Catalan growers could recover faster than the French, because the grafting techniques had already been developed when phylloxera claimed their vineyards. Inspired by the work of Josep Raventós in Sant Sadurní d'Anoia, they replanted largely with the local white varieties Parellada, Macabeu, and Xarel-lo. Raventós also experimented with wine making techniques learned in France to produce Catalan sparkling wine in 1872—originally called *"xampany,"* but now known as cava.

The general displacements of French wine makers as a result of the calamities of the nineteenth century encouraged *vignerons* to settle south of the Pyrenees and to introduce new techniques, including the use of oak barrels for aging. Two such wine makers were Spaniards by birth. The Marqués de Riscal returned to his homeland after learning about wine making in France in 1860, and the Marqués de Murrieta followed in 1872. They planted vineyards in the Rioja region and made Bordeaux-style wines that they aged in oak casks. Until then most Spanish wine makers still used *tinajas*, and table wines were distributed locally and drunk young. While monks from

Burgundy had introduced aging in oak barrels in the twelfth century, the lesson had not yet penetrated much of Spain's wine industry. The two marquises also introduced the revolutionary concept of selling their wines in bottles. Even until the 1970s, a common means of purchasing all but the highest-end wines was to bring an empty bottle to a wine shop and to request the *bodeguero* to fill it from the barrel (*barrica*) marked *tinto, blanco,* or *rosé.* Bodegas Vinícola de Navarra in Las Campañas was founded in 1880 by a Frenchman escaping phylloxera and was the first to commercialize wine in bottles in Navarra. In 1894, *viticulteurs* from Bordeaux settled near Barbastro, Somontano, to found Bodegas Lalanne and to plant vineyards with Cabernet Sauvignon, Merlot, and Moristel. Their bottles of Spanish wine won medals in Bordeaux and Brussels in 1908.

Pasteur's discovery in the 1860s of the importance of yeasts and bacteria in the fermentation process was a watershed event. This understanding initiated a scientific approach to viticulture and wine making, which fostered innumerable improvements that have led to the incredible range of wines which are characteristic of the modern era. New wine regions such as California, Australia, and Chile lacked the centuries-old traditions that can stultify original approaches to selecting and growing grapes or improvements in wine craft. Thus these new areas were free to benefit from wine science and experimentation and were in a position to challenge the conventional producers in Europe.

Both France and Spain have developed somewhat bureaucratic approaches to wine labeling—specifying which grapes are allowed to be used in wines for various regions as well as how the wine must be made. Such regulations favor the status quo, and tend to hinder experimentation and independence of thought. They also confuse consumers. Ironically, government agencies instituted the rules as initiatives to improve the quality of the wines. Through the 1970s, the wines of the Pyrenees region had a common problem. To the north, Languedoc-Roussillon was the oldest and largest wine producing region of France, accounting for about a third of all French wine and ten percent of the world's wine. The wines were consumed by French farm and factory workers or used for industrial alcohol. To the south, Spain had the most acres of vines of any nation in the world (more than 5,400 square miles), although its harvest was less than France and Italy because production levels were low. While available in prodigious quantities, virtually all of the wines from this region were perceived in the marketplace as being cheap, low quality plonk—watery, mediocre, nondescript, and boring. The quality of wines in Italy and other parts of France far exceeded that of the Pyrenees region.

With the rise of a quality wine industry in California, consumption of table wine from Languedoc-Roussillon began to drop in the 1960s and 1970s. Huge volumes of these wines were left to stagnate in southern France, stacking up in cases by the hundreds of thousands waiting for their uneventful blending and consumption. Ever resilient to changing circumstances, the French government began to encourage the restructuring of the vineyards, encouraging *vignerons* to plant better grape varieties and invest in modern technology. Legislation encouraged growers to replant the region, and winemakers to tighten the reigns on quality. Producers in every corner of the Midi started to uproot Grenache and Carignan and to replace them with Syrah, Mourvèdre, Cabernet Sauvignon, Cinsault (also called Hermitage), and Chardonnay. They also began to replant the hilly slopes along a Mediterranean coastal arc from Narbonne east to Montpelier, reclaiming *terroir* that had been abandoned to vineyards since phylloxera. At the same time they limited the quantities producers could harvest to give the region the reputation of an up-and-comer with competitive pricing. New labeling rules created the appellation *vin de pays d'Oc* in 1987, which stimulated the quadrupling of the number of producers within a decade. Wine makers began to make *vins de cépages*, which are made from a single variety of grape.

In Spain during the 1970s and 1980s, individual *bodegueros* realized that their future would be in quality, not quantity. They began to implement the technological revolution in wine making, including earlier picking of grapes, the introduction of temperature-controlled fermenting methods, and the use of stainless steel vats. These changes encouraged the renovation of old wineries, the establishment of new ones and the development of a highly organized quality wine industry. A prime example is the pioneering efforts of Miguel Torres, Jr., in Catalonia, beginning in 1962. In 1979 at the "wine Olympiad" in Paris, Torres' 1970 *gran reserva* black label from his family estate *Mas la Plana* took top honors, beating Château la Tour. It became impossible for wine enthusiasts to ignore the incredible changes that were taking place in the Pyrenean region.

Contemporary Spanish Wines

PYRENEAN SPAIN IS BEST KNOWN today for its powerful, age-worthy red wines, especially those made from its native Tempranillo grape that has a unique smoky, cherry, spicy fruit character. Catalonia is also known for its elegant sparkling cavas made using the traditional Champagne method with Spanish grape varieties. More and more Spanish wines are rising to world-class level and earning an enthusiastic international following. Others—whether silky, elegant reds perfect for drinking now or fresh, original whites or rosés with character, or rich dessert wines—provide fine drinking at reasonable prices. Visitors to Spain are delighted to find that wine shops routinely carry older vintages that are unavailable in similar shops elsewhere. This summary of the Spanish Pyrenees region is limited to wines that are produced north of the Ebro River, including those from Catalonia, northern Aragón, Navarra, Rioja Alavesa, and the Basque country. Due to my own preferences, and acknowledging the relative qualities of the wines, I tend to focus on reds.

Spanish red wines are traditionally aged in 225-liter oak casks (called *crianza, reserva,* or *gran reserva,* depending on the length of stay in wood). Others, sometimes called *vinos jóvenes,* or young wines, are consumed immediately with little or no aging and tend to be fruity. Because Spain has unique traditions and its labels can be confusing, it is important to understand some of its wine regulations. Beginning in 1926, the Spanish government began to designate *denominación de origen* (DO) areas, its equivalent of France's *appellation d'origine controlée* (AOC). Today there are more than fifty DOs (e.g., Penedès, Priorat), each of which refers to a specific geographical area that is controlled by a *Consejo Regulador.* This regulatory body specifies the geographical area within which the grapes for a demarcated wine may be grown, the permitted grape varieties, how the wine is to be matured, limits for alcohol and sugar content, and even such details as methods of pruning and the density of grape vines. In 1991, Spain established a new top category *denominación de origen calificada* (DOC), which adds the word *calificada* ("qualified"), indicating that the DOC has more exacting standards than those established for DOs. So far, only the Rioja region has met the definitive standards of the new category.

Like other European nations, Spain has two broad categories—table wine and quality wine. Among the table wines, *vino de mesa* is made from grapes grown on unclassified vineyards or blended and *vino comarcal* (VC) which may be labeled with the area in which it was produced. The highest classification of table wines is *vino de la tierra* (VdlT), which is from an officially demarcated region that might one day be elevated to a DO. Finding a small label on the back of a bottle with the phrase "guarantee of origin" does not necessarily ensure a quality experience. In addition, some excellent wines cannot qualify for a DO merely because the wine maker has used grapes that were not traditionally used in the region.

Catalonia

Catalan red—or "black wine" as translated from the Catalan *vi negre*—might have been well described as black in the past. Today, the combination of imported varieties like Cabernet Sauvignon and Merlot, with the traditional varieties Garnacha (Grenache), Cariñena (Carignan), Ull de Llebre (Tempranillo), and modern wine making processes are producing some excellent reds.

The DO Penedès is located near the Mediterranean coast of Spain, just south and west of Barcelona, and is centered on the town Vilafranca del Penedès where an interesting *museo del vino* is located. This area was instrumental in Spain's move toward modern wines and international varietals. Red wines predominate, except near Sant Sadurní d'Anoia, the capital of cava production and home of scores of cava producers. The reds of Penedès are typically heavy and fruity, perhaps because Cabernet Sauvignon is blended with the traditional Ull de Llebre. Other varietals used in Penedès red blends include Garnacha Tinta, Monastrell, and black Cariñena. Crisp, clean white wines and sparkling wines are made with the Parellada, Xarel-lo, and Macabeo (Viura elsewhere in Spain) varietals, with some fruity Malvasía used as well. Other white varietals are also being experimented with here, primarily by the Torres estate, where Chardonnay, Sauvignon Blanc, Riesling, and Gewurztraminer are made. *Mas La Plana* Black Label Gran Coronas (entirely Cabernet Sauvignon) is smoky and luscious, exemplifying the vision of Miguel Torres, Jr. Among the more affordable Torres wines that are widely available in the United States are Gran Sangre de Toro and Sangre de Toro, whose flavors burst from the vivid blends. Torres also produces Viña Sol, a fresh dry and fruity white wine made from Parellada and Chardonnay. Bodegas Jean León produces a crisp, clean Viña Sarda white, blended from Macabeo, Xarel-lo, and Parellada.

Penedès also produces cava or sparkling wines, mostly with native Catalonian grapes such as Parellada and Xarel-lo, but also with Macabeo and Chardonnay. DO Cava is not limited by geography, but most is produced in Penedès or Catalonia. The biggest producers provide reliable, and admirable cavas such as Codorníu Brut NV and Freixenet Brut Cordon Negro NV and are generally available in the United States at bargain prices. Codorníu provides a fascinating tour of its winery in Sant Sadurní d'Anoia, with buildings that have been declared a national landmark by the Spanish government. Many excellent cavas apparently are rarely available in the United States. In a winery adjacent to Codorníu, we purchased an outstanding Raventós I Blanc C Gran Reserva Personal M.R.N. Brut Nature Cava at a very reasonable price. We also enjoyed cavas in several of the fine restaurants of Catalonia, including Rovellats Brut Nature Grand Cuvée (El Bulli in Rosas) and Rovellats Gran Cru—Masía S XV (Mirador de las Cavas in Sant Sadurní). Other labels to seek out are Montsarra Cava Brut, Recardeo, and Tura D'Arnau.

The name of the DO Priorat, or priory, reflects the influence of the Carthusian Scala Dei monastery on the wine making of this tiny, historic enclave in the mountains west of Tarragon. The Priorat's red wines are made from Garnacha Tinta and Cariñena grapes (increasingly with additions of Cabernet Sauvignon and other international varietals) grown on steep, rugged hillsides where mechanical harvesting of grapes is virtually impossible. The harvests are minuscule, and many bottlings are under 1,000 cases per year. The wines are known for their huge concentrations of color, great personality, and immense power. They tend to have high glycerol content, making the wines round. Since the late 1980s, upscale *viñeros* like Alvaro Palacios and José Luis Pérez have produced some spectacular vintages in the Priorat. Palacios, descendant of a Rioja family, came to the Priorat looking for new challenges. While his reputation was made from his L'Ermita (primarily old-vine Garnacha Tinta) and his Finca Dofí (Garnacha Tinta blended with plenty of Cabernet Sauvignon, Merlot, and Syrah), his somewhat cheaper Les Terrasses is also excellent. Pérez produces two magnificent wines—Clos Martinet and Cims de Porrera. Every wine that we have tasted that had "clos" in its name—meaning "vineyard" in Catalonian—has been spectacular. Daphne Glorian's Clos Erasmus, J.M. Fuentes' Clos Martinet, and René Barbier's Clos Mogador are sensational, and worth the high price if you can find them. While some less-expensive Priorats can be a disappointment, there are many value-priced reds. Onix (Garnacha Tinta and Cariñena), made by the Vinícola del Priorat has generous flavors of raspberry and clove. De Müller's Legitim, a *crianza* made of Cabernet Sauvignon, Garnacha Tinta, and Cariñena, is also a pleasure. Solanes (90% Cariñena, 10% Garnacha Tinta), produced by Porrera Cooperative and Mas Martinet, is intense with berry tones and hints of vanilla. Barranc del Closos is an excellent claret-style wine with cherry notes. We also had the pleasure of experiencing René Barbier's Dolç de L'Obac (Cariñena and Garnacha Tinta), a dessert red, at the Michelin three-star El Racó de Can Fabes restaurant in Sant Celoni. Chef Santi Santamaria provided several glasses of this ambrosial 1998 vintage at the culmination of a wonderful tasting menu. It would be exceedingly difficult to find this in any wine shop, since only eight *barricas* (barrels) were made and it was voted Spain's top dessert wine that year.

The DO Costers del Segre was demarcated in 1988, and is comprised of four small areas near the city of Lleida. The DO owes its existence to the prestige of the Raimat estate, which is located to the west of Lleida, owned by the Raventós family of Codorníu, and was developed with assistance from the University of California at Davis. Much of the production of white grapes is destined for cava. The authorized reds are Cabernet Sauvignon, Trepat, Tempranillo (Ull de Llebre), Merlot, Monastrell (Mourvèdre), and Pinot Noir. Raimat makes a red Abadía (Cabernet Sauvignon, Tempranillo, Merlot) which has a fine reputation. We found one of the best wineries in Catalonia to be Castell del Remei. We enjoyed its 1780 (Cabernet Sauvignon, Tempranillo, Garnacha Tinta) at the restaurant El Racó de Can Fabes and its Oda (Cabernet Sauvignon and Merlot) at the Restaurant Mas Pau in Figueres. Its Chardonnay also has an excellent reputation.

Aragón

Aragón is a fairly large region and has four DOs. Only the DO Somontano, centered on the Roman town Barbastro, is located within the Pyrenees region. Situated in the foothills of the mountains, grapes grown in Somontano experience freezing temperatures during winter, scorching heat in summer, and strong winds. Historically, sturdy reds such as Garnacha Tinta and Tempranillo have done best, along with Moristel, but recently the regulatory body of the DO has allowed Cabernet Sauvignon and Merlot. Authorized white grapes include Viura, white Garnacha Blanca, Mazuelo, Parraleta, Alcañón (a native grape) and more recently Chardonnay. Somontano has not had a great reputation, and has been dominated by cooperatives that sell their wines in boxes in supermarkets.

Although a rather small viticultural district, wines from Somontano have a growing appeal for wine enthusiasts because of the dramatic improvements under way that are producing bright, fruit-filled wine styles. Carbonic maceration fermentation techniques are now commonly used in making the reds wines, which produce vibrant Beaujolais-like berry flavors. Somontano wines are uncommon in the United States. Our favorite is Señorío de Lazán *reserva* (Tempranillo, Cabernet Sauvignon, Moristel) produced by Bodega Pirineos. We enjoyed it at the Parador de Bielsa in the Monte Perdido National Park and found an excellent balance between fruit and tannins. We have also found Viña del Vero, produced by the Compañía Vitivinícola de Aragonesa (Tempranillo, Cabernet Sauvignon, Moristel), and Castillo de San Marcos (Tempranillo and Moristel), made by Bodegas Lalanne, to be serviceable everyday wines at budget prices. Other producers in Somontano that are said to be worth trying are Viñedos y Crianzas del Alto Aragón (Enate) and Bodegas Borruel (Barón de Eroles *reserva*).

Navarra

Located in the historical Basque region of Spain, Navarra is diverse in geography, extending from the Pyrenees to the Ebro River basin. The terrain is very mountainous in its northern portions, but the landscape becomes pastoral in the south. The climate is influenced by both the Mediterranean and the Atlantic, and the Pyrenees help to protect the area from France's Mistral winds.

During the post-phylloxera era, the predominant grape has been Garnacha Tinta which provides great concentrations of color, tannin, and alcohol. It has been used primarily for blending, and *viticultores* (growers) have been planting more Tempranillo to make longer-lived red wines more suitable to oak aging. Other red grapes include Graciano and Mazuelo (Carignan), together with the international Cabernet Sauvignon and Merlot. White grapes include Viura, Malvasía, Garnacha Blanca, and Chardonnay. Navarra has long been a producer of sturdy, fruity wines, red wines, and more recently its rosés were considered among the best in Spain. The current focus is on international-quality red wines, and many producers are rising to the challenge. Like the DO Somontano, there is some production of fruity Beaujolais-style wines fermented by carbonic maceration which are sold young without aging. Since 1981, the modernization of Navarran wines has been aided by Evena (*Estación de Viticultura y Enología de Navarra*) in Olite, a modern scientific enterprise with well-equipped laboratories that provides advice to all segments of the wine industry. Evena has helped to improve all aspects of wine making, including encouraging the planting of new varietals.

Bota Bags

Bota ("boot") bags—now sold to tourists in shops stuffed with tee-shirts and similar paraphernalia—are leather wine bags used originally by laborers. They are held high above the head at arm's length and squeezed with both hands. The wine should squirt into your mouth in a parabolic arc. The best *bota* bags are made from goat skin and pitch resin, which gives the wine a unique, Spanish flavor. Hilaire Belloc in his classic *The Pyrenees* praised the bota bag: "it is designed by Heaven to prevent any man abusing God's great gift of wine; for the goat's hair inside gives to wine so appalling a taste that a man will take of it exactly what is necessary for his needs."

There are numerous outstanding wineries today in Navarra, many of which are reasonably priced. Perhaps our favorite is Bodegas Guelbenzu in Cascante. Guelbenzu's Lautus (Tempranillo, Merlot, Garnacha Tinta, Cabernet Sauvignon) is aptly named since "lautus" is Latin for magnificent. The price of this upscale wine may be discouraging in the United States, where it seems to be marked up three times what we paid in a Pamplona wine shop. Guelbenzu also produces an excellent Evo (primarily Cabernet Sauvignon, blended with Tempranillo and Merlot), and a fine everyday

Guelbenzu Blue Label (Tempranillo, Cabernet Sauvignon, Merlot) that the winery describes as Evo's "younger brother" because it is essentially Evo with less aging. The Bodegas Julián Chivite is another excellent winery that pioneered modern techniques. Chivite's 125 Aniversario *gran reserva* (Tempranillo) is superlative, while its more budget-priced Gran Feudo (Tempranillo, Garnacha Tinta, Cabernet Sauvignon) is a fine everyday wine. Other wines that we have enjoyed from Navarra include Baron de Magaña *crianza* (Merlot, Cabernet Sauvignon, Tempranillo), Consecha Particular (Cabernet Sauvignon, Merlot, Tempranillo), Ochoa (Cabernet Sauvignon *crianza* and Tempranillo *crianza*), and Castillo de Monjardín. We found the wines from Bodega de Sarría to be disappointing, and received an unwarranted unwelcome greeting at its winery.

Rioja Alavesa

Wine has been made in the DOC Rioja since before the Roman occupation. For decades Rioja was known for its smooth, mellow Tempranillo reds aged in old wood that were available at reasonable prices. Today, however, wineries are increasingly making reds more in keeping with modern tastes. Aged in casks of new wood that impart a distinctive character, today's wines are potent, assertive, and well suited for laying down. Rioja is divided into three primary sub-regions: Rioja Alta, Rioja Alavesa, and Rioja Baja. Rioja contains at least 300 bodegas, many of which were founded since 1970. I include the Alavesa sub-region because it is north of the Ebro River which is traditionally Basque territory. Much of the production is *tintos jóvenes* (also called *vinos de cosecheros* or bulk wines) that are produced using semi-carbonic maceration and are favored beverages in Basque gastronomical societies. These are rarely exported. Alavesa also produces elegant reds primarily composed of Tempranillo, with small proportions of Garnacha Tinta, Mazuelo (Carignan), Graciano, and Cabernet Sauvignon. Red Riojas are classified at three levels of quality: *crianza* (vintage wines aged at least one year in *barricas* or barrels), *reserva* (richer wines, usually aged up to two years in oak), and *gran reservas* (the finest reds, aged two to five years in oak). Extended aging in Bordeaux-style 50-gallon barrels gives Rioja wines their distinctive soft, vanilla-scented character. Traditional white Riojas are produced in limited quantities using the Viura grape, sometimes blended with either Malvasía or Garnacha Blanca and aged for years in old American casks. Modern white Riojas are made in a fresh, dry style, while *reservas* can have a slight oaky nuttiness.

Since the 1980s, Contino and Granja Nuestra Señora de Remelluri have led the way toward estate-bottled and vineyard-designated wines, and now other wineries are following suit. We are particularly fond of the *reserva* made by Remelluri (90% Tempranillo with Graciano, Mazuelo, and Garnacha Tinta), and hand-carried several bottles back from Spain after enjoying a wonderful tour of the estate. Another favorite, which fortunately is imported into the United States, is Baron de Oña *reserva* (primarily Tempranillo). It is dark, complex, structured, and made in a modern style. We have also enjoyed wines from Bodegas Palacio, which is located at the outskirts of Laguardia, one of the most charming ancient towns in Rioja. Palacio's Glorioso *crianza* (Tempranillo) is a reasonably priced everyday wine available in the United States. We also purchased its Milflores at the winery, a *vino jóven* in a fruity Beaujolais style. The label suggested that it be consumed before the next harvest, so we enjoyed it a week later on a picnic next to a lighthouse overlooking the Bay of Biscay. For a splurge, Marqués de Riscal's Barón de Chirel *reserva* (similar proportions of Tempranillo and Cabernet Sauvignon) is outstanding. Another label worth seeking out is Bodegas Faustino Martínez *reserva*.

País Vasco (Basque Country)
The heartland of País Vasco is not generally known for its wines. This region produces indigenous slightly sour "green" red and white wines called *txacolí (chacolí)*, which an adventurous oenophile might sample. Made from the Ondarrubi Zuri (white) or Txacoliñ Zuri (red) grape and often sold in unlabelled bottles, it can be a quenching beverage to accompany grilled fish. There are now two DOs—Txacolí de Getaria and Bizkaiako Txakolina. We tried the white Uriondo from the DO Bizkaiako Txakolina. While an acquired taste, it was pleasantly refreshing and reminiscent of the ciders (*sidras*) of northern Spain.

Contemporary French Wines

FRANCE, OF COURSE, IS KNOWN THROUGHOUT THE WORLD for its excellent red and white wines. Pyrenean France is less acknowledged for fine wines, although regions such as Languedoc-Roussillon are rapidly improving and beginning to receive international recognition. Languedoc's red wines tend to be hearty and robust. They often have fragrant, peppery aromas and flavors, including strong herbal qualities of lavender, blackberries, and thyme. This region also makes wonderful sparkling wines (having invented what has become the traditional Champagne method) and some interesting dessert wines as well. This summary of the French Pyrenees region is limited to wines that are produced in the *départments* adjacent to the range, including Pyrénées Orientales (Roussillon), Aude in Languedoc, Ariège, Haute-Garonne, Hautes Pyrénées, and Pyrénées Atlantiques. Thus included are Minervois (including the parts of this AOC in Hérault) and Corbières in Languedoc, Roussillon, Madiran, Frontonnais, Jurançon, and Irouléguy. As with Spanish wines, I emphasize the reds both because of my personal preferences and in consideration of the relative qualities of the wines that are produced.

France's labeling rules can be very confusing and do not necessarily follow logical geographical boundaries. Like all European wine-producing countries, France has two general categories: unclassified table wine (*vin de table or vin ordinaire*) and quality wine. *Appellation d'origine controlée* (AOC) wines are the best in France, and AOC designation guarantees not only geographical origin but also minimum standards in the vineyard and winery. AOC wines come not just from a specified area, but from suitable vineyards within that area. Only recommended grape varieties can be used, planted to a certain density per acre and specified yields. An AOC wine must be made under specified conditions, and the finished wine must pass a tasting test and have a designated alcohol content. VDQS (*vin délimité qualité supérieure*) wines range from mid- to premium-quality and are found generally in smaller areas or areas that are in the process of establishing their reputations. VDQS is usually thought of as an interim step toward status as AOC, and has similar requirements.

French rules do not allow the label of any table wine to indicate its geographical origins. The category of *vin de pays*, or country wine, originated in 1973 and is a means of allowing areas that produce basic *vin de table* an opportunity to improve quality, price, and market. The category of *vin de pays* has some restrictions on geography, grape varieties, yields, and wine making requirements, but less so than traditional categories. Importantly for Languedoc-Roussillon, this category allows the use of nontraditional grape varieties such as Cabernet Sauvignon and Chardonnay. There are three tiers of *vin de pays*—regional, departmental, and zonal. For instance, *vin de pays d'Oc* refers specifically to the Languedoc region, many of whose inhabitants still speak Occitan (children today in Carcassonne learn their lessons half the day in French and half the day in Occitan). Hence the phrase, "d'Oc." *Vin de pays de l'Aude* refers specifically to wines from the *département* of Aude, which is within Languedoc. There are also wines from particular zones, for example, *vin de pays de la Cité de Carcassonne*.

Languedoc and Roussillon (the Midi)

The Midi is the hottest part of France, but its dry heat and the effect on vines is tempered by the Mistral and Tramontane winds. While the Midi includes four *départements*, only two—Aude in Languedoc and Pyrénées-Orientales (Roussillon)—can be said to be within the Pyrenees region. Hérault and Gard in Languedoc make increasingly excellent wines, but are too far east to be included here. There are at least ten AOC and five *vin de pays* appellations in Languedoc-Roussillon, and many other wines may be labeled by myriad sub-names that may apply to a wide area (Coteaux du Languedoc) or to an obscure and tiny patch of *terroir*.

Red wines are dominant, while sweet and dry styles of whites are growing in popularity and planting space. About 10 percent of Languedoc-Roussillon wine is now categorized as AOC (as compared to 30 percent in all of France) while another 10 percent is VDQS (as compared to 1 percent in all of France). Huge cooperatives are educating age-old producers, helping vintners produce wonderful wines at low cost. Experimentation abounds: the Beaujolais method of macerating grapes is increasingly used, lending fruitiness and quality to otherwise harsh wines. Eighty percent of the wine produced in Languedoc-Roussillon is *vin de pays*, most of which remains simple and light. The Carignan grape is probably the most common in the region and is found in most red wines, but the top labels add and are improved by blending Syrah, Grenache Noir, Cinsault, or Mourvèdre.

Many of our favorite wines from the French Pyrenees are from Minervois, a large AOC to the north and east of Carcassonne that includes parts of the *départements* of Aude and Hèrault. This region contained many of the first vines planted by Romans in this area, as evidenced by vestiges of wine cellars and countless amphorae that are unearthed there. The reds must include Syrah and Mourvèdre, and can be accompanied by Carignan, Grenache Noir, Cinsault, Terret Noir, Picpoul, or Lladoner Pelut. Minervois wines tend to be spicy and full of fruit, and are attractive both young or aged in wood. We have found the dark ruby-garnet and smooth wines from the town of La Livinière, which has recently been designated La Livinière-Minervois AOC, to be dependably excellent. *Vigneron* Giles Chabat's Clos de l'Escandil (Syrah, Mourvèdre, Grenache Noir) has incredible concentration and complexity, achieving a perfect balance. His terraced vineyard is situated above the village of La Livinière on the south-facing chalky slopes of "*Le Petit Causse*" in the foothills of the *Montagne Noire* where torrid daytime temperatures are tempered by cool nighttime winds blowing down from the mountaintop. All grapes in this low-yielding vineyard are hand-picked and grown organically. Château de Gourgazaud produces its Réserve Terroir du Petit Causse, another wonderful wine, in the same area. Other wines to seek out from La Livinière include Domaine Jacques (Maris Carte Noire), and Domaine Borie de Maurel (La Féline).

Several wines from Château d'Oupia are available in North America, and the more upscale Les Barons (Syrah, Mourvèdre, Carignan, Grenache Noir) is complex, well-rounded and full of spicy fruit. We visited Château La Grave in Badens and received a wonderful explanation about the winery from Tristan, the seven-year-old grandson of the *vigneron* who was busy with the *vendange*. La Grave's red Expression was excellent, and both of its Privilège labels (a *rouge* and a *blanc*) are superb. Other labels from Minervois that are worth trying include Château Tour Boisée (Marie Claude), Château Bonhomme (Les Alaternes), Domaine Cros (Tradition), and Château de Violet (Vielles Vignes en Vendanges d' Automne).

Corbières is our other favorite region in the French Pyrenees, just south of Minervois and within an easy drive from Carcassonne. The largest AOC in the Midi and located mostly in the *département* of Aude, 90 percent of its wines are reds produced from Carignan, Cinsault, Grenache Noir, Mourvèdre, Terret Noir, and Syrah. Its whites are produced from Clairette and Bourbulenc. We spent a delightful day exploring the wineries of Corbières. Châteaux La Voulte-Gasparets produces a Cuvée Réserve (Carignan, Grenache Noir, Syrah, Mourvèdre) that is rich and complex with much tannin. This wine is available in the United States, but La Voulte-Gasparets' outstanding Cuvée Romain Pauc is unlikely to be found outside of France. It is produced from vines planted in 1905, and no more than two bottles may be purchased at the winery. Another outstanding winery is the Cave Cooperative Embres at Castelmaure. Its Grand Cuvée is fantastic, and available at reasonable prices in North America. Castelmaure's Cuvée #3 (Syrah, Grenache Noir, Carignan) is probably not to be found outside of Corbières, and should be purchased at any opportunity. We also recommend the reds of Châteaux les Ollieux, which are exported to the United States. Finally, we found Cols des Vents - Max Savy to be a very drinkable bargain wine.

Fitou, located entirely within the geographical boundaries of Corbières, was granted its own AOC status for reds in 1948 before Corbières received its AOC designation. Fitou produces powerful, full-bodied red wines using a minimum 70 percent Carignan with Grenache Noir and Cinsault. We can recommend Domaine Les Mille Vignes' Cuvée de la Cadette, which is fruity and atypically somewhat light.

Within Roussillon are three AOCs: Collioure, Côtes du Roussillon, and Côtes du Roussillon Villages. Collioure is a tiny AOC next to the Spanish border that produces a very small amount of red wine from vineyards on the slopes of Mount Albères as they drop toward the sea. Wines from the established vineyards here have an excellent reputation, which we confirmed with a bottle of Cave de l'Abbé Rous "Vignes Rocheuses" (Grenache Noir, Syrah, Carignan) over a meal at the pleasant Château de Riell in Molitg-les Bains. Côtes du Roussillon is centered near the coast at Perpignan, extending inland to the foothills of the Pyrenees. Reds are produced from Carignan, Cinsault, Grenache Noir, and Mourvèdre. Côtes du Roussillon Villages is located in an area north of Perpignan in the Valley of Agly and includes only red wines. Domaine Piquemal unfiltered *rouge* has an excellent structure with both fruit and tannins that is sold at a very reasonable price in North America. We drank young bottles from two wineries whose dark, tannic complex wines that were excellent once they had breathed—Domaine de la Tour Boisée and Domaine de Bisconte. We also found Jean d'Estavel (Prestige) and Sarda-Malet to make good everyday wines.

Roussillon is also justly known for its *vins doux naturels* (VDN), which are made by adding grape brandy to partly fermented grapes which are then macerated for periods of several days to several weeks. The increased alcohol content releases color, aromatic substances, and tannins from the grape skins before pressing. The wine is then aged in wooden vats, resulting in a bouquet and flavor of stewed fruit, fresh figs, peaches, and candied cherries. They can age in the bottle very well, and after several years tones of roasted nuts and caramel emerge. *Vins doux naturels* received AOC status in 1936.

Banyuls is a *vin doux naturel* made from grapes grown in the Collioure AOC which uses a minimum of one-half Grenache Noir, along with Grenache Blanc or Gris, Macabeu, Malvoisie, and Muscat varieties. Production is centered in a small area just north of the Spanish border on the Mediterranean. We toured the Celliers des Templiers at Banyuls-sur-Mer and found each of the three sweet wines that we purchased to be appealing in its own way. The Vielle Réserve is semisweet, and is deep gold with honey tones. The Cuvée du 3ème Millénaire was sweeter, a deep red, and had hints of honey. The Rimatge was sweet with pronounced yet smooth tannins and spicy aromas of cinnamon, cherries, and blackberries.

Rivesaltes is a *vin doux naturel* that is made from Grenache Noir, Macabeo, Malvoisie and Muscat. We enjoyed a wonderful bottle of Rivesaltes produced by Domaine Força-Réal in Côtes du Roussillon. Its deliciously rich port-like Hors d'Age Villa Passant is aged in oak and has caramel and coffee flavors among the various fruit tones. We also tried Domaine Piquemal's Muscat de Rivesaltes (entirely Muscat), which seemed a fair dessert wine. *Vins doux naturels* are largely unknown in the United States, and we recommend trying any of these excellent wines.

Blanquette de Limoux AOC received an appellation in 1938. Now called Crémant de Limoux, these sparkling wines are produced in a hilly region near Limoux southwest of Carcassonne where monks invented the *méthode champenoise* in the sixteenth century. The sparkling wines today are made from a minimum 90 percent Mauzac Blanc, blended with Chenin Blanc and Chardonnay. "Blanquette" refers to a white fungus that develops under the leaves of Mauzac Blanc grapes. We have enjoyed bottles of four producers and found each to be exquisite and refreshing: Grand Cuvée de Antech; Domaine J. Laurens Blanc de Blancs Brut, Tête de Cuvée; Saint-Hilaire Blanc de Blancs Brut; and Maison Vergennes Le Berceau. These effervescent wines are increasingly available in the United States and offer outstanding values.

Wines labeled *vin de pays* from the Midi represent many of the interesting new-wave wines being produced there. Many include grape varieties or *cépages* that are nontraditional, and some wines are made from a single grape. We have experimented with dozens of *vin de pays* wines in both France and the United States with mixed results. Many wines such as the La Bastide Merlot are thin and tart. Others such as the very dark Domaine Coussergues Cuvée Charles VIII (Syrah, Cabernet Sauvignon and Merlot) seemed to be merely adequate. Still others such as Les Jamelles Syrah are very pleasing. This overview of the hundreds if not thousands of wines from Languedoc-Roussillon cannot possibly be complete, and the best course would be to try as many as you can. You will surely find labels and styles that please.

The Southwest

The grape varieties of the Southwest are from a dim, almost mythical past and often have difficult Basque names. The local *vignerons* produce wines with these grapes that taste like no others. This region is more exposed to the climate of the Atlantic than the Mediterranean, having cooler summers than Languedoc-Roussillon and generally more rainfall. This results in wines that have lower alcohol content and which can be complex with varied flavors.

Madiran AOC is located in the cooling hills of Gascony. The principal grape is the Tannat, which can be blended with Cabernet Sauvignon and Cabernet Franc to complement and soften its tougher attributes. Madiran was one of the areas worst affected by phylloxera, and whose recovery was long delayed because the farmers could not afford to replant. After World War II, Madiran was reduced to less than 20 acres of vines. When the production of a wine is so rare so as to be known only to a few connoisseurs and the local growers, the French call it a *"confidentiel"* wine. Despite its rarity, the French government granted Madiran full AOC status in 1948.

Madiran is a complex, tannic red wine that seem to inspire love or hatred. It has excellent aging ability, and most vintages should not be drunk before five years. We drank a bottle of Odé d'Aydie (Tannat and Cabernet Sauvignon) from Château d'Aydie, a winery that produces what many think of one of the best Madirans. It had a flinty, metallic character without much fruit and plenty of tannin. It was interesting, and cheered a surprisingly ordinary luncheon at Michel Guérard's Michelin three-star restaurant in Eugénie-les-Bains. We found that whatever imperfections there may have been in the wine, they were less so than a vastly over-rated and pretentious meal at a glorified health spa. Subsequently we discovered a bottle of Odé d'Aydie in a wine shop in St. Jean-Pied-de-Port and learned that Guérard had marked the price up by a factor of almost five. A bottle of Domaine Capmartin's Cuvée de Couvent (entirely Tannat), which is available in the United States, seemed in many ways to be similar. The deeply rich and tannic wine had an earthy, mineral quality that while intriguing is not something that we would drink regularly.

Jurançon AOC was registered in 1936 and has been made for over a thousand years. Jurançon *crus* were certified by the Navarra Parliament in the seventeenth century when this region was part of Navarra. It is an increasingly rare but outstanding sweet white wine that is produced to the southwest of Pau, Pyrénées Atlantiques. The vineyards are comprised of small parcels located in hilly terrain with an average elevation of 900 feet. In order to utilize the best land—which is often very steep—the vines can be planted in terraces sometimes taking the shape of an amphitheater. Béarn enjoys a fine Indian summer and the south wind permits *"le passerillage"* or an over-ripening of the grapes to concentrate sugar. The authorized grapes are local to the region. Gros Manseng, Petit Manseng, and Courbu produce full-bodied, spicy wines with an aroma of lemon and orange and a golden color. The best quality sweet wines are produced from Petit Manseng grapes and have a capacity to age well. In addition to sweet Jurançon, the area produces a dry Jurançon *sec* that is a less interesting version of the outstanding sweet wine. Several are available in North America. We recommend Domaine Larredya, located in La Chapelle Rousse, whose Jurançon is buttery with tones of apricot and pineapple. While the French often drink these wines as aperitifs, for American tastes these may be more suitable as dessert wines, similar to late harvest wines.

Côte Frontonnais AOC is an appellation located north of Toulouse on the east bank of the Garonne River in Haute-Garonne. It produces some of the Southwest's most enjoyable wines at reasonable prices, which are consumed in great quantities in Toulouse. The most abundant grape used is negrette, a variety that the Knights Templar brought to the Southwest after discovering it in Cyprus during the Crusades. Negrette can be blended with a number of other grapes, including Cabernet Sauvignon, Cabernet Franc, Cinsault, Malbec, Merlot, Syrah, and Gamay. We had a Château Cahuzac produced by Viticulteurs Fabas that was excellent.

Irouléguy wines can be red, white, or rosé and are primarily of local interest in the Basque country, especially the foothills of the Pyrenees in the Valley of the Nive. The reds are made from Tannat, Fer, Cabernet Sauvignon, and Cabernet Franc. The whites are made from Gros Manseng, Petit Manseng, Courbu, Lauzat, Baroque, Sauvignon, and Sémillon. During a visit to Les Vignerons du Pays Basque cooperative in Saint Étienne-de-Baigorry, we tasted two rosés and three rouges, and most were marginally drinkable. Only the Domaine Mignaberry, which was complex and full of tannins, evoked any real interest. There may be better examples of these wines in the French Basque country, but they are difficult to find in North America.

APPETIZERS

Appetizers

Tomato Bread

(Pa amb Tomaquet)

(Catalonia)

WHEN THE FIRST TOMATOES WERE INTRODUCED to Europe in the sixteenth century, the Spanish readily adopted them into their diets as they did with so many other introductions from the New World. Before the end of the sixteenth century, the chef at Spain's royal court had combined tomatoes with olive oil and onions to make the first tomato sauce. The concoction was enthusiastically received by the court which lead to its wide adoption in Iberia.

This simple Catalan recipe is a delicious snack, commonly eaten throughout northern Spain with slices of regional cheese, cured sausage, or mountain ham. In L'Escala, along the coast, tomato bread is preferred with preserved sardines or anchovies. The popularity of this particular combination has spread to other areas of northern Spain as well.

IF USING A LONG LOAF OR BAGUETTE, slice bread in half, lengthwise. For a round loaf, cut into ½-inch slices. Toast both sides of bread until surface is firm and slightly browned. If using a broiler, toast for 2 to 3 minutes on first side, and 1 to 2 minutes on the second side.

Cut garlic clove in half and rub cut surface over both sides of toasted bread. Cut tomato in half and rub cut surface over both sides of bread, pressing, to allow juices to soak in. Drip or drizzle a few drops of olive oil over the bread, and finish with a sprinkling of salt to taste.

> 1 loaf country bread, such as a French baguette, or a large round loaf
> 1 to 2 large cloves garlic
> 1 large very ripe tomato
> 3 tablespoons extra-virgin olive oil
> Salt
>
> MAKES 10 APPETIZER SERVINGS

If using a halved long loaf, cut into 1½ to 2-inch-wide slices before serving.

Fresh Tomato and Garlic Sauce

(Catalonia, northern Spain)

THIS LIGHT UNCOOKED SAUCE is the essence of Catalan tomato bread, *Pa Amb Tomaquet*, in a bowl. It provides the same fresh flavors of ripe tomato, garlic, and olive oil, without the squeezing, pressing, and dribbling at the table. We enjoyed a small bowl of this excellent sauce with a basket of fresh bread, before our dinner at the *Parador de Bielsa*, located in the heart of the Pyrenees mountains. The following morning at breakfast, we were delighted to find a fresh batch on the buffet table, and spooned it liberally on our eggs and toast.

THE TOMATOES CAN BE BLANCHED in hot water for 30 seconds, or roasted over a fire or in an oven broiler, to remove the skin. If roasting, when the skin is slightly blackened on all sides, remove the tomato from the heat and peel skin off. Chop tomato in large pieces and remove seeds.

Place tomatoes, garlic, olive oil, and salt in a blender and quickly purée. Mixing too long will break down the tomato cells and the mixture will take on a curdled appearance. Alternatively, push tomatoes and garlic through a food mill and blend in a processor for a few seconds to finish. Serve immediately or let flavors combine for an hour at room temperature.

Spoon over fresh crusty bread or as a sauce for fish or chicken.

4 fresh ripe tomatoes

2 to 3 medium cloves garlic

1 to 2 tablespoons olive oil

1/4 teaspoon salt, or to taste

MAKES 1½ TO 2 CUPS

Tomatoes Roasted with Garlic and Herbs

(southwest France)

THE FIRST TOMATOES INTRODUCED into Europe in the sixteenth century were lumpy and red. The Spanish immediately found ways to use this new kitchen ingredient. The French, however, did not take to tomatoes until Napoleon III's Empress Eugénie, daughter of a Spanish nobleman, introduced Spanish tomato dishes into France in the 1850s. The French called tomatoes *pomme d'amour*, or love apples. This was derived apparently from a mispronunciation of *pomme des Mours* (eggplant, or apples of the Moors), a favorite Moorish vegetable that is from the same family (Solanaceae) as tomatoes.

Today roasted and dried tomatoes, such as the following dish, are standard food items throughout the Mediterranean regions of Spain, France, and Italy.

PREHEAT OVEN TO 300° F.

Mix minced or crushed garlic and olive oil in a small bowl. Add basil or desired herb(s).

Slice tomatoes in half, lengthwise. You may press or scoop out seeds, but it isn't necessary. Place tomato halves, cut side up, on a baking sheet. Spoon a bit of the oil, garlic, and herb mixture over each tomato. Sprinkle salt lightly over tomatoes.

6 to 8 cloves garlic, minced or
    crushed through a garlic press
1/4 cup or more olive oil
1 tablespoon chopped fresh basil,
    or thyme, oregano, or rosemary
18 to 20 firm plum tomatoes
Salt

MAKES 6 TO 8 SERVINGS

Place baking sheet in oven for 2 to 3 hours. Check after 2 hours. Tomatoes are done when they have collapsed to about half their original height, or slightly less. They should still be moist and somewhat plump. The tomatoes will shrink a little more as they cool. Do not allow to roast dry.

Continued

Serve alone as an appetizer, warm or cold with fresh bread, or paired with cheese or anchovies.

•┄•

The strong aroma of roasting garlic will fill your house, as these gestate in the oven.

Although the number of tomatoes may appear to be more than you think you will need or anyone can eat, I have learned through experience that three pieces per person is somehow never enough. A single person can inhale four of these little morsels, effortlessly.

Anchovy-Olive Spread
(Garum/Anchoïade/Tapenade)

GARUM IS A FISH SAUCE that the ancient Romans used as a flavoring much like salt. Extremely pungent, it was made by fermenting fish in a brine solution for several days in the sun. In his *Natural History*, Pliny describes this seemingly vile concoction as "Consisting of the guts of fish and the other parts that would otherwise be considered refuse; these are soaked in salt, so that *garum* is really liquor from the putrefaction of these matters." The Romans combined the resulting liquid with various other flavorings such as oil, pepper, wine, and spices. *Garum* is probably the progenitor of *anchoïade* and *tapenade*.

Anchoïade, from Roussillon and Provence, is made from anchovies, preferably the whole fish rather than fillets, and black olives. *Tapenade* is similar to *anchoïade*, but also includes capers (called *tapena* in Provençal). While *tapenade* seems to be an ancient concoction harkening back to the Romans, it was invented only about a century ago at the Maison Dorée.

A simple vegetable side dish can be created with this spread by serving it atop ripe summer tomatoes, roasted potatoes, or eggplant.

SOAK ANCHOVIES in a bowl of water for 1 or 2 hours to remove some of the salt. Dry on paper towels before using. Mix together anchovies, olives, garlic, oil, and lemon juice in a food processor or blender, or by hand with a mortar and pestle. Blend or mix into a well combined paste. Place in a serving bowl.

Spread this over slices of toasted bread or crackers. If desired, top each portion with a slice of manchego cheese, ripe tomato, or both.

---

1 can (2 ounces) anchovy fillets
   packed in oil
16 oil-cured or brine-cured black
   olives, pitted
2 cloves garlic, minced
3 tablespoons extra-virgin olive oil
1 tablespoon lemon juice

MAKES 1½ TO 2 CUPS

Continued

In its simplest form, this spread contains only anchovies, garlic, olive oil, and lemon juice or vinegar.

Other items that both French and Spanish cooks may add to the basic list of ingredients include a few drops of Armagnac, pimientos, capers, tomato paste, egg yolk, mustard, cumin, or fresh herbs, such as thyme, fennel, bay leaves, mint, and rosemary.

Catalan Roasted Vegetable Spread/Pâté (Escalivada/Escalibada)

THIS IS A VERY EASY DISH that can be cooked on an open fire or in the oven. The name is derived from the Catalan word *escalivar*, which means to cook or roast on hot cinders. Technically, a true *escalivada* is a collection of vegetables, usually sweet peppers, eggplant, and onions roasted on coals or embers. Although this is most often eaten as an appetizer, it can also be served as a side dish.

ROAST EGGPLANT (skin side to heat) and red and green peppers over a fire or in an oven broiler. Turn occasionally to blister and blacken all skin of peppers and eggplant. Remove peppers and eggplant and place in a bowl. Cover bowl with a plate or foil to allow vegetables to "sweat" for 10 to 15 minutes. Remove peppers and peel off their skins. Slice peppers open and remove stems and seeds. Cut into large pieces. Remove the skin from the eggplant in the same way and cut into chunks.

The tomato can be roasted similarly to remove the skin. When the skin is slightly blackened on all sides, remove the tomato from the heat and peel skin off. Chop tomato in large pieces and remove seeds.

1 small regular eggplant, cut in half lengthwise
2 red bell peppers
1 green bell pepper
1 large tomato
1 medium onion, cut in half
3 to 6 whole cloves garlic
12 anchovy fillets, cut into ¹/₄-inch sections
Salt and pepper

MAKES 4 OR MORE CUPS

The onion and garlic can also be roasted with the other vegetables, but place these farther away from the heat source to let the onion cook through slowly and to keep the garlic from burning. When onion and garlic are softened, remove parchment and trim ends. Slice the onion.

Continued

Place peppers, eggplant, onion, garlic, tomato, and anchovy fillet pieces in a food processor. Process in short bursts until it is the consistency of coarse relish. Add salt and pepper to taste. Refrigerate for several hours to allow flavors to combine.

In this recipe, I chose to process the *escalivada* vegetables into a spread. It is, however, more traditional to thinly slice these vegetables after they have been roasted, and layer or toss them together to create a roasted vegetable salad.

A bit of balsamic vinegar drizzled over the sliced version before serving, brightens the sweetness of the vegetables.

With crusty bread, this can be a fresh, flavorful appetizer, by itself or paired with other appetizer items such as the cod fritters or croquettes. *Escalivada* is a good accompaniment to fish or chicken, and excellent when layered with meats or other vegetables (carrots, peas, asparagus) to create a terrine.

Piperade

PIPERADE IS A BASQUE SPECIALTY, a stunning sauté of red, green, and yellow bell peppers scrambled with eggs fortified with chili pepper. While I have substituted cayenne, the Basques actually use their beloved *piment d'Espelette* or Espelette pepper. In southwestern France this chili pepper is such a cultural and culinary icon that it gained controlled-name status in 1999, much like Minervois wines or Ossau Iraty cheese from ewes in Béarn and the Basque country. Since World War II, enough were grown for Espelette peppers to be threaded into braids or tresses and hung to dry on buildings, much like ristras in the American Southwest. In 1967, the village of Espelette established the Celebration of Peppers, which is held the last Sunday in October.

PLACE 3 TABLESPOONS OIL in a skillet over low heat. Add onions and peppers and cook, stirring occasionally until onions are limp, approximately 15 minutes. Stir in garlic, cayenne, and basil. Add tomatoes and continue to cook until most of the liquid has evaporated and tomato pieces begin to break down. Mix in parsley, and season with salt and pepper to taste.

Pour in beaten eggs, and stir once while eggs are still liquid. Cook until eggs are just set and tender.

Continued

---

4 tablespoons olive oil

2 medium or 1 large onion, thinly sliced

3 green and/or red bell peppers, sliced in strips

2 cloves garlic, minced

1/2 to 1 teaspoon cayenne or *piment d'Espelette*

1 tablespoon chopped fresh basil, or 1/2 teaspoon dried (optional)

4 medium tomatoes, chopped

1 tablespoon chopped fresh parsley

Salt and pepper

6 eggs, beaten

4 slices ham

MAKES 4 SERVINGS

While eggs are cooking, pour remaining 1 tablespoon of oil into a separate pan set over medium heat. Fry ham on both sides.

Accompany each serving of piperade with a slice of ham.

•••

In Béarn, a slice of Bayonne ham is the classic partner served with piperade. If you don't feel like ham, slices of bread fried in oil and garlic or toasted and coated with a thin layer of anchovy paste are other good partners.

Potato and Chorizo Omelet

(Tortilla de Patatas con Chorizo)

THIS CLASSIC DISH IS WILDLY POPULAR throughout Spain but does not extend deep into antiquity because one of its main ingredients—potatoes—did not arrive in Europe before the sixteenth century when *conquistadors* brought it back from the Peruvian highlands. Tortilla always means omelet in Spain (where Mexican corn tortillas are rare), and unless you specify a simple egg-only *tortilla francesa* (French omelet) a tortilla will always be round with a cake-like appearance. The *tortilla española* or *tortilla de patatas* can be considered a heartier cousin to the Italian frittata.

The *tortilla de cartujana*, invented by Carthusian monks, is said to have been the first omelet. It consisted of eggs and a bit of cream, and was introduced to France by Napoleon's soldiers. A Spanish chef for the Hapsburgs, Francisco Martínez Montiño, is credited with having invented the *tortilla de agua*, eggs fried in oil and a bit of water, which was later renamed *tortilla francesa*. He cooked it in the court of King Philip III in the early seventeenth century. The *tortilla española* is considerably more recent and was not invented until well into the nineteenth century. It is one of the national dishes of Spain and there are few Spanish bars that do not serve a *tortilla española* as a tapa, which for a light meal goes well with a green salad and glass of wine. It is often made into a sandwich or taken on picnics. It can be served hot or cold.

IN A 9-INCH SKILLET, which will be the size of your omelet, heat a tablespoon of oil over medium-low heat and add onions and sauté for several minutes until they are soft and begin to darken. Remove onions and set aside.

Adding enough oil to coat the skillet, fry a layer of potato slices on both

---

Olive oil for frying

1 small onion, finely chopped or in thin slices

4 medium potatoes, sliced ⅛ inch thick

Salt and pepper

5 eggs

4 ounces Spanish-style chorizo, finely diced

MAKES 8 APPETIZER SERVINGS

---

sides. Sprinkle a small pinch of salt and pepper over the potatoes, if desired, keeping in mind that the chorizo will add some salt to this dish. Place cooked potatoes aside on paper towels to absorb excess oil. Repeat this process for remaining potatoes. Alternatively, it may be less authentic, but easier to cook potatoes by placing the raw slices in a single layer on an oiled baking sheet. Place the sheet of potatoes in a 350°F oven for about 20 minutes. Flip potatoes over and bake for 10 to 20 minutes more depending on when they become fork-tender.

In a bowl, beat the eggs, add the cooked onions and chorizo while mixing. Add a pinch of salt if desired. Fold in potatoes and let sit for 10 minutes.

Remove any food particles remaining in the skillet. Add enough oil to skillet to generously coat the bottom and sides. Reheat pan over medium-high heat. When oil is hot quickly pour in entire potato and egg mixture. Press potatoes down with spatula to even out the layers, and cover. Reduce heat to medium-low to prevent scorching. Shake frequently to keep tortilla omelet from sticking. When bottom is browned, slide the tortilla onto a large plate, place another plate on top of tortilla and invert them, so the browned side is facing up. Add enough oil to the skillet to coat all sides. Slide the uncooked side of the tortilla on to the bottom of the pan and cook, uncovered, until browned.

Slide finished tortilla onto a large plate. Cut into wedges or 1 to 2-inch squares for tapas or *pinchos*. The center should be slightly moist. Serve warm or at room temperature.

The *tortilla española* normally consists of potatoes, onions, and eggs.

The chorizo I include in this recipe is the large, ready-to-eat, Spanish-style sausage, which should not be mistaken for the small, raw, Mexican or Latin American-style, link sausages.

Other items such as bacon, mushrooms, or roasted sweet peppers, will also lend greater flavor and color to your tortilla.

Salt Cod and Potato Fritters
(Bunyols de Bàcalla or Buñuelos de Bacalao)

THIS BASQUE RECIPE extends across the Atlantic Ocean to North America. We visited the historic town of Twillingate in northern Newfoundland a few years ago during a time when commercial cod fishing was not allowed because the fish stocks were too low. Twillingate's proud fishermen sought another means of sustenance, and during the summer entertained tourists in the town hall with a repertory theater of local songs, fisherman's stories, and "Newfie" humor. Their wives cooked and served a simple and satisfying supper that included as the main course cod and potato fritters very similar to this recipe. Historians say that Basques first began to fish the rich cod grounds near Newfoundland perhaps as early as the fifteenth century. Nearby at Red Bay, Labrador, archaeologists have discovered the remains of a sixteenth-century Basque whaling station. The western Newfoundland town, Port aux Basques, was named in the 1500s by Basque fishermen and used as a haven in storms and a base for fishing and exploration. Some local fishermen believe that Basques were plying the waters off Newfoundland as far back as the Roman era.

This recipe is based on the golden crusted, creamy centered, cod-potato balls we enjoyed as tapas in several areas of northern Spain.

REMOVE SALT FROM COD by soaking for at least 2 days, changing the water about 3 times a day. Cut cod into more manageable pieces and place in a saucepan with enough water to cover; add a bay leaf, if desired. On medium heat, bring

---

1 pound salt cod

1 bay leaf (optional)

3 medium potatoes (1 to 1½ pounds), quartered

3 tablespoons olive oil

2 cloves garlic, minced

1 cup whole milk

⅓ cup flour

2 eggs, separated

3 sprigs or 2 tablespoons minced fresh parsley

Salt and pepper

2 or more cups oil for frying

MAKES 5½ TO 6 CUPS OR
20 TO 30 FRITTERS

---

to boiling point. Cover, remove from heat, and set aside to steep for approximately 10 minutes. Remove cod pieces from water and set aside to let drain.

Place quartered potatoes in hot cod water, bring to a boil and cook potatoes till fork-tender. Drain and remove potatoes.

In a skillet, heat 1 tablespoon olive oil over medium-low heat, add minced garlic, and sauté for 1 to 2 minutes. Do not allow to brown. Remove and set aside.

In a saucepan, bring milk with remaining 2 tablespoons olive oil to a boil. Turn off heat and quickly whisk in flour to prevent lumps from forming. Mixture should resemble a thick paste. Whisk yolks into hot mixture.

Flake and shred cod in a food processor or with a fork. Place in a bowl with potatoes, garlic, and parsley. Mash contents together, add milk and yolk batter and continue to mix. Salt and pepper to taste.

Place egg whites in a mixing bowl and beat until stiff or soft peaks form. Gently mix ⅓ of whites into cod-potato mixture to lighten it before folding the rest of the egg whites into the mixture.

Pour enough oil into a skillet or fryer to fill it to a depth of at least a ½ inch. Heat oil to 375°F. on medium-high heat. Cod-potato mixture should be thick enough to shape. If not, place in refrigerator to chill slightly. Using tablespoon-size portions, roll cod-potato mixture into balls or small thick patties, and fry in batches, being careful not to lower the oil temperature by placing too many cod balls in at once. Turn once to brown on all sides. Remove and drain on paper towels.

Serve with *Allioli* (page 175) for dipping or pair with *Sardinas* (page 76).

Due to the time needed to soak the cod, and several steps involved, this is not a spur-of-the-moment dish. However, all the steps through combining the cod and potato mixtures can be done a day ahead. Just prior to forming and frying the fritters, whip the egg whites and fold into the cod-potato mixture.

For a richer taste, substitute half-and-half or cream for half the milk.

Pan-Fried Sardines

(Sardinas Fritas)

FOR MILLENNIA, fishermen have netted shoals of shimmering silvery fish off the coasts of Sardinia, from which sardines take their name. The strong flavor of this fleshy fish appeals to the Mediterranean palate. Both sardines and anchovies are abundant during summer along the Costa Brava of Spain and the Côte Vermeille of France. In the ancient trading port of Collioure, France, we enjoyed grilled fresh sardines at the café-bar Les Templiers on the rue Camille Pelletan. Amidst paintings by Matisse and Picasso and views of lateen-rigged fishing boats in the harbor, this sumptuous yet simple fare was a delight. However, just south of Collioure, on Spain's Costa Brava, the traditional Catalan dish is fried anchovies, *anxoves fregides*, rather than sardines.

BEAT EGG in a medium to large bowl. Place flour in a wide dish or pan for dredging. Place sardines first in the egg and then dredge in flour. Set them aside.

Heat olive oil in a large skillet over medium heat. Add garlic and sauté until lightly browned. Remove garlic. Increase heat to medium-high and place sardines in hot skillet. Fry until brown and crisp on both sides. Remove and place on paper towels to drain.

1 egg

4 to 6 tablespoons flour for dredging

2 dozen fresh sardines, 4 to 5 inches long, cleaned (instructions on cleaning, page 78)

¼ cup oil

3 cloves garlic, minced or crushed

SAUCE:

Remove pits from olives. Using a mortar and pestle or food processor, mash or purée the olive meat, anchovy fillets, and garlic. Add mixture to sour cream, blending well.

Serve fried sardines with the sauce.

.•..•..•..•..•..•..•..•..•..•..•..•..•..•..•.

Sauce:

4 kalamata or oil-cured black olives

3 anchovy fillets

2 cloves garlic, chopped or crushed

4 to 5 tablespoons sour cream

MAKES 4 APPETIZER SERVINGS

In this recipe, the dipping sauce is essentially a *garum* or *tapenade* with the addition of sour cream to provide a creamy base to soften the pungency of the other ingredients in the sauce.

Fresh Marinated Anchovies or
Sardines (Boquerones en Vinagreta)

SARDINES AND ANCHOVIES (*boquerones* in Spanish) are relatives of herrings and have been prominent in Mediterranean diets since time immemorial. Anchovies are somewhat smaller than sardines, and pass through the Bay of Biscay in early fall en route to Norway where they fatten up before returning each spring. Both fishes are abundant during summer along the Mediterranean coasts of southern France and northern Spain. Marinating sardines in vinegar and/or wine is a traditional method of preparing the strong flavored fish, and can also be used with anchovies, which Miramar Torres describes as being "plump, sweet and subtle in taste." In southwest France, the seaside town of Collioure is well known for its excellent seafood. Similarly, along the Costa Brava of Spain, the fishing port town of L'Escala is famous its *boquerones* and fresh seafood.

TO CLEAN ANCHOVIES/SARDINES: Cut off heads. Holding each fish belly up, pierce the skin and run the knife along the belly to open body cavity. Place opening under a thin stream of water, allowing the water to help push organs out. Pull all contents out. Continue to rinse under water stream, lightly rubbing away any dark lining that might remain. Drain and place in a bowl or dish.

Mix together vinegar, bay leaf, garlic, onion, salt, and parsley. Pour marinade over fish to cover. Allow to marinate at least overnight in refrigerator. Can be marinated for several days.

To serve, remove and drain fish. Lightly pat dry with paper towels. Place on a platter and serve.

1 pound fresh anchovies or sardines
(about 30 at 3 inches long)

1 cup white wine vinegar

1 bay leaf, crumbled

2 cloves garlic, crushed

1 small onion, thinly sliced

$^{1}/_{4}$ to $^{1}/_{2}$ teaspoon salt

1 sprig or tablespoon fresh parsley, chopped

MAKES 4 TO 6 SERVINGS

Garlic Squid

(Chipirones al Ajillo)

SQUID AND CUTTLEFISH ARE CEPHALOPODS, a class of mollusk. Both have been renowned for excellent eating since classical Greek times. Fried squid was mentioned as far back as the fifth century B.C. in a play by Aristophanes. Historically cheap, they are sometimes called "poor man's lobster." The common squid of Europe—the *calamar* or *Loligo vulgaris*—has a long body 12 to 20 inches in length and a pouch that is suitable for stuffing. The young, smaller squid are called *chipirones* throughout the Pyrenean region, and have a more tender texture than the larger adults. Cuttlefish (*Sepia officianalis*) are about 12 inches long and have squatter, flattened bodies. They also tend to have thicker meat. Recipes for squid and cuttlefish can be found in the fourteenth-century Catalan cookbook *Libre de Sent Soví*.

The following is a simple, classic, and extremely popular preparation for chipirones.

PLACE SKILLET OR PAN over medium heat and add olive oil, garlic, and pepper flakes. Sauté 1 minute. Do not let garlic brown. Make sure squid are patted dry with paper towels. Increase heat to medium-high, immediately adding the squid. Sauté quickly until the squid are just cooked and their flesh looks opaque, 1 to 3 minutes depending on size and thickness of the individual pieces. Sprinkle with salt, top with minced parsley and serve hot.

3 tablespoons olive oil

3 cloves garlic, minced

1/2 teaspoon red pepper flakes

1/2 pound small squid (*chipirones*), or larger squid, cleaned and cut in bite-size pieces

Sea salt

1 tablespoon minced fresh parsley

MAKES 2 APPETIZER SERVINGS

Shrimp prepared in this way is an equally popular tapa in Spain, and can easily be substituted for squid in this recipe.

Fish Terrine

(Pastel de Pescado)

THIS BASQUE DISH is essentially a fish pâté or pudding, called *budíns* in Spain. The food writer Pepita Aris notes that there was a "budin-mania" when *la nueva cocina vasca* became popular in the late 1970s and early 1980s. This culinary movement eschewed long and difficult recipes and focused instead on simple cookery using local ingredients. Inspired by *la nouvelle cuisine* in France, it readily took root in the Basque Country partly due to this region's abundant use of butter and cream, which is unique in Spain. This recipe is based on one by Karlos Arguiñano, talented chef and head of the Academia de Cocina in Zarautz, Spain. Serving this with the "salsa rosa" or the tartar sauce included here, while not part of the ancient recipe, is a contemporary Basque addition.

PREHEAT OVEN TO 350°F.

Wash and coarsely chop leeks or onions. Over medium heat, add oil to a skillet and sauté leeks for several minutes, until they are no longer opaque. Add garlic and sauté for another minute. Pour in wine and reduce heat slightly to allow liquid to simmer. Stir occasionally until liquid is nearly gone. Place leeks in a food processor or blender and process to a coarse purée.

Chop cooked shrimp into large dice. Flake poached fish with a fork. In a large bowl mix together tomato purée, cream, leeks, and fish. Taste and add salt and pepper, if desired. Stir in whole eggs and yolks. Add shrimp.

Terrine:

3 to 4 medium leeks or 2 medium onions

Olive oil

2 cloves garlic, minced

1/2 cup white wine

1/2 pound shrimp, lightly cooked (poached)

2 pounds hake or similar white fleshed fish, poached

1 cup tomato purée

1 cup heavy cream

Salt and pepper (optional)

3 whole eggs

2 eggs, separated

1/4 cup dry bread crumbs

In a separate bowl, beat egg whites until stiff peaks form, and fold into fish mixture, adding one-third or half of the whites at a time.

Grease a baking pan or mold and scatter or press bread crumbs along bottom. Pour fish mixture over bread crumbs. Bake in a hot water bath or *bain marie* for 40 minutes. Remove from oven and let sit for 5 to 10 minutes. Slide a knife along the sides to loosen terrine from mold. Place a plate on top and invert to coax the preparation to fall away from the mold.

Sauce:
¼ cup mayonnaise
¼ cup ketchup
2 tablespoons mustard
Pinch of *piment d'Espelette*, or cayenne powder
1 tablespoon Armagnac or brandy

MAKES 6 TO 8 SERVINGS

SAUCE:
Whisk mayonnaise, adding ketchup and mustard until all ingredients are blended. Stir in the *piment d'Espelette* and Armagnac or brandy. Spoon a bit of sauce over each serving of fish terrine.

•—•

While the shrimp adds texture and interest to the final terrine, for those allergic to shrimp, this can be omitted without any loss of flavor.

When placing the filled mold into the hot water bath in the oven, I find it is easiest and safest to first place the empty outer pan onto the oven rack, then place the filled mold into the pan, and lastly, carefully pour hot water into the outer pan until it reaches about halfway up the sides of the fish mold.

On occasion, to avoid the extra steps of preparing the mold and the water bath, I have baked the terrine mixture in a pie crust, at the same oven temperature, until the crust is golden and the center is no longer liquid.

Mushrooms with Roquefort and Banyuls

THIS RECIPE EMPLOYS BANYULS, a *vin doux naturel* from the Côte Vermeille, in the portion of Languedoc-Rousillon just north of the Spanish border on the Mediterranean. In making this sweet wine, grape brandy is added to the partly fermented grapes, which increases the alcohol content and stops fermentation to preserve part of the natural fruit sugar. Banyuls is aged in wooden vats, and the final product is a wonderful mélange of roasted nut and subtle fruit flavors such as cherries, figs, blackberries, and peaches. The Grenache and other grapes that comprise Banyuls are grown on lovely steep hills above the rocky bays of blue sea and beaches of this Catalan coast. The Celliers des Templiers in picturesque Banyuls-sur-Mer offers tours that allow visitors to sample many different versions of this distinctive beverage. The nearby fishing village of Collioure is the jewel of the Côte Vermeille, and for centuries has impressed travelers and artists with its simple beauty. This dish features the tasty marriage of the incomparable sweet Banyuls wine and a powerful cheese in a perfect balancing act.

PREHEAT OVEN TO 350° F. Prepare the individual bread loaves by cutting the top off each roll, creating a 2 to 3-inch hole at the top. Make a bowl by partially hollowing out the center of each roll (excess bread can be saved and dried for bread crumbs). Do not make walls or bottoms of bread bowls too thin or they will melt through when hot filling is added. Place rolls on a baking sheet and toast in oven for 10 to 15 minutes.

Melt butter in a skillet over medium-high heat. Add mushrooms, sautéing for several minutes, until well cooked.

4 small, individual-size, round, French bread rolls

2 tablespoons butter (or olive oil)

1 pound mushrooms, coarsely chopped

Salt and pepper

1/2 cup sweet Banyuls or port wine

1/3 cup plus 1 heaped tablespoon crumbled Roquefort cheese

3/4 cup cream or half-and-half

MAKES 4 SERVINGS

Sprinkle in salt and pepper to taste. Stir in Banyuls or port wine. As liquid begins to bubble, add the Roquefort cheese and cream. Reduce heat to bring sauce to a simmer. Continue stirring to help melt all the cheese.

Spoon mushrooms and sauce into each roll, dividing evenly. If desired, place bread tops back on each roll and serve.

Superb fall or spring dish, alongside game or any roasted meat.

Toasted walnuts can be added into the mixture or used as a garnish.

Country Pâté

(Pâté de campagne)

(southwest France, Catalonia)

 AMONG THE WONDERFUL FOODS that France has bestowed upon us, pâté is one of the most satisfying and versatile. It is equally at home at an elegant soirée or a picnic. While more often served cold, pâté can also be served hot, usually as a first course or appetizer. It can be satiny-smooth and easily spread or, like this country or farm-house pâté, coarsely textured.

Traditionally, pâtés are well-seasoned meat preparations made from a mixture of fine-ly ground and/or coarsely chopped meats such as poultry, pork, game, ham, or veal, usu-ally featuring the livers. Lighter pâtés, made from fish or vegetables, have since evolved. Pâté is French for pie, and usually refers to seasoned meat mixtures cooked in a crust wrapping. Mixtures simply cooked in a clay mold, or as a free-standing mound in a tra-ditional clay or earthen container, are called *terrines* after the French word for earth, *terre*. Even in France the terms are sometimes used interchangeably or applied incorrectly, as in this case, in which *pâté de campagne* is technically a terrine.

To ensure that the finished product is moist, rich, flavorful, and retains its shape after the lengthy cooking process, fat, herbs and seasonings, and egg are common ingredients. To help achieve maximum depth of flavor, the terrine or pâté mixture is often marinat-ed in wine or spirits, and after being fully cooked allowed to season for several days to further develop the flavors. The following is a good basic recipe, based on rustic coun-try pâtés we have tasted in southwest France and northern Spain.

PREHEAT THE OVEN TO 350° F.

Place onion and garlic in a food processor, running it for several seconds, until they form a coarse purée. Add tocino* to the onion in the processor and, if grinding your own meat from a pork shoulder or loin, mix in lean meat together with any fatty pieces until ground up. If previously ground meat is being used, include it when adding the livers.

Rinse and pat dry pork and chicken livers. Cut away as much grisly connective tissue as possible. Add livers to food processor and pulse several times to blend into meat mixture.

Place mixture in a large bowl and mix in diced pork. Pour in Armagnac, followed by eggs, bread crumbs, thyme, salt and pepper. With a large spoon or bare hands, mix to combine. If using hazelnuts or walnuts, mix in last.

To sample the mixture for the correct amount of seasoning, fry a small spoonful and taste it. Adjust the seasoning.

Line the inner surface of a loaf pan with salt pork strips, spoon in the meat mixture, and lay salt pork strips over the top. Cover the pan tightly with foil. Place in a *bain marie* or water bath, with hot or simmering water poured to about halfway up the sides of the loaf pan. Bake for 1½ to 2 hours. Lift the foil to check that the pâté is cooked completely through by pressing on the middle with a spoon. It is cooked when the liquid that emerges is clear, as opposed to pink and cloudy.

Remove from oven. Open foil top enough to pour excess liquid into a container and reserve the rendered fat. Leave the foil on and if desired add an extra thickness of foil. Wrap a board or any other heavy flat item, that just fits in the loaf pan or baking dish, in plastic and/or foil. Place the board directly on top of the meat, with weights on top, to press any pooled liquid out of the meat as it cools. This will produce a solid even pâté, which does not crumble apart

1 small onion, cut in quarters

3 cloves garlic

¼ pound tocino*, pancetta, or salt pork

½ pound lean pork, ground or finely chopped

¼ pound pork liver

2 whole chicken livers, sinew removed

3 tablespoons Armagnac or cognac

2 eggs

6 ounces lean pork, from shoulder or loin, cut in ¼-inch dice

½ cup dry bread crumbs

½ teaspoon dried thyme (or 3 sprigs fresh thyme)

½ to 1 teaspoon salt

1 teaspoon coarsely ground black pepper

¼ cup hazelnuts or walnuts, slightly toasted and coarsely chopped (optional)

14 strips thinly sliced salt pork (about 8 ounces)

MAKES 1 LOAF OR 8 HALF-INCH SLICES

when sliced. Allow to completely cool this way. Refrigerate. Remove weights and any liquids or congealed fat that were pressed out.

The pâté can be stored in the pan for two weeks or more by re-melting the rendered fats collected and pouring over the pâté to cover. Alternatively, the pâté will keep for a week or more, if removed from the baking dish, tightly wrapped in plastic, and refrigerated. If needed, to dislodge the pâté from its container, place the pan or dish in hot water and slide a knife along the sides to loosen.

* Tocino: Fatty layer, just under pork skin, with thin striping of meat.

If using ground pork that is somewhat fatty, use ¾ pound and omit the fatty tocino.

In this recipe, I use salt pork strips to line the loaf pan instead of the more traditional pig's caul, the web-like fatty lining around a pig's stomach. A caul is an ideal tool to keep the pâté moist and prevent it from sticking to the pan. In the United States, cauls are fairly unique items, which must often be special-ordered from the butcher. Substituting salt pork strips adds seasoning to the mixture as it performs the other functions of the caul during cooking. Alternatively, you can simply butter the pan before pouring in the pâté mixture.

SOUPS AND STEWS

Soups and Stews

Garbure

(southwest France, Basque)

THIS CLASSIC BEAN AND VEGETABLE SOUP has been proclaimed by many one of the great national dishes of France. *Garbure* is a source of culinary pride throughout the Basque country and the Pyrenees, especially in and around Béarn. Each year, in the small French Basque town of Anglet, along the Bay of Biscay, a Brotherhood of the *Garbure* (*Confrérie de la Garbure*) holds a celebration paying homage to this traditional vegetable soup. *Garbure* is also extremely popular in many parts of southwest France, most notably Landes and Gascony. The basis of this hearty, peasant dish is a pot of white beans, salted meat, and cabbage, to which seasonal produce is added. In the fall and winter, roasted chestnuts, pumpkin, and root vegetables are included; in spring, fava beans; and in summer, haricots verts (green beans), tomatoes, sweet peppers, and leafy greens may be added.

PLACE BEANS IN A LARGE BOWL or pot and fill with water at least 2 inches past the top of beans. Soak overnight. Drain and rinse. Place in a large pot, adding enough water to cover beans. Boil until a foam rises to the top. Remove from heat and pour off foamy top liquid.

Add ham bone or salted meat, thyme, bay leaf, and parsley. Fill with enough water to cover all. Bring to a simmer and cover. Cook for 1 hour on low heat.

Continued

---

2 cups or 1 pound white beans

1- to 2-pound meaty ham bone, or any salted meat, such as salt pork, sausages, Bayonne ham, or pieces of confit

3 sprigs fresh thyme or ¹/₂ teaspoon dried

1 bay leaf

4 sprigs fresh parsley

1 medium onion, chopped

2 medium carrots, chopped in ¹/₂- to 1-inch pieces

INGREDIENTS CONTINUED

CONTINUED FROM PREVIOUS PAGE

4 cloves garlic, coarsely chopped

3 leeks, chopped in ¹/₂- to
  1-inch pieces

1 turnip, chopped in
  ¹/₂- to 1-inch pieces

1 small cabbage (2 pounds),
  coarsely chopped

Salt and pepper

Brown or country bread

MAKES 6 OR MORE SERVINGS

Stir in onion, carrots, garlic, leeks, and turnip, adding more water if needed. Simmer 15 minutes, then add cabbage and cook for 45 minutes more. Remove ham bone. Season soup with salt and pepper to taste.

Place slices of bread in each dish and spoon the soup over it. Accompany the soup with pieces of ham, bacon, duck, or sausage.

It is customary for French kitchens to prepare and stock duck or goose confit, to be applied as a key flavoring in a variety of dishes, mostly soups and stews.

Confit is the antithesis of a food that would be promoted by today's health-conscious society. A meat is first heavily coated in salt and left to marinate for 12 hours or more, then cooked and preserved entirely in its own fat. Delicious, but truly not for the faint-hearted.

As confit is not common to most American kitchens, I have substituted a ham bone in this recipe, and named other meats that can be used to enrich your *garbure*.

Garlic Soup

(Sopa de Ajo/Soupe à l'ail)

(Basque, southwest France)

ALTHOUGH GARLIC SOUP WITH EGGS identifies this particular version as the classic Basque sheepherder's soup, simple garlic soups are made in kitchens throughout southwestern France. The use of *piment d'Espelette*, the sweet yet hot red pepper, is characteristic to many Basque dishes. In France, red chilies were established as a tradition only in the Nive Valley, especially in the Basque village of Espelette. In the fall, the white buildings in and around the town of Espelette will often be covered with strands of bright red peppers hanging to dry before being ground into the *piment d'Espelette* powder. These chili peppers were introduced into the Nive Valley by Gonzalo Percaztegi in 1523, the same year that corn first made its appearance there.

When Columbus brought chili peppers to Europe after his second voyage in 1493, they were first grown in monasteries in Spain and Portugal as curiosities. But soon the word got out that they were a cheap substitute for black pepper, which was so expensive that it had been used as currency. The best thing about chilies—in addition to their heat and flavor—was that they could grow in temperate climates and did not have to be imported from India. Chilies quickly spread throughout the Old World, where they permanently spiced world cuisines.

HEAT OLIVE OIL IN A LARGE PAN or pot over medium heat. Add garlic cloves, and stir to soften and lightly brown the exterior on all sides. Remove and set aside. Place bread slices in the same oil and fry each side until golden brown. Pour stock into the pot with the bread. Add paprika and *piment d'Espelette*. Mash or push softened garlic cloves through a sieve and into the

---

1/4 cup olive oil

6 to 8 cloves garlic

6 slices, 1/4 inch thick, day-old
   French bread (baguette)

6 cups beef stock or chicken stock

1 teaspoon sweet paprika

1/4 teaspoon *piment d'Espelette* or
   cayenne

Salt to taste

4 eggs

MAKES 4 SERVINGS

---

stock. Simmer for approximately 15 minutes, stirring occasionally. Taste and adjust seasoning as needed.

Gently break each egg into the simmering liquid and let them poach for a few minutes, until whites have cooked through, approximately 2 minutes.

Ladle some of the bread and an egg into each serving of soup. Serve with toasted or pan-fried bread.

In the non-Basque areas of southern France, a basic garlic soup will also include fresh thyme and possibly other herbs. The bread may be fried in butter rather than olive oil, and the soup may be finished with the addition of a few spoonfuls of cream prior to being served.

Onion and Garlic Soup

EACH OF THE "ONIONS" in this recipe are in the genus *Allium* of the lily family, native species of which are found on every continent. They are prized for their pungent flavors and odors. Onions have been cultivated in China, Egypt, and India for about 5,000 years and were among the primary vegetables consumed in Europe since the Middle Ages. There are two main classifications of onion (*Allium cepa*): young green onions (also called scallions) and mature dry onions. Dry onions come in a wide range of sizes, shapes, and flavors including yellow-skinned Spanish onions and red-skinned or Italian onions. Garlic (*Allium sativum*) has long been credited with providing physical strength and was fed to Egyptian slaves building the giant pyramids. The edible bulb or "head" is made up of cloves, each section being encased in its own parchment. Shallots (*Allium ascalonicum*) are thought to have originated in Ascalon, an ancient Palestinian city. Shallots are favored for their mild onion flavor and have multiple cloves more like garlic than onions. Leeks (*Allium ampeloprasum porrum*) are native to the Mediterranean countries and have been prized by gourmets for millennia. Nero is said to have eaten prodigious quantities to improve his singing voice. Looking like giant scallions, leeks are milder and more subtle than onions or garlic. "Scallion" is applied to young shoots of many members of this family, but true scallions (*Allium fistulosum*) have a milder flavor than immature onions and have straight sides along the base with no hint of a bulb.

This soup is surprisingly easy to prepare for one so robustly flavorful.

Recipe and ingredients on following page

¼ cup olive oil

1 medium yellow onion, chopped or sliced

1 medium red onion, chopped or sliced

2 to 3 shallots, chopped or sliced

1 leek, chopped (white and light green parts only)

4 to 6 scallions, chopped

6 cloves garlic, chopped

2½ to 3 cups chicken stock

½ cup white wine

3 to 4 sprigs fresh thyme, or 1 teaspoon dried

Salt and pepper

½ cup heavy cream or half-and-half

MAKES 4 SERVINGS

HEAT OLIVE OIL IN A LARGE SKILLET or pan over medium heat. Add yellow and red onions, shallots, and leek. Sauté until yellow and red onions become translucent, then add scallions and garlic. Continue to cook and stir until most of the onions have browned a bit and become limp.

Pour in chicken stock, white wine, and add thyme. Simmer until liquid has reduced by about half, approximately 20 minutes, stirring occasionally. Add salt and pepper to taste. Remove from heat and place in a blender to purée to a smooth consistency. Stir in cream and serve. If reheating soup before serving, do not allow to boil.

Leek and Cod Soup

(Porrusalda)

PORRUSALDA, OR LEEK SOUP IN BASQUE, is a very traditional dish. It includes pumpkins, an interesting component in a soup composed of both Old World (carrots, leeks) and New World (potatoes, pumpkin) ingredients.

In Spain, the first use of potatoes as food was recorded in 1530. The families of Basque sailors along the Bay of Biscay were the first Europeans to grow potatoes in their gardens, and Basques fishing for cod introduced them to the Irish by the mid-seventeenth century.

Pumpkins were widely eaten by native Americans from Canada to northern South America for centuries before Columbus arrived. European settlers in North America readily adopted them as a staple in their diets. The first definite record of pumpkins in Europe occurred in 1591. Pumpkins require a fair amount of hot weather for best growth and are successful in much of the Pyrenean region, unlike northern Europe.

SOAK THE COD IN COLD WATER at least 24 hours in advance. Change the water, several times a day. Then cut in pieces.

Place a large pot over medium-high heat. Add olive oil and sauté leeks until they brown slightly, 10 to 15 minutes. Add garlic and sauté until they begin to take on a slight tan color, 1 to 2 minutes.

Toss in potatoes, carrot, pumpkin, and cod pieces. Immediately, pour in enough water to cover, 4 to 5 cups. Add about 1 teaspoon salt or less to the water, as the cod might still contain salt. Bring soup to a boil, and reduce heat to a simmer. Cook, uncovered, until potatoes are the

---

½ pound salt cod

4 tablespoons olive oil

6 leeks, white and pale green parts only, chopped in ½-inch sections

4 cloves garlic, chopped or minced

4 potatoes, chopped in 1-inch pieces

1 medium carrot, chopped in ½-inch pieces

½ pound pumpkin, chopped in ½-inch pieces (about 1 cup)

Salt and pepper

MAKES 4 SERVINGS

desired softness. Stir once or twice. Depending on the size of the potato pieces, simmer for 15 to 25 minutes.

Taste and add salt and pepper, if needed. Serve alone or with good bread.

•·••·•·•

Two basic types of *porrusalda* exist, with and without cod. Excluding cod from the soup makes it no less genuine.

Many cooks will not include garlic or sauté their leeks, and may stir in olive oil only at the end, into the nearly finished product. I find that the simple steps of pan-frying the leeks and garlic add greatly to the flavor of these vegetables, as does the oil in the *porrusalda*.

Basque Tuna Stew
(Marmitako)

Marmitako is a simple and flavorful *guiso marinero* or fish stew. It was apparently invented aboard fishing boats in the Bay of Biscay where it was prepared as a complete meal to nourish sailors during their arduous fishing tasks. While usually considered a Basque dish, Cantabrians lay claim to it as well. *Marmitako* is prepared in large earthenware casseroles called *marmitas* from which the dish is named. Fresh tuna is one of the favorites of Basque cuisine. While other tunas could be used in *marmitako*, the Basques prefer to use fresh *bonito del norte*—albacore (*Thunnus alalunga*)—whose white meat is considered better quality than *atún*—skipjack tuna (*Katsuwonus pelamis*)— which is usually eaten canned in Spain. *Marmitako* is a seasonal dish, and most often eaten during August when *bonitos del norte* enter the Bay of Biscay to feed on migrating anchovy. Chef Martín Berasategui, who served us a wonderful meal in his eponymous restaurant in Lasarte near San Sebastian, notes that this dish predates the arrival of potatoes in the Basque kitchens several hundred years ago. The original recipes used bread, which is present in some modern recipes as a testimony to the past. Excellent *marmitakos* can be found in Biscayan ports such as Bermeo, Lekeito, or Ondarroa where the dish can be either an entrée or a complete meal.

Recipe and ingredients on following page

2 tablespoons olive oil

2 medium onions, thinly sliced or
chopped

1 green or red bell pepper, cut in
strips or chopped

4 cloves garlic, minced or chopped

3 teaspoons sweet paprika

1/4 teaspoon *piment d'Espelette* or
cayenne

2 medium tomatoes or 4 roma
tomatoes, peeled, seeded, and
chopped

2 slices dried French bread

4 medium potatoes, cut in 1/2 to
3/4-inch dice

1 cup dry white wine

2 cups fish broth

1 bay leaf

1 1/2 to 2 pounds fresh tuna, cut in
bite-size pieces

2 tablespoons chopped fresh parsley

Salt and pepper

MAKES 4 SERVINGS

HEAT OLIVE OIL IN A LARGE SKILLET or pan over low or medium-low heat. Add onions and peppers, stirring occasionally. When the onions become translucent, add garlic, paprika, and *piment d'Espelette* and continue cooking until onions are limp. Stir in tomatoes and dried bread, increasing the heat to medium. Cook for about 5 minutes, mixing to break the bread into small pieces. Add potatoes, white wine, fish broth, and bay leaf. Stir to combine all ingredients.

Bring liquid to a boil and reduce heat to a simmer. Cook for approximately 20 minutes, or until potatoes are soft. Stir in tuna and parsley, and cook for approximately 3 more minutes. Do not overcook the tuna. Season with salt and pepper to taste.

Serve hot with fresh crusty bread or slices of bread toasted in a skillet with a bit of olive oil or butter.

Garlic and Salt Cod Stew with Pil-Pil Sauce (Zurrukutuna)

WHEN THE FRENCH MASTER CHEF Paul Bocuse launched *nouvelle cuisine*, many of his most talented disciples were chefs from the Basque country. In 1976, they formed the *Grupo de la Nueva Cocina Vasca*, and dedicated themselves to using only the best ingredients and cooking them to maximize their natural flavors. They focused on simple cooking and respect for tradition. Among these chefs are Juan Marí Arzak, Pedro Subijana, and Jesús María Oyarbide (who moved to Madrid to found Zalacaín). This movement has swept the more sophisticated restaurants throughout the Pyrenean region.

Zurrukutuna is an excellent example of how the *nueva cocina vasca* movement has updated and paid homage to a rustic ancestral Basque dish. This soup was originated and made popular in humble country kitchens, and by Basque sheepherders, who made this soup from ingredients that kept well and were readily available, such as preserved salted cod, bread, garlic, leeks, and dried peppers. Chefs leading the school of *nueva cocina vasca*, including Juan Marí Arzak, Martin Berasategui, and Pedro Subijana, all pay respect to *zurrukutuna*, each with his own very fine interpretation of it. We very nearly swooned over Chef Subijana's version while lunching at his outstanding restaurant, Akelare, located in the hills above San Sebastian and overlooking the Bay of Biscay. The velvety smooth opaque garlic soup, jeweled with droplets of bright orange and green herb-infused oils, provided an unbelievably rich, flavorful background for the morsels of shredded cod that studded the soup. We later learned that Chef Subijana considers this dish as one of the specialties at Akelare.

The following is a very delicious simple recipe for this popular soup.

Recipe and ingredients on following page

1 pound salt cod with skin

6 dried choricero peppers or 6 teaspoons sweet paprika and pinch
of cayenne

³/₄ cup olive oil

2 heads garlic, cloves separated,
peeled, and coarsely chopped

1 guindilla or anaheim pepper

1 leek (white and light green
portions), chopped

6 to 8 slices (¹/₄-inch-thick) French
bread

1 egg yolk

¹/₄ to ¹/₂-teaspoon gelatin (optional)

MAKES 4 SERVINGS

DESALT COD BY SOAKING IN WATER for 24 to 48 hours, changing water several times a day depending on amount of salt remaining in the flesh. Divide cod into two portions.

To rehydrate choricero peppers, place in a bowl of water overnight. If you don't have the time to do this, boil an inch or two of water in a saucepan and remove from heat. Place choriceros in water and cover. Let peppers sit for 20 to 30 minutes. When rehydrated, scrape pulp from the skins and save. Discard skins, seeds, and stems. If using paprika powder, add paprika and cayenne to ¹/₃ cup of hot water and set aside until needed.

Boil 5 cups of water in a saucepan. Remove from heat and immediately add one portion of the cod. Let steep for 10 minutes. Remove cod and reserve poaching liquid.

Heat ¹/₂ cup of olive oil in a skillet or pan and add chopped garlic and guindilla or anaheim pepper. Stir occasionally. When garlic begins to tan, remove and set aside. Repeat this process with the leek. Pour the garlic and leek–flavored oil remaining in the pan into a small cup and reserve for the pil-pil sauce.

Add bread slices to the residual oil coating the pan, to brown both sides. This step is essentially making large croutons. Add some fresh oil to the pan, if needed. Remove bread and crumble into smaller pieces.

If needed, add more oil to the hot pan and fry both sides of uncooked portion of cod until edges brown slightly. Add the bread, choricero or paprika purée, garlic, and leeks. Pour in 3 cups of the reserved poaching liquid and simmer for 20 to 30 minutes. Just before removing mixture from the heat, whisk in the raw egg yolk, blending well. Strain liquid through a sieve and purée solids through a food mill, with a food processor, or blender. Return purée to the liquid and mix together. Taste and adjust seasoning, as needed.

Pil-Pil Sauce

Place the poached portion of cod, skin side down, in a hot pan with just enough of the reserved oil to coat the pan. After 1 minute, flip cod over and continue to cook, reducing the heat to low. Continuously move the pan in swirling motions to keep the fish from sticking. The oil should begin to mix with the gelatin in the juices from the cod skin and form a white custard-like sauce. As the oil in the pan becomes part of the sauce, gradually add oil, one spoonful at a time until all the oil has been accepted into the sauce.

If this doesn't work, and your oil remains separate, the gelatin in the fish juices can be supplemented with a bit of store-bought gelatin. First, place gelatin in a small cup with a teaspoon of cold water, for several minutes. When it has swelled into a single mass, add a bit of gelatin to the pan, continuing to swirl the pan, the oil, and the cod. Add a drop or two of the poaching water if enough liquid is not released from the fish.

To serve, spoon puréed soup into each bowl. Place chunks of the fried cod with each serving and top soup with a dollop of pil-pil.

⋅•⋅

A step can be saved by frying bread crumbs or using pre-made croutons instead of preparing baguette slices.

To achieve a more rustic soup, in the style of the original creation, do not strain out or purée solids at the end.

Peas and Mussel Soup

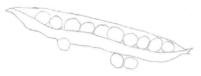

(southwest France)

BLUE MUSSELS (*moules* or *mejillones*) are a favored shellfish throughout the Pyrenean region. These bivalves aggregate in large colonies, from the high intertidal to the shallow subtidal areas on the rocky shores of open coasts, attached to rock surfaces and piers in sheltered harbors and estuaries. Although the same species (*Mytilis edulis*) is abundant in North America, it is all too often unappreciated there. Mussels have been cultivated in southern Italy since ancient times. Today the most likely provenance of mussels in this region are Galicia and Bouzigues, Languedoc, where they are cultivated in bays or lagoons, on giant wood rafts that are firmly anchored and can produce almost 100 tons per year. Tidal flows provide the nutrients, and the seawater ensures that the mussels will have their particularly briny taste that is so favored by connoisseurs. They are harvested all year, but are especially large in September and October.

I created this particular recipe to duplicate the wonderful sweet pea and cream purée, studded with rich briny mussels, that we love at Petits Plats in Washington, D.C.

IN A LARGE SKILLET OR PAN, heat oil over medium heat. Add garlic and sauté for about 1 minute. Do not brown. Pour in white wine. When hot and bubbling, toss in the mussels and cover. Cook for approximately 2 minutes. Uncover and shake pan or toss mussels with a large spoon for an additional minute, to ensure all have been cooked. Remove pan from heat when almost all mussels have opened. Discard any unopened mussels.

1 tablespoon olive oil

2 cloves garlic, minced or crushed

1/2 cup white wine

3 dozen mussels, cleaned, scrubbed, and drained

3 cups peas, fresh or frozen

1/2 to 3/4 cup heavy cream

Salt and pepper (optional)

MAKES 4 SERVINGS

Reserve the liquid, transferring it to a saucepan over medium-low heat. If using fresh peas, add to pan at this point and simmer for 2 to 3 minutes. Otherwise, add cream to broth and simmer until it begins to thicken and the liquid is reduced slightly, 1 to 2 minutes. Add frozen peas and heat until liquid begins to bubble. Remove from heat.

Pluck 2 dozen of the cooked mussels from their shells and set aside, discarding shells. Remove the top shell from the remaining dozen, and set them aside in their half shell.

Purée peas and cream mixture in a blender or food processor. Taste, and, if desired, add salt and pepper. If reheating soup before serving, do not allow to boil.

To serve, place approximately 6 of the cooked mussels in individual soup bowls and ladle puréed soup into each bowl. Serve mussels on the half shell as a garnish with soup.

Red Beans of Tolosa Stew

(Alubias de Tolosa)

BEANS HAVE LONG BEEN AN IMPORTANT component in the Pyrenean diet from Asturias (*fabada asturiana*) to Toulouse (*cassoulet*). They are easily stored and in centuries past could enable a rural family to eat well during winter. Tolosa is a Basque town in Guipúzcoa, Spain, near the French border and San Sebastián. Known for manufacturing the familiar Basque berets, on Saturdays it also hosts a colorful farmers' market in the village square where visitors can sample local produce. Red beans of Tolosa, are often referred to as black beans, and their cultivation is concentrated primarily in Guipúzcoa. The Basque consider this bean variety to be simply the best tasting that can be had. Tolosa has long been famous for its stews made of these local red beans. Periodically, the area's chefs have contests to vie for the recognition of preparing the best. As with many widely made classic dishes, the recipe for *alubias de Tolosa* will vary with each Basque cook; however, this version is fairly representative. The town of Gernika also lays claim to having outstanding beans for this recipe. This dish is often served with pickled guindillas, a pencil thin, regional, spicy, green pepper.

PLACE BEANS IN A LARGE BOWL or pot and fill with water at least 2 inches past the top of beans. Soak overnight. Drain and rinse. Place in a pot, adding enough water to cover beans. Boil until a foam rises to the top. Remove from heat, and pour off foamy top liquid.

Heat olive oil in a large pot or casserole dish over medium-high heat. Quickly brown the surface of the ribs. Add salt pork or bacon, and onion, stirring quickly for 3 minutes. Add garlic, and

2 cups (1 pound) small red or
  black beans
4 tablespoons olive oil
1 pound pork ribs
¹/₄ pound salt pork or bacon
1 medium onion, chopped
3 cloves garlic, chopped
2 links chorizo sausage, whole or
  chopped in sections
2 links morcilla (blood) sausage,
  whole
Salt and pepper (optional)

MAKES 4 TO 6 SERVINGS

sauté until garlic begins to turn a straw color. Pour in beans and add enough water to cover all. Cover and simmer on low heat for 1 to 1½ hours, stirring occasionally, until beans are cooked through and centers are no longer tough.

Add chorizo and continue to cook for 30 minutes. At this time, cook the morcilla separately in a pan with just enough water for them to simmer, and cook, covered, for 30 minutes.

When the beans are done, season with salt and pepper, if needed. Just prior to serving, remove and cut into sections, pork ribs, salt pork/bacon, and chorizo sausages, if whole. Also cut morcilla sausage into sections.

Serve the beans, including a piece of pork rib, chorizo, and some morcilla in each serving.

White Beans and Sausage
(Fabada Asturiana/Botifarra amb Mongetes/ Haricots aux saucisses)

(Asturias, Catalonia, and southwest France)

BEANS ARE AN EXTREMELY POPULAR staple along both sides of the Pyrenees. Each region has its own version of a white bean and sausage "stew." Only slight differences identify a bean dish as Catalan, Asturian, or Gascon. The differences are chiefly in the type of sausage traditionally used in each. The Botifarra sausage defines a Catalonian white bean stew, while the Toulouse sausage is used in Gascony, and blood sausage and chorizo are included in *Fabada Asturiana*. Tomatoes are used to some extent in all versions. Interestingly, the Aztecs, who may have cultivated tomatoes in Mexico as early as 700 A.D., often mixed tomatoes or other ripe fruits with chilies to make a sauce to accompany cooked beans.

TO REHYDRATE BEANS, place in a large pot and fill to the top with water. Let the beans soak overnight. If preparing it all on the same day, immerse beans in a pot of water and bring to a boil. Reduce heat to a low simmer and cover, adding water occasionally to keep beans covered. Simmer approximately 1 hour. Beans should double in size. Pour out the extra water not absorbed by beans.

Pour enough olive oil in a large stew pot to cover the cooking surface. Over medium-high heat brown sausages on all sides. Remove when well browned.

Place bacon or ham into the pan and cook for several minutes. Reduce heat to medium-low or low. Add onions and continue to sauté until they become translucent and begin to brown. Add garlic and sauté for another minute. Stir in tomatoes, and cook until well blended

---

1 pound dried navy beans

Olive oil

4 to 6 sausages, garlic or smoked

4 to 6 ounces bacon or ham

2 medium onions, chopped

4 cloves garlic, crushed or minced

1 can (14 ounces) tomatoes or 4 medium tomatoes, peeled and chopped

Salt and pepper

MAKES 4 TO 6 SERVINGS

---

with garlic and onions. Dump beans into this mixture and stir. Pour in enough water to just cover the beans. Simmer for 2 to 3 hours, stirring occasionally to keep bottom from scorching (shorten this time, if beans were previously cooked). After $1\frac{1}{2}$ to 2 hours add the sausages.

Season to taste with salt and pepper before serving.

In Catalan regions a *sofregit* sauce of slow-cooked onions combined with garlic and tomato is the base for this soup.

In Gascony, carrots and a *bouquet garni* of herbs (bay leaf, thyme sprigs, and parsley sprigs) are added.

Catalan Beef Stew

(Estouffat / Estofat)

THE CATALAN WORD FOR STEW, *ESTOFAT*, is related to the word for smother, *ofegar*, as a stew is covered, or smothered, and cooked for hours. This French Catalan dish is a regional specialty that is prepared and served only on special occasions. Interestingly, beef is essentially absent from Spanish Catalan cuisine, with the exception of veal. Although the Spanish Pyrenees region is rich in dairy cows, farmers cannot afford to raise beef cows to maturity on the precious little pasture acreage available.

We were fortunate to find *estouffat* on the menu of the Restaurant Au Grill, when we visited Villefranche-de-Conflent, a walled village in the Têt Valley (also known as the Conflent) that dates from 1092. With the Moorish threat having receded, the Count of Cerdagne granted the charter for this settlement at the confluence of the Cady and Têt rivers. We walked the stone ramparts of this Medieval town with yellow and red Catalan flags snapping in the breeze, imagining what life might have been like centuries ago in this cobblestone town. The Restaurant Au Grill was an inviting, intimate eatery that seemed to cater to residents as well as tourists, and we both decided to order this traditional beef stew with a half bottle of Roussillon *vin rouge*.

IF POSSIBLE, SOAK BEANS overnight in a pot with 2 to 3 times more water than beans. Otherwise, add the same amount of water to dried beans and simmer for I hour to rehydrate them. Pour out the soaking water and replace it with just enough water to cover the beans. Add I onion, the bouquet garni, ½ teaspoon salt, and crush and add I garlic clove.

1½ cups dried white cannellini or navy beans

3 large onions, chopped

Bouquet garni of fresh thyme, oregano, sage, and bay leaf

Salt

4 cloves garlic

2 pounds beef, cut in 1½-inch pieces

½ pound salt pork or bacon, diced

2 leeks, cut in ½-inch rounds

½ pound carrots, cut in pieces

1 turnip, chopped in large pieces

INGREDIENTS CONTINUED

Cover and simmer, while preparing the other ingredients.

Chop and mash 1 garlic clove, and use it to rub over the beef chunks. Set aside.

Place a large pot or Dutch oven over medium heat. Cook the salt pork or bacon. When the fat is rendered and the pieces are browned, add beef, 2 remaining onions, leeks, carrots, turnip, cloves, and cinnamon. Pour in all the wine, add tomatoes, 2 remaining garlic cloves, crushed, and a sprinkling of salt and pepper. Stir once or twice to combine all ingredients. Bring liquid to a boil, cover, and immediately reduce heat to a low simmer. Cook for 3 hours.

Place the cèpes or porcinis in a bowl and add 1 cup hot water. Soak for 15 to 20 minutes to rehydrate.

CONTINUED FROM PREVIOUS PAGE

3 cloves

¼ teaspoon ground cinnamon

1 bottle of (750 ml) red wine (3 cups)

1 pound tomatoes, peeled, seeded, and chopped

Pinch of pepper

3 ounces dried cèpe or porcini mushrooms

1 pound garlic or smoked sausage, whole or cut in large rounds

3 tablespoons Armagnac or brandy

Makes 8 servings

Fry the sausage in a pan until browned, and add to the beans. Mix beans, sausage, and cèpes into the pot containing the meat and vegetables. Stir in the Armagnac. Cook for 30 minutes more.

Serve over slices of bread fried in olive oil and garlic, or roasted potatoes.

Of course countless variations exist for *estofat*. Cinnamon is very characteristic, and a bit of chocolate is sometimes included. The beans are not a mandatory ingredient in all beef *estofats*.

Accompany this stew with a good Minervois wine.

FISH AND SEAFOOD

Fish and Seafood

Lemon Shrimp

THERE ARE SEVERAL SPECIES OF CRUSTACEANS available in the Pyrenean region, fished from the Mediterranean and the Atlantic. The largest are called *langostinos* or *langoustines*, which are actually slim-bodied members of the lobster family. Red in color, their wide, heavier tails distinguish them from shrimp and prawns. The next in size is the red shrimp (*crevette rose*), which can be up to four inches in length. Red shrimp are difficult to transport alive, and are usually available boiled or frozen. Finally, North Sea prawns (*crevette grise*) are only about two inches in length and have an excellent, distinctive taste. The frozen shrimp and prawns that are sold in North American markets rarely provide the precise species or provenance of the product, which can come from any ocean.

In northern Spain it is most common to find the simple and classic preparation of shrimp or prawns quickly sautéed in a bit of garlic and olive oil. For a change, I created this shrimp marinade composed of common Mediterranean ingredients. This recipe is based on a technique to marinate shrimp with lemons, learned from Barry Morgenstern, a friend who trained at the famous Cordon Bleu in Paris. The marinade quickly infuses deeply into the hot shrimp, imparting bright flavors deep into each morsel. Once all the ingredients are assembled this is an extremely easy recipe, in which all the work can be done in advance.

Recipe and ingredients on following page

Zest of 1 lemon

$1/2$ cup lemon juice, from
approximately 2 large lemons

2 cloves garlic, crushed

1 tablespoon wine or sherry vinegar

2 tablespoons olive oil

12 black olives, kalamata or
oil-cured, pitted, and halved

6 anchovy fillets, coarsely chopped

1 small red onion, thinly sliced

1 bay leaf, crumbled

Pinch of *piment d'Espelette* or
cayenne

1 to $1^{1}/2$ pounds large shrimp

2 to 3 teaspoons salt

1 ripe avocado, pitted, peeled, and
sliced (optional)

MAKES 4 SERVINGS

PREPARE MARINADE IN A LARGE BOWL
by combining lemon zest, lemon juice,
garlic, vinegar, oil, olives, anchovies, red
onion, bay leaf, and *piment d'Espelette*.

Peel and clean shrimp, leaving tails on.
Partially fill a pot with water, add salt,
and bring to a boil. Add shrimp and
boil for $1^{1}/2$ to 2 minutes, or until
shrimp pinks and the flesh looks
opaque. Remove immediately. Drain and
place hot shrimp into marinade. If additional
liquid is needed to cover most of
the shrimp, add a few tablespoons of
the shrimp poaching water to the marinade.
Cover and refrigerate for at least 2
to 3 hours, turning the shrimp once.

Serve with avocado slices (if desired), on
a salad, or by themselves as a shrimp
cocktail.

Garlic Shrimp
(Gambas al Ajillo)

GARLIC SHRIMP IS VERY POPULAR as a tapa throughout Spain. We first enjoyed a wonderful interpretation of this dish as part of a tasting menu in the Restaurante Arzak in San Sebastián, a location where the Arzak family has cooked since 1897. Juan Marí Arzak was one of the founders of *la nueva cocina vasca*, an approach to Basque cooking that focuses on simplicity using only the freshest local ingredients. Chef Arzak's daughter, Elena, now shares the kitchen helm and is the fourth generation to cook there. This recipe, though, is adapted from another internationally acclaimed chef, Ferran Adrià of El Bulli near Rosas on the Costa Brava. Adrià is part scientist, part alchemist, part conceptual artist, and part magician. He is one of the most influential chefs in Spain, and offers one of Europe's most thrilling eating adventures. This recipe is fairly simple, yet provides a great deal of flavor.

REMOVE HEADS AND TAILS of shrimp. Over high heat, place shrimp heads in a skillet and lightly sauté, 1 to 2 minutes. Remove and place sautéed pieces in cheesecloth and squeeze to extract juices. Set extracted liquid aside and discard solids.

> **20 medium to large shrimp, whole**
> **¼ cup olive oil**
> **3 cloves garlic, minced**
> **1 guindilla pepper**
> **4 to 5 sprigs parsley, chopped**
>
> MAKES 4 SERVINGS

Add olive oil to a skillet over medium-high heat, sauté minced garlic with the guindilla pepper. When some of the garlic begins to lightly brown, remove it and the pepper and set them aside. Add shrimp to the same oil and sauté until shrimp is no longer translucent and begins to turn pink, about a minute on each side, depending on the size of the shrimp. Remove shrimp and set aside.

Continued

Allow oil to cool a bit. Then add the extracted shrimp liquid to the warm, but not hot, oil and mix to combine well. If oil is hot the liquid will form lumps. Toss shrimp in the sauce. Top with chopped parsley and the lightly browned garlic and serve.

⋆•⋆•

Guindilla peppers are thin peppers 2 to 3 inches long. When green, they are slightly pungent with a green bean flavor, and only slightly hot. As they mature and redden, guindillas develop a sweeter taste and slightly more heat.

Native to northern Spain, guindillas are popular in Basque regions, as well as in Galicia. They are usually fried in olive oil with garlic and served alongside seafood and fish dishes.

In place of guindillas, you can substitute another mild green pepper, such as the Anaheim.

Cream of Cod

(Brandade de morue)

A CELEBRITY FROM LANGUEDOC, this dish is rich and famous beyond its origins in southern France. Considered a special dish due to the dedication originally required to transform cod into a fluffy, rich, creamy purée, the original recipe is a time-consuming labor of love. The invention of the blender, followed by the food processor, allowed those wishing to prepare *brandade de morue* to do so without slaving for hours over a mortar and pestle. Many French housewives now purchase their cod *brandade* pre-made in supermarkets.

USING COLD WATER, rinse surface salt from cod. Place cod in a bowl and cover it in cold water for at least 24 to 48 hours. You may wish to first cut the fish into smaller pieces to help leach out the salt faster, and to allow it to fit in the bowl more easily. Keep refrigerated, removing to change the water several times a day throughout the process.

Place cod in a saucepan and cover with water. Bring to a boil, cover, and immediately remove from heat or reduce to a very low simmer. Steep cod in hot water for 10 minutes. Let cool. When it is cool enough to handle, remove fish from poaching liquid and break it up into small nuggets.

> 1 pound salt cod
> 1 to 2 medium potatoes, peeled and chopped in chunks
> 1/2 cup whole milk or half-and-half
> 1/2 cup olive oil
> 2 cloves garlic, minced and/or crushed
> Juice from 1/2 lemon (3 tablespoons)
> Salt and pepper
>
> MAKES 4 SERVINGS

Boil potato chunks in a pot of water until soft enough to be pierced with a fork. Drain and crush or coarsely mash potatoes. Keep potatoes warm until needed.

Continued

If possible, place milk and olive oil in separate saucepans over a very low heat and keep them mildly hot, but not scalding, until needed.

In a food processor, mix the cod, garlic, and lemon juice together. After a few seconds, or when they are just combined, pour in olive oil and milk in thin streams, together or alternating between them. The mixture should start to appear light and fluffy.

Add the crushed potato in thirds, as you continue to process the cod. Taste it, and if you reach your desired thickness, while retaining a light, creamy texture, before all the potato is used, stop at that point. Add salt and pepper to taste. If the mixture becomes too thick after adding the potato, mix in about ¼ cup more of heated milk or half-and-half.

Spread this over bread or use as a stuffing for sweet roasted peppers, eggplant, or boiled cabbage.

•·•·•

In northern Spain where cod is a primary food, it is commonly used to stuff sweet piquillo peppers for *Pimiento del Piquillo Relleno*.

Lemon is actually not found in the short list of original *brandade* ingredients. Modern recipes include lemon juice to help the purée reach its final creamy emulsified texture.

If your mixture achieves the consistency of a thick custard before adding the potato, you may wish to stop. This is the closest to the most traditional recipe for this dish.

The addition of the potato is second tool in modern recipes, to help this dish reach the correct fluffy custard-like consistency. I personally feel the potato adds to the rich mouth feel and sweetness of this dish.

Black Rice

(Arròs Negre)

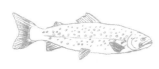

THIS RECIPE USES A SAUCE made from the squid's or cuttlefish's own ink, which makes the dish totally black and imparts an unusual, wonderful flavor. Squid and cuttlefish in Spain and France are usually caught on lines with bait rather than by gillnet. They tend to have more ink than squid purchased in North America, generally caught in gillnets. Squid caught in gillnets often panic and expel much of their ink.

Black Rice, or *arròs negre*, originated along Spain's Costa Brava, in the Catalan district of L'Empordà (near the French border), but is now beloved throughout Spain. Based on rice, it is really a paella dish in all but name. While lunching at the internationally renowned El Bulli, located on the Costa Brava coast very near to L'Emporda, one of the dishes we enjoyed was labeled "Black Rice which is not rice," a delightful take-off on the classic original. It consisted of bean sprouts cut to the size of rice grains, lightly cooked in a squid ink sauce and accompanied by pan-fried *chipirones*, or baby squid.

The following recipe is based on an outstanding *arròs negre* we sampled in San Francisco while dining at B44, a bistro specializing in regional Catalan cuisine. I pursued the chef and owner, Daniel Olivella, to obtain the recipe to his wonderfully flavorful dish. Chef Olivella is a Catalan native from the town of Vilafranca del Penedès, located in the heart of premium Catalonian wine-producing country, and very near Barcelona. He returns to the area every summer for new culinary inspiration and to participate as a member of the human tower team for Vilafranca. For over 100 years the "building" of a human tower was an annual feat performed to pay respect to the town patron St. Felix. In the past 20 to 30 years the teams have become extremely competitive and perform throughout the summer. Every two years, 50 to 60 teams participate in a regional competition held in the Tarragona bull ring. Vilafranca del Penedès has been ranked as one of the top two teams over the past 10 years.

Chef Olivella's particular interpretation of this dish was inspired by black rice preparations from the coastal town of Vilanova i la Geltrú, just south of Barcelona. He very graciously took the time out of his busy schedule to write his recipe out for me.

Recipe and ingredients on following page

1 pound fresh or frozen whole
  cuttlefish
1 pound fresh or frozen whole squid
4 cups or more fish stock
4 to 6 tablespoons olive oil
2 onions, chopped
1 green bell pepper, seeded, and
  chopped
1 red bell pepper, seeded, and
  chopped
4 cloves garlic, finely chopped
4 ripe tomatoes, peeled, seeded,
  and chopped
4 cups fish stock
2 cups uncooked short-grain rice,
  well rinsed and drained
18 clams, scrubbed, rinsed well,
  and drained
1/2 pound peas
Salt
1/2 to 3/4 cup *Allioli* (page 175)

MAKES 6 SERVINGS

RINSE AND CLEAN CUTTLEFISH/SQUID, removing the ink sacs* and setting them aside. Cut cuttlefish and squid into 1 1/2 to 2-inch pieces.

Break sacs to release the ink by mashing or pounding them with a mortar and pestle. Add a few tablespoons of fish stock to the ink, while continuing to grind and break down the ink with the mortar. This process will extract more color and flavor from the ink. Set ink aside.

Add 2 to 3 tablespoons olive oil to a wide, deep skillet over low heat. Add onions and peppers, and sauté until limp. Add half the garlic and sauté for a minute more before adding tomatoes. Create a *sofregit* or *sofrito* (also see page 138) by slowly cooking mixture over low heat, stirring occasionally, until tomato breaks down and all ingredients combine into a thick sauce. Remove and set aside.

Heat 4 cups fish stock until nearly boiling. Reduce heat to low and cover, to keep hot until stock is needed.

Pour remaining 2 to 4 tablespoons olive oil into the skillet or a large paella pan. Over medium-high heat, sauté the cuttlefish and squid until half cooked. Add rice, sautéing for 2 minutes. Stir in the tomato mixture, ink, and hot fish stock. Reduce heat to a very low simmer and let mixture cook, uncovered, approximately 10 minutes. Stir in whole clams and green peas, and cook for 10 minutes more, or until the mixture is the consistency of a thick rice pudding, and the rice has absorbed much of the liquid. Do not overcook the rice, or allow it to completely absorb all the liquid. Add salt to taste.

Serve immediately with a dollop of *Allioli* over each serving.

* *

* Alternatively, buy a package of frozen squid ink, available through seafood merchants or gourmet specialty shops. Fresh or frozen, whole, uncleaned squid and cuttlefish can be found at various grocers specializing in Portuguese or Mediterranean foods.

Ideally, one should use a pan wide enough to hold the rice in a fairly thin layer. This allows all the grains to cook more evenly.

Sofrito is the Castilian word for the Catalan *sofregit*, a thick onion and garlic–based sauce, derived from very slow cooking. A *sofrito* is a common Catalan base for flavoring stews, soups, and other sauces.

Use large cuttlefish or squid, for their larger ink sacs. I prefer cuttlefish for its thicker meat, which remains more tender through the cooking process, and it tends to have a sweeter taste than squid.

This dish would be complemented by a Spanish cava; Segura Viudas, Montsarra, and Codorníu are a few producers of cava commonly found in the United States.

Hake with Clams, Asparagus, and Peas (Merluza a la Koskera)

HAKE (*MERLUZA* OR *COLIN*) IS A FLAVORFUL cod-like fish that is one of the most popular fishes in Spain. It is eaten to a lesser extent in France, where it is also called *merluche* when salted and dried. The twelfth-century Hispano-Muslim advice on food contained in the *Kitab al-agdhiya* notes that doctors of that era recommended eating fish because fish has a humor that found a natural affinity with man. Both the anonymous fourteenth-century Catalan *Libre de Sent Soví* and Robert de Nola's *Libre del Coch* indicate that hake was a typical fish of that time. Hake is a relatively delicate fish, and should be handled carefully when turning over or moving.

This particular dish is a traditional Basque specialty. Its origin is traced to a street named Calle 31 de Agosto, located in the historic *Koskera*, or *Koxkera*, neighborhood of the *Parte Viejo* or old quarter of San Sebastián. Hake Koskera is very representative of the Basque style of cooking, in which ingredients not usually seen together are joined in the same dish to form wonderful combinations. Today, this light preparation of hake in a green sauce of garlic and parsley is a common Basque staple.

SALT FILLETS AND SET ASIDE for 10 to 15 minutes, then dredge in flour. Pour olive oil in a large pan or skillet, over medium-high heat. When hot, sear hake fillets about 2 minutes on each side and remove.

4 hake fillets (6 to 8 ounces each)

Salt

Flour for dredging

5 tablespoons olive oil

4 cloves garlic, minced

2 shallots, minced

1/4 cup chopped fresh parsley

1 teaspoon red pepper flakes (optional)

1/2 cup white wine

2 dozen cockles or 16 small little-neck clams, well washed and drained

1 cup peas, fresh or frozen

8 ounces asparagus, preferably tips

MAKES 4 SERVINGS

If needed, add more olive oil, followed by garlic, shallots, parsley, and pepper flakes. Sauté until garlic and shallots soften, 1 to 2 minutes.

Pour white wine in with the garlic mixture, then add cockles or clams. Cook for approximately 4 minutes, stirring occasionally. Add peas and asparagus, mixing to combine. Moving cockles/clams to one side, return fillets to pan and cook for another 4 to 5 minutes, or until fish is just cooked through and cockles/clams have opened. Remove any unopened shells before serving.

Variations of this recipe may include hard-boiled eggs or mushrooms, and depending on the season, may omit or replace the asparagus.

Monkfish with Golden Garlic

(Rap amb All Cremat)

MONKFISH (*RAPE* OR *BAUDROIE*) ARE HIGHLY PRIZED fish in the Pyrenean region. Also called anglerfish, these ugly saltwater creatures live on the ocean bottom often near the coast and have appendages resembling lures used to entice their prey. Caught in either trawls or gillnets, these fish are valuable even to fishermen in North America, where monkfish has been gaining popularity. In their range along the European and North American coasts, there are actually two similar species that are not separated during either selling or processing. White-bellied monkfish are the predominant species in the North Sea while black-bellied monkfish are predominantly found in the Mediterranean with some living along the Atlantic coast of Iberia. Males can grow to three feet in length, while females can be twice as large.

When cooked, monkfish flesh is unlike any other fish and is similar in texture to lobster. In Languedoc, sea bass is cooked in a very similar style, with the browned slices of garlic left intact and the juice of one lemon stirred directly into the garlic and thyme sauce. The paste or roux base for this sauce is essentially a *picada*, which is very useful for adding flavor to and thickening soups or stews.

There are numerous variations on monkfish or sea bass with browned garlic. After tasting and trying several, I offer the following recipe, which was inspired by Colman Andrew's simple yet satisfying preparation of this dish.

¹/₄ cup or more olive oil

8 or more cloves garlic, sliced

2 slices French or Italian bread

Salt and pepper

1¹/₂ to 2 pounds monkfish fillets, sliced in 1¹/₂- to 2-inch sections

Flour for dredging

2 cups fish stock

2 to 3 sprigs fresh thyme

3 tablespoons chopped fresh parsley

Pinch of cayenne

2 to 4 tablespoons white wine or sherry

1 lemon, cut in wedges

MAKES 4 SERVINGS

PLACE A LARGE SKILLET OVER LOW or medium-low heat, add enough olive oil to cover the surface. Sauté garlic slices until light golden brown. Remove and set aside.

Place bread slices in the remaining hot oil, adding more oil if needed. Increase heat to medium or medium-high and fry bread on both sides until lightly browned. Remove and set aside.

Salt and pepper fish pieces. Dredge pieces in flour, shaking off excess. Fry in remaining olive oil, adding more if needed, over medium heat, until crisp and browned on each side. Remove and set aside.

Pour fish stock into the hot skillet, stirring to deglaze the pan of cooked juices and food particles. Add thyme and simmer stock for several minutes to reduce the liquid. Pour any juices from the browned monkfish into the simmering stock.

As the stock simmers, place the fried garlic, bread slices, and parsley into a food processor, with cayenne, a pinch of salt and pepper, and 2 tablespoons wine. Process the mixture into a purée, adding 1 to 2 more tablespoons of wine or fish stock, as needed, to help form a thick paste.

Remove thyme sprigs from stock. Stir in the paste, blending it into the stock to make a smooth thick sauce. Continue to simmer on low heat. If fish has cooled or is not cooked through, place in simmering sauce to heat through or finish cooking. The sauce will thicken as it simmers. If it becomes too thick, stir in some water, wine, or stock. Check and adjust seasonings.

When done, serve fish accompanied by sauce, and with generous wedges of lemon.

This recipe works well with any firm, white-fleshed fish.

Some Catalan cooks add several ripe tomatoes into the simmering fish stock or lemon juice to the sauce, to lend a pungent edge to the flavor.

Mushrooms with Clams

(Setas con Almejas)

CLAMS ARE BIVALVE MOLLUSKS that have surely been eaten by humans for tens of thousands of years. A wide variety of marine clams are available in the Pyrenean region. My favorite are razor clams (*couteau* or *navaja*), which are long and thin and dig in the sand to escape collectors. Their flesh is so sweet and subtle that I prefer eating them with little adornment. Cockles (*coque* or *berberechos*) have little flesh and must be thoroughly cleaned in saltwater to remove sand. They are often eaten raw in Spain and have a delicate ocean flavor. Praire clams (*mye*) can be found along the coasts of France, and are actually quahog clams that have been introduced from North America. The grooved carpet shell (*clovisse* or *almeja*) is the most popular clam in the Pyrenean region and is available all year. This dish can be made with any of these clams. For that matter, any combination of edible mushrooms can be used: chanterelles, porcini, shiitake, or button just to name a few.

This recipe is related to the classic dish of *Almejas a la Marinera*, in which fishermen cook their clams in white wine. This dish, with slight variations, is very popular throughout northern Spain, from Galicia to the Costa Brava. The trait that identifies this version as Pyrenean, is combining the clams with mushrooms.

Heat olive oil in a skillet over medium heat. Add onions and garlic, and sauté until onions are soft and translucent, then add mushrooms. Cook until most of the juice has evaporated, stirring frequently. Mix in the parsley, followed by the red pepper flakes. Add white wine and season with salt to taste. Bring mixture to a simmer and add clams. Cover and let simmer for 5 minutes, stirring occasionally. Remove from heat and discard any unopened clams. Spoon sauce over clams and serve immediately.

$1/2$ cup olive oil

1 large Spanish onion, finely chopped

4 cloves garlic, minced

2 pounds mixed mushrooms, coarsely chopped

2 tablespoons chopped fresh parsley

$1/2$ teaspoon red pepper flakes

1 cup white wine

Salt

2 pounds whole clams, washed and drained

MAKES 4 TO 6 SERVINGS

Trout with Bacon, Sherry, and Cream (Trucha del Cincla a lo Fino)

THE STREAMS THAT DRAIN the French and Spanish Pyrenees are excellent habitat for trout, and this is a common dish in this region. Ernest Hemingway spent much time trout fishing in Navarra during his Parisian years, as reflected in many short stories and *The Sun Also Rises*. When we stayed at the Parador de Monte Perdido, in the heart of the Pyrenees, we enjoyed this recipe using trout fished from *El Río Cincla*, which was established in 1918 as Spain's first national park. Today the companion Parc National des Pyrénées allows for common management of a huge and contiguous portion of the range. The small parador located just outside the town of Bielsa in the Pineta Valley has a hunting lodge atmosphere, and we sampled the local Somontano wines in front of a roaring fire in the lounge. The chef, Julian Roque, is French, reflecting the fact that the border is only a few miles away. He borrowed the best of both culinary worlds to create this delicious adaptation of the classic *trucha a la Navarra*, pan-fried trout using ham of the Spanish Pyrenees.

RINSE AND PAT DRY each trout. Dredge both sides of each fish in flour, shaking off excess.

In a large skillet or pan, fry bacon pieces until partially cooked, but still limp. Remove bacon pieces and set aside. Pour out some of the excess fat released by the bacon, allowing some to remain in pan. Fry trout in pan, in batches, over

---

4 whole trout, cleaned

Flour for dredging

6 ounces bacon, chopped

2 tablespoons olive oil

2 medium onions, chopped

1 large potato chopped in ¼-inch dice (about 1½ cups)

6 ounces Bayonne or country ham, chopped

4 ounces mushrooms, preferably a mix

1½ cups dry sherry or white wine

½ cup heavy cream or crème fraîche

Salt and pepper

MAKES 4 SERVINGS

---

medium heat, approximately 5 minutes on each side. Skin should be crisp and browned. Remove trout and set aside.

If needed, add olive oil to the pan, and sauté onions until they become translucent. Add bacon, diced potatoes, ham, and mushrooms, continuing to stir until potatoes soften, and onions and mushrooms become golden. Pour in sherry or white wine to deglaze the pan, stirring up any browned morsels stuck on the bottom. Let simmer to reduce by about a half. Stir in cream and continue to simmer. Taste and adjust seasoning.

Place trout into the sauce and cook for 2 minutes on each side to reheat.

Serve each fish with the sauce and all the bits swimming in it spooned generously over each. Accompany this with green beans and fresh country bread to soak up all the sauce.

Crème fraîche can be made by blending a tablespoon of buttermilk or sour cream into a cup of heavy cream. Cover and allow the mixture to stand in a warm spot for 8 to 12 hours. Once it has thickened, refrigerate it. It can keep for up to two weeks.

Marinated Trout with Mint and Ham (Trucha a la Navarra)

FLY FISHERMEN FROM AROUND THE WORLD have considered the icy rivers of the Pyrenees among the best trout waters in the world. In Navarra, Ernest Hemingway favored fly fishing in the *Rio Irati*. Don Ernesto and Alexander Dumas had the highest praise for the individual specimens and the abundance of trout in Navarran waters. Cantabria, Aragón, Asturias, and upper Catalonia are also well known for their excellent trout rivers. The brown trout (*Salmo trutta*), recognized by its red and black spots, and salmon trout, a type of brown trout which has creamy pink flesh due to its crustacean eating habits, are the most common varieties caught and consumed in Navarra.

This well-known Spanish dish hails from the mountainous region of Navarra, where it has been eaten for several hundred years. As with many historic dishes, it is a simple one, originally made with ingredients readily available in rural mountainous areas—a freshly caught brown trout was pan fried in bacon or pork fat, and seasoned with garlic, serrano ham, and herbs. Sometimes the trout would be *en escabeche*, or marinated in wine or vinegar.

RINSE EACH TROUT AND PAT DRY. Separate ribcage bones from the flesh of each fish by inserting a small sharp knife just behind each row of ribs at their base. Cut upward while pressing against the bones. Clip away separated ribs with scissors. Line the cavity of each fish with a tuft of mint leaves and place them in a dish or sealable watertight plastic bag. Add garlic, thyme, white wine, and any remaining mint. Cover

4 whole trout, cleaned*

1/2 cup well-packed chopped or crushed mint leaves

2 cloves garlic, crushed

1 teaspoon dried thyme or 2 to 3 sprigs fresh thyme

1 cup dry white wine

Salt and pepper

4 slices serrano ham (similar to prosciutto ham)

4 slices bacon, chopped

Flour for dredging

1 lemon, cut in wedges

MAKES 4 SERVINGS

dish or seal bag and allow to marinate in refrigerator for at least 4 hours.

Remove trout from marinade and pat dry. Salt and pepper each fish inside and out. Stuff a slice of ham in each trout cavity. Roll each slice of ham and place one in each trout cavity. In a large skillet, fry bacon pieces and remove, allowing the bacon fat to remain. Dredge both sides of each fish in flour, shaking off excess. Fry trout in the bacon fat over medium heat for 5 to 7 minutes on each side. Skin should be crisp and browned.

Serve trout as is, topped with bacon pieces and lemon wedges, and accompanied by fried or roasted potatoes.

To use marinade as a sauce, pour it into a saucepan. Add bacon pieces and bring to a simmer. Reduce liquid by half and add salt and pepper to taste and pour over potatoes.

* If the trout are large (over 10 inches) you may with to double the marinade ingredients.

To add more depth of flavor, add thin slices of lemon, sliced shallots, onions, a bit of vinegar, and/or cured olives in the marinade bag. Olive oil can be used instead of bacon fat for frying.

Much of the preparation for this dish can be done in advance by varying the steps slightly: After adding the ham stuffing, wrap a whole bacon strip around each trout. Lightly oil one side of large pieces of foil—one for each trout. Make well-sealed foil envelopes around each fish, folding the sides and corners at least twice to keep juices from escaping. When you are ready throw these on a hot grill or on a baking sheet in a 350°F oven for 15 to 20 minutes, until the packets are puffed out.

Stuffed Crab Donostiarra

(Txangurro a la Donostiarra)

DONOSTIA IS THE BASQUE NAME for the city of San Sebastian, Spain, the Basque culinary capital. This recipe in the style of Donostia is the most popular version of *txangurro al horno* or oven-baked crab. *Txangurro a la Donostiarra* is the creation of Felix "Shishito" Ibarguren, one of the most renown Basque chefs during the *Belle Epoque* in San Sebastian or Donostia. This was a period from the late nineteenth century through World War I when San Sebastian was one of Europe's most cosmopolitan cities, filled with famous artists, celebrities, and Parisian high society. Chef Ibarguren's recipe was unique in his dedication to the innovative use of the locally caught *centollo* or spider crab found along the coast of the Bay of Biscay in the heart of Basque country. Prior to his *centollo* recipes, imported lobster was almost exclusively the crustacean used for finely prepared dishes. The *centollo* is clawless, sweet, and very similar to snow crab, in which the best meat is found in its thick spidery legs. Another popular Basque crab used for this dish is the *buey de mar*, literally translated as "ox of the sea", similar in appearance to the American west-coast dungeness crab. Since *centollo*, *buey de mar*, and snow crab are difficult to come by, any sweet crab, such as the dungeness, will make a fine substitute.

IF STARTING WITH LIVE CRABS, boil enough water to immerse crabs in a large pot. For each quart of water, stir in 1 to 2 tablespoons salt. When the water is at a rolling boil, quickly drop crabs in. Depending on the type of crab (thickness of shell, size of each crab, etc.), boil them for 10 to 15 minutes. Remove crabs and set aside to cool.

When cool enough to handle, remove carapaces, by prying and pulling up the rear edge first. Clean and rinse carapaces and set them aside until the end. Crack open the legs and body of the crabs and extract the meat. Collect and save any juices from the crabs.

Place a large skillet over low heat and add olive oil and 1 tablespoon butter. When hot, add onion, leeks, garlic, and carrot. Stirring occasionally, cook until onion and leeks begin to caramelize, 10 to 15 minutes. Stir in tomatoes, increase the heat to medium, and cook for 5 to 8 minutes to reduce most of the liquid. Pour in hot fish stock, any crab juices collected, liquor, and white wine. Stirring occasionally, simmer for several minutes until liquid is reduced by about one-third. Stir in the crabmeat, and pinch of cayenne. If the mixture is still fairly liquid, stir in a tablespoon of bread crumbs to thicken the sauce. Taste, and add salt and pepper, if needed.

Preheat oven to 500° F or turn on broiler.

Using cleaned crab carapaces as bowls, place them on a baking sheet or pan. Spoon equal portions of the crab mixture into the carapaces. Mix parsley into bread crumbs. Sprinkle bread crumbs evenly over the top of each. Cut the remaining 2 tablespoons of butter into small pieces and drop a few over the bread crumbs in each "bowl." Place in oven for 8 to 10 minutes, or until bread crumbs are browned. If placing under a broiler to brown, reduce time and check after 3 to 4 minutes. Serve hot.

2 pounds crabmeat or 4 one-pound crabs

2 or more tablespoons salt

2 tablespoons olive oil

3 tablespoons butter

1 medium onion, chopped

2 leeks, chopped

1 or 2 cloves garlic, chopped

1 medium carrot, chopped

2 medium tomatoes, peeled, seeded, finely chopped; or 1 cup purée

2 cups fish stock, heated

1 to 2 tablespoons brandy/cognac/Armagnac

1/2 to 1 cup white wine

Pinch of cayenne

2 to 4 tablespoons bread crumbs

Salt and pepper

1 tablespoon chopped fresh parsley

MAKES 4 SERVINGS

While preparing and serving the crab in individual carapace "bowls" will delight your guests, the steps involved to prepare fresh crabs from scratch may not be practical for all.

Preparation time can be cut in half if you purchase pre-shelled lump crabmeat from your seafood merchant, and bake the finished product in individual ceramic dishes.

Seafood Operetta

(Zarzuela)

THROUGHOUT THE AGES, numerous types fish and seafood stews have been invented along the Mediterranean coastline. *Zarzuela* is a famous Catalan dish invented in the sophisticated culinary atmosphere of Barcelona during the nineteenth century. *Zarzuela*, or *sarsuela* in Catalonian, means "seafood operetta," as it is considered a musical performance of seafood. The parade of freshly caught pelagic delicacies in this dish embrace the philosophy of "too much is not enough." The reputation of this wonderful dish has been somewhat tarnished by lesser kitchens which will use this dish as a vehicle for disguising seafood that is less than fresh. For better or worse, this dish quickly became popular throughout Catalonia, as every cook created his or her own *zarzuela* in attempts to dazzle guests with their composition.

The thick onion, tomato, and garlic base made for this stew is a *sofregit*, a Catalan sauce that is the essential flavoring in an overwhelming variety of Catalan dishes including soups, stews, and sauces. The name *sofregit* is based on a Catalan word, *sofregir*, which means to lightly fry, as these sauces are created by frying the ingredients slowly over low heat. Today the most widely used *sofregit* contains tomatoes and onion, and varies with the addition of other vegetables and herbs. The first Catalan cookbook, *Libre de Sent Sovi*, written in approximately 1324, shows that *sofregits* date back to at least the Middle Ages, when they were usually made from onions and leeks, and occasionally flavored with bacon. Tomatoes became an essential *sofregit* ingredient after their introduction to Europe, following the discovery of the New World.

HEAT 2 TABLESPOONS OF OLIVE OIL in a large, deep pot over low to medium-low heat. Sauté onions until light brown and limp, 15 to 20 minutes. Add garlic and stir for 2 more minutes before mixing in the tomatoes. Increase heat to medium, and continue to cook until the loose liquid from the tomatoes has evaporated and tomatoes soften and break down. Set aside.

Add 2 to 3 tablespoons of olive oil to a large skillet or pan over medium-high heat. When the pan is hot, add the fish and quickly fry both sides until the edges are slightly browned; remove and set aside on a plate. Quickly fry the shrimp or prawns, scallops, and cuttlefish/squid the same way. Do not attempt to cook them through.

Add the fish to the onion and tomato mixture. Pour Armagnac over all and ignite, to burn off the alcohol, taking care that the flames do not ignite anything else.

When the alcohol has burned out, add bay leaf, red pepper or cayenne, and saffron (if available). Mix in the fish stock and white wine and bring to a boil. Reduce heat to a simmer and let cook for 10 minutes. Add shrimp mixture, mussels, and clams. Simmer for another 5 minutes, or until mussels and clams are open, turning shrimp/prawns and scallops once to make sure all sides are cooked by the broth. Discard any mussels or clams that remain unopened. Stir in parsley. Taste, and season with salt and pepper if needed.

Serve hot with fresh crusty bread or slices of bread toasted in a skillet with a bit of olive oil or butter.

⁑⁕⁕⁕⁕⁕⁕⁕⁕⁕⁕⁕⁕⁕⁕⁕⁕⁕⁕⁕⁕⁕

Although the nature of this recipe is that no single recipe exists, the basic ingredients of onions, garlic, tomatoes, cognac or other spirit, such as rum, and white wine, or sherry are regulars in most *zarzuela* caldrons.

1/4 cup or more olive oil

1 large or 2 medium onions, chopped

3 cloves garlic, minced or crushed

3 large tomatoes, peeled, seeded, and chopped or one 14 ounce can tomatoes, chopped

1 pound firm white fleshed fish, such as hake, monkfish, or grouper

12 large shrimp or prawns, with shells

1/2 pound sea or bay scallops

1/2 pound fresh (or frozen) cuttlefish or squid, cut in bite-size pieces

1/4 cup Armagnac, cognac, or brandy

1 bay leaf

1/4 teaspoon red pepper flakes or cayenne

Pinch of saffron (optional)

2 or more cups fish stock or clam juice

1 cup white wine or dry sherry

12 mussels, scrubbed clean

12 clams, scrubbed clean

1/4 to 1/2 cup chopped fresh parsley

Salt and pepper (optional)

MAKES 4 TO 6 SERVINGS

Tailor this dish to whatever seafood is available or that you prefer.

POULTRY AND
FEATHERED GAME

Poultry and Feathered Game

Basque Chicken

(Poulet basquaise/Pollo a la Vasca)

WE FOUND THIS DISH on the menus of nearly every French Basque restaurant serving regional cuisine. I particularly enjoyed it at the small, unpretentious *brasserie* Realis la Nive in the charming and historic St.-Jean-Pied-du-Port, which was once the capital of Basse-Navarre. St. Jean is located about 10 miles south of the junction of three major paths from northern Europe to Santiago de Compostela, and consequently thrived on the tourist traffic of pilgrims between the tenth and sixteenth centuries. The modern tourist traffic virtually ends by early October, and we spent the day enjoying the photogenic old quarter on the Nive River without being engulfed by the summer hordes. As an *apéritif*, we sampled Izarra—a green syrupy Basque liqueur that my husband described as tasting of baby aspirin, crème de menthe, and mouthwash. Fortunately the Basque chicken was sumptuous, and we quickly forgot about our misadventure with Basque liqueurs. To be truly authentic use a white wine from Irouléguy, located in the heart of the French Basque region.

SALT AND PEPPER CHICKEN. Add enough oil to a large deep skillet or large pot to cover cooking surface. Place over medium-high heat. Brown chicken pieces on each side. Remove and set aside.

Continued

Salt and pepper

1 chicken (about 3 pounds), cut into 8 pieces

Olive oil for sautéing

1 medium to large onion, chopped

4 cloves garlic, minced or crushed

Pinch of *piment d'Espelette* or cayenne

1 to 2 red bell peppers, seeded and chopped

3 medium to large tomatoes, seeded and chopped or 1 (14-ounce) can tomatoes

1 cup white wine

¼ cup chopped fresh parsley (optional)

MAKES 4 TO 6 SERVINGS

Add a few more tablespoons of oil to skillet, if needed, and sauté onion for several minutes, until it becomes translucent. Add garlic and *piment d'Espelette*, and stir for a minute more. Do not let garlic brown. Stir in peppers and tomatoes, and cook for an additional 5 to 10 minutes. Blend in white wine and add browned chicken pieces.

Lower heat to bring mixture to a simmer. Cover, leaving a crack for some steam to escape. Let simmer, stirring occasionally, for 30 minutes or more; until chicken is well cooked. Season with salt and pepper to taste. Stir in chopped parsley during the last 5 minutes of cooking, if desired.

Serve with fried or roasted potatoes.

<hr>

Each Basque cook seems to have his or her own variation of this basic recipe. Some flour the chicken before browning, to thicken the sauce as it cooks, others add a cup of chicken stock to create a more fluid sauce.

Additional ingredients that frequently appear in Basque chicken recipes include Bayonne, serrano or smoked ham, green peppers, mushrooms, fresh thyme, bay leaf, lemon juice, or a bit of sugar to take the acid edge off the sauce.

Basque Rice with Chicken
(Gachucha)

RICE, WHICH IS IN THE GRASS FAMILY, was apparently first cultivated in India, China, and other tropical Asian countries nearly 10,000 years ago. Persia acquired rice from South Asia around 1000 B.C. and brought it to the western part of its empire. Invading Arabs brought rice into Spain and Languedoc during the eighth century. Rice cannot compete with dry land cereals in areas of low rainfall unless irrigation water is readily available, but the Arabs used new irrigation techniques such as waterwheels and irrigation ditches. They found ideal conditions for planting rice south of Valencia and on the Mediterranean coast where traditional varieties of rice have attained some of their highest yields in the world.

As a result of historical parallels with rice and Moorish influences on its preparation, this Basque rice dish, *gachucha*, and the national dish of Spain from Valencia, paella, are made in very much the same way. The name for rice in Arabic—*ar-rozz*—became *arroz* in Spanish.

REHYDRATE THE CHORICERO in hot water for 20 to 30 minutes. Bone chicken and cut meat into 1½-inch chunks. If you prefer leaving chicken on the bone, chop into manageable-size pieces. Open the rehydrated choricero or ancho pepper and remove seeds. Gently scrape the flesh from the pepper and set it aside, discarding the skin.

Heat oil in a large, deep skillet or paella pan over medium-high heat. Fry chicken pieces on all sides to a light brown. Add chorizo/sausage and ham and cook all for 1 to 2 minutes more. If using bacon, fry separately and drain some of the extra oil when done. Remove all meat

1 choricero (or ancho) pepper or
   1 to 1½ teaspoons paprika plus
   a pinch of cayenne
1½ to 2 pounds chicken (or 1 to
   1½ pounds boneless)
3 tablespoons oil for frying
½ cup (4 ounces) diced chorizo or
   smoked sausage
½ cup (4 ounces) diced bacon or ham
1 medium onion, chopped
2 cloves garlic, minced or crushed

INGREDIENTS CONTINUED

2 cups uncooked short-grain or
risotto rice

1 medium tomato or
¹/₄ cup tomato purée

1 bay leaf

1 teaspoon dried thyme or
2 fresh sprigs

2 cups chicken stock

¹/₂ cup dry white wine

¹/₂ cup fresh or frozen peas

1 to 2 tablespoons fresh chopped
parsley

1 pimiento pepper or red bell pepper,
roasted, peeled, seeded, and sliced

Makes 4 to 6 servings

from pan and set aside. Add onions to the oil in the pan and sauté until they begin to soften, add garlic, and cook for another minute.

Stir in rice, tomato, choricero pulp (or paprika and cayenne), bay leaf, and thyme. Return meat to the pan, either mix in or place on top of rice. Heat the stock and pour it in, along with the wine. If using fresh peas, add peas. Reduce heat to low and cover tightly. At this point the pan can be transferred to a 350° F oven to finish or kept on low heat on the stove. If using frozen peas, after 15 minutes, add them on top of the rice and replace cover. Cook rice approximately 5 minutes more or until rice the liquid is absorbed and the rice is tender. Total cooking time for the rice should be 20 to 25 minutes.

Mix peas and chopped parsley into rice and top with pimiento slices before serving.

The ingredients that earmark a rice dish as Basque *gachucha* are chorizo, bacon, onion, garlic, tomato, and pimiento pepper. Basque cooks on both sides of the Pyrenees will individualize this dish with other meats and flavor nuances. In this case, chicken, white wine, and peas have been added.

Game Hens with Garlic and Lemon

(French Catalonia)

THIS RECIPE IS MADE IN FRENCH CATALONIA with guinea fowl, although Cornish hen, pheasant, or free-range chicken could substitute. Helmeted guinea fowl (*Numida meleagris*), also called *pintade, faraona,* and African pheasant, is the fowl of choice in France for special meals. Native to much of Africa, they were first domesticated by the ancient Egyptians and Carthaginians and have been raised on farms in France for centuries. With striking white spots on its black feathers, a mature guinea fowl is similar in size to a pheasant and slightly smaller than a chicken. Guinea fowl flesh is white like chicken, but its delicate and fragrant taste is more reminiscent of pheasant, without an excessive gamy flavor. They are meaty birds. With only five percent fat, they are substantially leaner than chicken. For this reason, guinea fowl are often cooked with bacon or sausage to keep the flesh from becoming too dry.

Having experimented with various methods and combinations for a sweet and savory method of preparing fowl, I decided that my favorite was my adaptation of a recipe Colman Andrews obtained in Banyuls-sur-Mer, home of the *vin doux naturel* that bears its name. This recipe is a wonderful balance of savory, sweet, and tart ingredients mixed in a very Catalan manner.

Recipe and ingredients on following page

Recipe and ingredients on following page

Salt and pepper

2 to 6 game hens (4 to 5 pounds total), cut in quarters or depending on size, in half

Olive oil for sautéing

1 medium onion, chopped

2 heads garlic, cloves separated and peeled

4 to 6 ounces bacon or sausage, coarsely chopped

1 cup white wine

2 cups chicken stock

1 lemon, grate zest and extract juice

1/2 cup sweet Banyuls or port wine

1/2 cup cream or half-and-half (optional)

MAKES 4 TO 6 SERVINGS

SALT AND PEPPER THE HENS. Pour enough oil into a large deep skillet or pot to cover. Place over medium-high heat. Brown the bird pieces on both sides. Remove and set browned pieces aside.

Lower heat to low and add onions, garlic cloves, and bacon to the hot skillet. Sauté until onions become translucent and begin to lightly brown. Add white wine, chicken stock, lemon juice and zest. Place browned hen pieces into this mixture.

Let simmer, uncovered, for approximately 1 hour. Add Banyuls or port and cook 15 minutes more. Add salt and pepper to taste.

Optional: Remove garlic cloves and place in a blender or processor. Add cream and purée. Blend purée into the mixture in the skillet or pot.

Serve with crusty bread, fried or roasted potatoes.

Quails Roasted in Parchment

(Cailles en papillotes)

MANY FOOD CRITICS BELIEVE that we live in a dismally monotonous age with regard to poultry. Until a few hundred years ago, innumerable bird species were considered edible—swans, flamingos, herons, peacocks, magpies, owls, you name it. Of course, such fare was primarily the province of the wealthy. Quail may still seem exotic to some, but farmers have developed techniques to raise them commercially, so they are widely available and reasonably priced. This method of cooking quail in parchment, or *en papillote*, bakes the birds inside a wrapping of greased parchment paper. In Ariege, France, quail are wrapped and cooked in grape leaves. Cooking these birds inside their own little bag essentially steams them, enhancing the fowls' natural sweetness while keeping them moist. During baking the parchment puffs up into the shape of a dome, and at the table the secret contents are not revealed until the parchment is slit open and peeled back. This technique provides an experience your guests will long remember.

BRUSH TOP OF PARCHMENT with duck fat or butter. Place a tablespoon of Armagnac inside the cavity of each bird. Sprinkle both the inside and outside of each bird with a pinch of salt, pepper, and garlic. If using parsley, sprinkle over the exterior of each bird.

Place each bird on one half of a large sheet of parchment paper. Toss a ½ cup of mushrooms over each bird. Fold the parchment paper in half to completely cover the ingredients. Create a well-sealed

---

4 sheets parchment paper (each large enough to form an envelope around one bird)

¼ cup duck fat (or butter)

2 ounces Armagnac or cognac

4 quails or other small game birds

Salt and pepper

2 cloves garlic, finely chopped

2 tablespoons chopped fresh parsley (optional)

2 cups sliced mushrooms, divided into ½-cup portions

MAKES 4 SERVINGS

---

envelope by creasing and folding all side edges. Begin a second series of toothed folds, by first turning down a corner at a 45° angle to form a triangular fold. Along the next ¼ to ½-inch, fold down the corner formed by the last crease, making sure to overlap some of the previously folded section. This overlapping will double fold each preceding part and create a tight seal.

Place packets over a hot grill, slightly removed from the flame. When paper browns, turn over and brown the other side. Remove when packets are puffed from the steam caused by cooking. Cooking time should be approximately 5 minutes on each side. If baking in an oven, preheat oven to 350° F. Place packets in baking pan, and bake until each packet has puffed out from steam, 20 to 30 minutes.

Serve birds in their packets, to be sliced open by each diner.

•·•·

If quails are unavailable, cornish game hens, easily found in American food stores, will roast deliciously in parchment.

While not traditional, aluminum foil is an excellent substitute for creating "papillote" envelopes, if one lacks parchment paper.

Quails or Ortolans with Foie Gras and Grapes

(southwest France)

RURAL RESIDENTS OF THE PYRENEES spend a great deal of time hunting, especially during the autumn and winter. This recipe, which few people in North America are likely to prepare with ortolans, is included to provide an example of some of the unique culinary tastes in this region (it should be noted that this dish can no longer be served in commercial establishments in France). The ortolan bunting (*Emberiza hortulana*) is a small songbird that scratches on the ground to eat seeds and is very similar to North American sparrows. Hunters in southwest France each autumn place grain in wire traps called *matoles* to lure and capture them live. The ortolans are fed grain to make them as fat as possible and then drowned in Armagnac. The buntings are plucked and roasted whole without removing any internal organs. Although it is now illegal to serve ortolans, they are considered a fine delicacy, properly consumed only under the cover of a napkin, which allows one to privately enjoy all the exquisite vapors of this rare dish.

The following excerpt from an article by Thomas Matthews for *Wine Spectator* sums up the mystique and controversy surrounding the consumption of ortolans. The meal took place in 1995 at Le Cirque in New York, and was labeled "The Dinner of the Millennium."

"But the biggest outcry came when Ducasse served a surprise course for the press only: roast ortolan.

Ortolans are songbirds, once common in southwestern France, now rare and protected by law. For centuries, the French have considered them delicacies, and an elaborate ritual of preparing and eating them became part of any gourmet's rites of passage. Today it's illegal in France to serve them commercially. But Ducasse managed to find 50 ortolans (they are about the size of lemons and cost $50 each) and brought them to the United States in a diplomatic pouch. He also brought along a $15,000, 1,000-pound gas-fired rotisserie and a chef, Marc Valet, to Le Cirque to cook the birds.

Ducasse carefully set the stage. Handing out large napkins specially embroidered for the event with the chefs' names, he explained that the ortolans would come out sizzling in small casseroles. Each diner would put a napkin over his or her head, grasp the bird by the beak and eat it whole from the neck. (A restaurateur in the Rhône told me he once saw Bocuse eat two dozen ortolans at a sitting, tiny beaks rimming his plate like a crown.) The napkin was essential: It captured all the savory aromas and hid the guilty diner from the eyes of the law and the Lord.

Peter Kump, president of the Beard Foundation, visibly emotional, rose to say that he had long heard of ortolans, but had never eaten one before, and described his sensations in almost mystical terms. Valet said that probably never again would he roast 50 ortolans at one time. Some of the journalists were squeamish. Most ate with relish. One decided to bite the hand that fed her. The next day's Daily News splashed the birds on the cover with the headline 'Rare Bird Killed for N.Y. Feast' and quoted animal rights activists calling the ortolan dish 'inappropriate and probably unethical.'

'Even if there were only 500 ortolans left in the world, we should eat 50 of them,' Ducasse responded. 'Keep the species alive, yes, but also a tradition of hunting and eating that's lasted for centuries and become almost a myth. In 1994 in France, it's likely that not even 500 people ate an ortolan. It's part of our soul, and it's disappearing.'

Fin de siècle. An era is coming to an end, a way of life with its roots in the Middle Ages, that began with ortolans and reached a peak with this century's great French cuisine."

Skylarks, robins, blackbirds, thrushes, and other songbirds are sometimes eaten in parts of the Pyrenean region. Small game birds with grapes and foie gras is a classic combination in southwest France.

PREHEAT OVEN TO 425° F.

Lightly salt the inside of birds. At the rear and anterior ends of each bird, gently loosen skin from meat by moving a finger just under skin. In ½-teaspoon increments, place small pats of foie gras in spaces just under skin, at both ends.

Melt butter and rub over each bird. Sprinkle with a little salt. Spoon wine or sherry into the cavity of each. Arrange birds in a roasting pan, making sure bottom of pan is buttered or oiled. Scatter grapes in the pan around the birds.

---

2 small quails or other small
  game birds
Salt
4 teaspoons foie gras
3 to 4 tablespoons butter
3 tablespoons white wine or sherry
2 cups green grapes, whole or
  halved

MAKES 1 OR 2 SERVINGS

Place pan in oven and immediately reduce temperature to 350° F. Cooking time depends on the size of birds. Roast for 20 to 25 minutes per pound. Cook small birds such as ortolans or thrushes for only 10 minutes.

Spoon the butter and drippings over each bird and serve with roasted grapes. Serve over toasted bread or potatoes.

If truly preparing tiny bunting-sized birds, spoon the foie gras into the body cavity of each bird instead of attempting to form pockets under the skin.

Traditionally, these little birds are roasted in butter. If concerned about the health aspects of larding butter over foie gras, olive oil can be used instead.

Duck with Pears

(Ànec amb Peres)

(Catalonia, southwest France)

DUE TO THE RICHNESS OF ITS DARK MEAT, duck is commonly served in France with a sweet and sour sauce, often accompanied by fruit. This recipe is based on dishes from Languedoc and Gascony. As with other traditional dishes, many variations exist of duck with pears. Depending on the fruits in season, you may find duck with pears, peaches, or cherries on a table in southwest France or northeast Spain.

In Spanish, this Catalan dish is called *pato con peras* and includes raisins, pine nuts, 2 heads of garlic, several onions, and Aguardiente, instead of Armagnac.

PREHEAT OVEN TO **425°** F. Pierce the fatty skin of the duck all over with a fork. Sprinkle the inside and outside with salt and pepper. Tie legs together with string. Line bottom of roasting pan with the onion, carrot, and garlic. Place duck, fatty side up, on a rack in the roasting pan and bake for 30 minutes. Lower heat to 350° F for the remainder of the cooking time. Calculate total roasting time allowing 15 to 18 minutes per pound.

Meanwhile, heat wine in a saucepan with the sugar and lemon peel. Slice each pear into 8 wedges. Poach pears in wine and sugar for approximately 8 minutes, or until tender and easily pierced by a knife. Depending on the ripeness of your pears, cooking time could range from 7 to 15 minutes. Discard lemon

---

1 duck (5 to 6 pounds)

Salt and pepper

1 medium onion, cut in chunks

1 large carrot, cut in chunks

2 to 4 cloves garlic, chopped

1¹/₂ cups white wine

¹/₄ cup sugar

Peel of ¹/₂ lemon

2 large pears, peeled and cored

¹/₂ tablespoon butter and 1 tablespoon sugar (optional)

2 tablespoons Armagnac or brandy

¹/₄ cup red wine vinegar

2 teaspoons cornstarch (optional)

MAKES 4 SERVINGS

peels. Remove pears from liquid and set aside. Optional: Place pears on a buttered baking sheet, sprinkle tops with sugar, and place under a broiler for a minute to caramelize or brown the sugar.

After removing duck from oven, make sure any juices in the cavity are poured into the roasting pan. Place duck on a serving platter. Spoon Armagnac or brandy into the cavity, and cover it in foil to keep warm.

Remove and discard vegetables, and spoon out duck fat from roasting pan. Add vinegar to the remaining pan drippings to deglaze. Pour liquid from the roasting pan into a saucepan over medium heat. Boil for a minute. Add the white wine poaching liquid and continue to boil until reduced by about half. Add salt and pepper to taste. Optional: For a thicker sauce mix cornstarch into 2 tablespoons of cool water, and whisk into the simmering sauce.

Carve the duck, and pour some of the sauce over the sliced meat. Serve meat with several wedges of poached pear, accompanied by remaining sauce in a pitcher or gravy boat.

Peaches can easily be substituted for pears in this recipe. Peaches should be poached in halves or quarters, for only 4 to 5 minutes. A tablespoon or two of peach brandy may be added to enhance the peachiness of the sauce.

In place of spooning the Armagnac or brandy directly into the hot bird, you may wish to add it directly into the sauce, along with the poaching wine.

Other variations include:
- adding thyme, parsley, and/or bay leaves with the vegetables in the roasting pan;
- sprinkling a handful of toasted pine nuts over the poached pears just before serving.

Magret of Duck with Walnut Garlic Sauce

(Languedoc, southwest France)

SOUTHWEST FRANCE IS WELL KNOWN for many food products, ducks and walnuts being two of them. *Magret* is the breast meat from the large Muscovy or Moulard ducks in the southwest of France that are force-fed for foie gras. The *magret* is much thicker than the breasts of other ducks and has a nutty, rich taste, similar to a good steak. *Magret* has long been a delicacy commonly available only in southwest France, the land of foie gras. Happily, it is now served throughout France, and fine dining establishments in the United States. As with a good steak, *magret* is usually served with a rare center.

This walnut and garlic sauce or *aillade*, a variation on *allioli*, originates from the Languedoc region. In the language of the Occitan, the culture which gave rise to the region's name, Langue d'Oc, this sauce is called *Alhad Tolosenca*. In Languedoc, this would be made with the local sweet, extremely flavorful, pink garlic "d'Albi," which is primarily grown in and around Lautrec. The *ail rose de Lautrec*, which is planted in early winter and harvested in June and July, is the most popular variety. The walnut oil, or *huile de noix*, adds an exceptionally fine flavor to the sauce. It is pressed in autumn, when the nuts are first spread out to dry on wooden balconies of farm houses and then taken to mills in sacks for crushing by huge millstones. The southwest region of France is well known for the resulting walnut oil.

WALNUT GARLIC SAUCE:
Using a blender or food processor, process walnuts into a purée. Add garlic, salt, and 2 tablespoons of cold water. Continue blending. Add lemon juice and process for 5 to 10 seconds to purée all

Walnut Garlic Sauce:
2/3 cup walnuts, in small pieces
3 to 4 cloves garlic, chopped
1/8 to 1/4 teaspoon salt
2 teaspoons lemon juice
1/2 cup walnut oil

Magret/Duck Breasts:
4 duck breasts, boned, with skin on
Salt and pepper
2 to 3 shallots, finely chopped

MAKES 4 SERVINGS

ingredients together. Begin adding walnut oil in a thin stream. If the food pusher in your processor has a small hole in the middle, feed the oil through it. Make sure the mixture stays thick, and all the oil is incorporated before more is added. To let flavors combine, let the sauce sit for approximately an hour.

If you find that your mixture has separated, pour out the excess oil that floats to the top, and save it for another use. The remaining mixture will be the consistency of a thick sour cream. Give it a stir and serve it in dollops with the duck. It will taste just as good.

MAGRET/DUCK BREASTS:
Score the skin with a sharp knife, making cross-hatch marks ½ to 1 inch apart, across its surface. Season both sides of each breast with salt and pepper.

INDOOR METHOD: In a hot skillet over medium heat, place the breasts skin side down. Cook approximately 8 minutes, or until the skin is browned. The skin will have released more than enough fat to coat the bottom of the pan. Toss in shallots, and turn each piece over. Cook for 5 to 6 minutes more, depending on the desired level of rareness. Transfer to a platter lined with paper towels, to absorb excess fat. Cover with foil to keep warm and allow the meat to rest for 2 minutes.

OUTDOOR METHOD: If possible build a fire using grape vines. Another type of wood or charcoal fire will also work well. Grill the seasoned duck breasts over the fire, as you would a steak. When cooked to the desired level, scatter chopped shallots in a plate and place meat over them. Cover with foil or another plate. Place in a warm spot near the fire for 10 minutes. After 5 minutes spoon any juices released over the meat and re-cover.

Slice duck breasts and serve with walnut garlic sauce.

•◆•"◆•

True *magrets* are difficult to come by in the United States, and the price is very dear when found. The breast of an easily available Long Island duck serves as a fine substitute.

Partridges with Chocolate Sauce

(Perdices con Salsa de Chocolate)

(Catalonia, Aragón)

 RED-LEGGED PARTRIDGES (*perdices*) are game birds that have been considered feast dishes for royalty and clerical officials since the Middle Ages. Widespread and abundant in vineyards, fields, and hillsides, they have been eaten by rural huntsmen since time immemorial. The season begins in many areas the second Sunday in October, but these birds are now raised commercially and can be obtained throughout the year. A common proverb implies that eating partridges symbolizes happiness: *Fueron felices y comieron perdices* (they were happy and ate partridges).

There are many different ways to prepare the lean flesh of this succulent fowl. This one uses chocolate, and represents an amalgam of a classical Spanish game bird with a New World preparation. Conquistador Hernando Cortéz encountered *mole poblano* in Mexico, in which chickens or turkeys are cooked in a chocolate chili sauce. Chocolate, of course, was not known in Europe before Columbus. Unlike the *moles* of Mexico, this dish does not use capsicum peppers and is not hot, but surely owes its inception to Mesoamericas. The Catalan, more so than other cooks of the Pyrenees region, will routinely use chocolate to add depth to various savory sauces and stews.

ADD 2 TABLESPOONS OLIVE OIL to a skillet over high heat. In 2 batches, brown birds on all sides. Remove and set aside. Place pearl onions in the remaining oil and brown. Shake the pan occasionally to brown onions on all sides. Remove onions and set aside.

If needed add more oil to the hot pan. Lower the heat to medium. Sauté chopped shallots and garlic. Cook for about 3 minutes. Do not let garlic brown. Add oregano and pepper and stir for a minute. Pour in wine and broth, and add bay leaf. Bring to a simmer and add birds. Cover and let simmer for 15 minutes. Next, turn birds over and add pearl onions, cover and simmer for 15 minutes more, longer if onions are not yet tender.

When done, remove birds onto a serving platter and surround with the pearl onions. Cover with foil to keep warm while finishing sauce.

Continue boiling the cooking liquid to reduce by half. Meanwhile, place chocolate in a small bowl, adding some of the hot broth. Stir to melt and blend chocolate into the liquid. Taste cooking liquid and add salt, if needed. Whisk the melted chocolate into the liquid. Stir in vinegar and taste. The amount of vinegar depends on amount of sauce and strength of chocolate used. To make thicker sauce, place the cornstarch or flour into a small dish with just enough cold water to dissolve it. Stir into the hot sauce to thicken.

Pour sauce over the birds and serve with a chestnut purée.

Another layer of flavor can be added by wrapping a strip or two of bacon around each bird before browning.

4 tablespoons olive oil

4 quails or other small game birds

1/2 pound pearl onions (about 3 dozen)

3 shallots or 1 smallish onion, finely chopped

4 cloves garlic, minced

3 sprigs fresh oregano or 1/2 teaspoon dried

1/4 teaspoon black pepper

1 cup white wine

2 cups chicken stock

1 bay leaf

2 ounces semisweet chocolate

Salt

1 to 2 tablespoons wine vinegar

1 tablespoon cornstarch or flour (optional)

MAKES 4 SERVINGS

Pheasant with Banyuls and Walnuts

(southwest France, Catalonia)

IN OCTOBER AND NOVEMBER hunters will shoot pheasants in the foothills and areas surrounding the Pyrenees. This autumnal recipe highlights French Catalan ingredients with the inclusion of walnuts, duck fat, and sweet Banyuls wine. Banyuls is a *vin doux naturel* or naturally sweet wine from Banyuls, Collioure, Port-Vendres, and Cerbère, in Rousillon, found at the southern corner of France that borders both the Mediterranean Sea and the Pyrenees mountain range.

SEASON PHEASANT QUARTERS with salt and pepper, and dredge each piece in flour. Place duck fat or butter in a large pot or casserole over medium to medium-high heat. Quickly brown each piece on all sides. Remove meat and set aside. Reduce heat to medium.

Add onions to the pot, sautéing for several minutes until browned. Pour in the Banyuls or port, stirring the bottom to remove any cooked particles clinging to the cooking surface. Add thyme, bay leaf, and parsley. Return pheasant pieces to the pot, adding ½ to 1 cup of water or chicken stock if more liquid is needed to braise the meat. When the liquid reaches a simmer, reduce heat to low, and cover. Cook for 45 minutes or until meat is tender.

> 2 pheasants, plucked, cleaned, and cut into quarters
> Salt and pepper
> ¼ to ½ cup flour for dredging
> 2 to 3 tablespoons duck fat or butter
> 1 large onion, chopped
> 1 cup Banyuls or port wine
> 3 to 4 sprigs fresh thyme
> 1 bay leaf
> 3 sprigs fresh parsley
> ½ to 1 cup chicken stock (optional)
> 1 cup heavy cream
> ½ cup walnuts, broken into pieces
>
> MAKES 4 OR MORE SERVINGS

When cooked, remove and discard bay leaf, and thyme and parsley stalks. Take pheasant pieces from the pot and set them aside as you finish the sauce.
Continue to simmer the juices in the pot to reduce to ½ or ⅔ cup. Stir in cream and walnuts. Taste and, if needed, add salt and pepper. Return pheasant pieces and any juices to the pot to heat through and cover each piece in sauce.

Serve this with bread, noodles, or rice to help soak up the rich sauce.

━━━

Guinea fowl can be substituted for pheasant in this and most recipes. Both birds are very short on fat, and their meat can be dry if not cooked properly. For this reason, most recipes for such game birds will include a fatty enhancement, such as bacon, butter, or cream. Using a moist cooking method, such as braising, will also help prevent the meat from drying out.

Fresh domestic or wild mushrooms are also a delicious enhancement to this dish. First chop them, and sauté in olive oil or butter; then add them to the pot 20 to 30 minutes before the meat is done.

Wood Pigeons and Artichokes

(Béarn and Landes, southwest France)

WOOD PIGEONS (*PALOMBES*) ARE HIGHLY PRIZED in southwestern France. Each autumn hunters in Béarn, Landes, and the Basque country harvest between one and two million of these plump birds. While some are taken in August and September, mid-October becomes a spectacle in low western passes in the Pyrenees such as Col d'Organbidexha where thousands of hunters vie to harvest some of the 10 million wood pigeons that migrate south. They use now-traditional techniques developed over 600 years ago by monks to ambush this common pigeon, throwing whitened wooden disks. This apparently scares the birds to swoop to ground level to escape what they think is an attack by a bird of prey. Amidst the waving of large white flags and the din of horns and drums, the birds are herded into the center of the pass where they are netted or shot. A hunter returning home with a full bag of this tasty delicacy is welcome indeed and is only too happy to let some of his Armagnac go into the marinade.

REMOVE AND SAVE THE LIVERS. Salt and pepper the birds. Place duck fat or butter in a skillet over medium-high heat. Quickly brown the skin of the birds on all sides. Cut each pigeon in half, lengthwise. Save the fat in the pan.

4 wood pigeons or doves (including livers), plucked and cleaned

Salt and pepper

2 tablespoons duck fat or butter

1/3 cup lemon juice (about 2 large lemons)

1/3 cup Armagnac, cognac, or brandy

1 cup white wine

1 to 2 cups chicken stock (or enough to simmer artichoke hearts)

8 artichokes, hearts only, cut into quarters

2 tablespoons butter

MAKES 4 SERVINGS

To make the marinade, combine the lemon juice, Armagnac or brandy, wine, and a ¼ to ½ teaspoon each of salt and pepper (to taste). Place the birds in the marinade, making sure the flesh is well covered in the liquid. Marinate ½ to 3 hours.

As the pigeons are marinating, prepare the artichokes and livers. Pour chicken stock into a saucepan and bring to a simmer. Poach livers in the stock for 1 minute. Remove and set livers aside. Let the stock continue to simmer. Place the artichoke heart pieces in the stock, cooking until soft enough to mash or purée easily, 8 to 10 minutes.

Meanwhile, over medium-high heat, sauté the livers in the fat or butter remaining in the pan that the birds were browned in. When the livers are almost done, add 1 or 2 tablespoons of the marinade, cooking until the liquid has evaporated.

Preheat the oven to 375° F.

Purée sautéed livers together with artichoke hearts, and 2 tablespoons of butter. During this process, add a little cooking stock, a tablespoon at a time, until a smooth consistency is achieved. Add salt and pepper to taste. Spoon the mixture into the bottom of a baking dish.

Take the birds from their marinade and pat dry with paper towels. Arrange them over the purée. Place the dish in oven for 20 to 30 minutes, depending on how much they cooked during the browning process.

Serve birds over the purée. Accompany with potatoes or fresh bread.

·—·

Since wild wood pigeons are hard to come by in North America, I have cooked quails and guinea fowl in this style with great success.

The Armagnac or cognac in the marinade adds perfume to the meat.

If artichokes are unavailable, substitute another vegetable purée that will stand up to the additional cooking time in the oven. Root vegetables, such as parsnips and carrots, or celery hearts work well with the flavors in this dish.

MEATS AND
FURRED GAME

Meats and Furred Game

Lobster and Rabbit with Lemon Butter (Mar i Muntanya)

In the Catalan district of L'Empordà, chefs have a long tradition of dishes called *mar i muntanya*, which literally means "sea and mountain." Similar in conception to "surf and turf" in North America, these dishes rely on ingredients from both the sea and the land. As evidenced in this recipe, the juxtaposition of very different ingredients in one dish can result in some unusual, even brave, combinations. Other *mar i muntanya* dishes include pork with mussels and chicken with scampi. A now-classic recipe from L'Empordà that originated early in the nineteenth century is lobster with chicken, nuts, and chocolate. The following recipe is based on a dish created by Ferran Adrià, the chef of El Bulli in the Costa Brava resort town of Rosas which has become a culinary mecca. Part alchemist and part magician, this dish showcases Adrià's creative talents.

In a pot large enough to comfortably hold lobsters or lobster tails, fill with enough water to cover them when ready. Boil water. Place whole lemon in a strainer, and dip it into the boiling water for 30 seconds, remove and let cool. Grate lemon to make 1 tablespoon zest. Squeeze lemon to make 1 tablespoon juice. Mix lemon zest with lemon juice.

Lemon Butter:

1 lemon

3 tablespoons butter

Salt

Lobster and Rabbit:

2 lobsters (only tails needed)

Loin cuts from 1 rabbit, for 6 medallions

1 teaspoon salt

Marinade:

Pinch of ground black pepper

4 to 6 cloves garlic, crushed

1 teaspoon rosemary

2 sprigs fresh thyme or ¼ teaspoon dried

Pinch of crushed bay leaf

¼ cup white wine

½ cup or less olive oil

1 teaspoon paprika

Makes 4 servings

Add to butter and mix until well blended. Add salt to taste.

Allow water to return to full boil and add the lobsters for 30 seconds. This is not intended to cook them, but only to easily separate the meat from the shell. Remove and let cool. Peel shell from lobster tails.

Make shellfish stock from lobster shells: place shells in a hot pan for a minute, tossing to heat evenly. Pour a cup, or more, if more stock is desired, of hot poaching water over shells, cover and simmer for 30 minutes. Set aside.

Season both the rabbit loins and lobster tail meat with salt. Marinate by placing in a dish with pepper, garlic, rosemary, thyme, bay leaf, wine, ¼ cup olive oil, and paprika. Mix all ingredients and coat rabbit and lobster well. Cover and refrigerate for 3 hours.

Remove both meats from marinade, pat dry with paper towels. Reserve marinade. Place rabbit loins and lobster tails in two separate skillets, with 1 to 2 tablespoons olive oil in each, over medium heat. Cook until meat is browned and cooked. Remove meat and cover with foil to keep warm.

Divide marinade and ½ cup shellfish stock between the skillets, to de-glaze each pan. Then, if desired, combine liquids into one pan. Boil for several minutes to reduce the sauce slightly. Pour sauce through a sieve to remove solids.

Slice both rabbit loin and lobster tails into round, thin medallions. Alternate rabbit and lobster slices on serving plate. Drizzle with sauce, and serve with lemon butter.

Accompany this with potatoes or chestnut or pumpkin purée.

⁕•⸱⸱•⸱•⸱⸱•⸱•⸱⸱•⸱•⸱⸱•⸱•⸱⸱•⸱•⸱⸱•⸱•⸱⸱•⸱•⸱⸱•⸱•⸱⸱•⸱•⸱⸱•⸱•⸱⸱•⸱•⸱⸱•⸱•⸱⸱•⸱•⸱⸱•⸱•⸱⸱•⸱•⸱⸱•⸱•⸱⸱•⸱•⸱⸱•⸱•⸱⸱•⸱•⸱⸱•

The original recipe calls for accompanying the finished lobster and rabbit medallions with ⅛-inch slices of eggplant fried in a tempura batter, and apple chunks pan-fried in olive oil.

In an effort to cut down on the steps involved, I omitted the accompanying vegetables above, but mention them for the sake of completeness, and as options for more ambitious cooks.

Roasted Rabbit with Herb Stuffing and Allioli

(Lapin farci aux herbes/Conejo al Allioli)

RABBIT (*LAPIN* OR *CONEJO*) AND HARE (*LIÈVRE* OR *LIEBRE*) are very common in both the fields and on the tables of the Pyrenean region. The French on average eat as much rabbit each year as lamb. Spain was named Ispania for its innumerable rabbits, which were called *spahn* by the Carthaginians. Game has always been important in Pyrenean diets and hunting is a favorite pastime in the rural parts of this region especially during autumn and early winter. For centuries rabbit has been a component of thick meat stews in the countryside, to which beans, cabbage, and root crops such as carrots are added. Hares are usually larger than rabbits and can have tough meat in older animals. For this reason, the best hares are young animals about eight or ten months old—*lièvre de l'année* or "three quarter hares" that are still tender. Rabbit flesh tends to be tender even in adults, but those from the wild may be exceptionally gamy. The farm-raised rabbits that you will purchase from a market will likely be mostly white meat and mild in flavor. Rabbit has only about 5 percent fat, so it is a very healthful meat. The herb stuffing is adapted from a Gascon recipe by Pierre Koffmann. Instead of Bayonne ham, prosciutto can be substituted, or bacon for a smokier, though less traditional flavor.

We had similarly roasted, but unstuffed, rabbit at *Español*, a modest restaurant in Bujaraloz, Spain, located on the A2 highway between Zaragosa and Lerida; and at the charming dining room at the *Masía del Cadet*, very near the monastery at Poblet. In both cases, the rabbit was indescribably delicious, served simply with generous amounts of *allioli* as the accompanying sauce.

Recipe and ingredients on following page

1 whole rabbit (including liver, heart, kidneys), 3 to 4 pounds

5 tablespoons or more olive oil or duck fat

1 slice Bayonne ham or 2 slices bacon, chopped

¼ cup finely chopped shallots or onion

1 apple, peeled, cored, and diced

¼ cup chopped assorted fresh herbs (thyme, chervil, dill, chives, etc.)

½ cup bread crumbs

2 cloves garlic, minced

¼ cup chicken or vegetable broth, or white wine

Salt and pepper

2 to 3 large potatoes, chopped in 1½-inch pieces

4 carrots, chopped in 1 to 1½-inch pieces

MAKES 2 TO 3 SERVINGS

PREHEAT OVEN TO 400° F.

Over medium-high heat, fry liver, heart, and kidneys found in the rabbit, in 1 or 2 tablespoons olive oil or duck fat. Remove and set aside. If using bacon, rather than Bayonne ham, fry chopped bacon, remove and set aside. Add shallots or onion to remaining olive oil or bacon fat, sauté until pieces become translucent, remove, drain on paper towels if desired, and set aside. Add apple pieces to the pan and sauté until tender, 5 to 7 minutes. Remove and set aside.

Chop liver, heart, and kidneys into fine pieces, and place in a large bowl. Add herbs, bread crumbs, garlic, shallots, apple, and bacon or ham. Toss all ingredients together to blend well. Gradually add broth or wine to the stuffing to moisten the bread crumbs as you continue to mix.

Place stuffing in the cavity of the rabbit and sew up edges to enclose. Tie ends of the legs together and cover tips with foil. Brush the outside with olive oil or duck fat. Sprinkle the exterior meat with salt and pepper.

Drizzle remaining olive oil over the bottom of the roasting pan. Place potatoes and carrots in the pan, sprinkle with salt and pepper, and toss to coat all sides with oil. Place rabbit on a rack and set it in the roasting pan with the vegetables around it.

Place the pan into the oven for 30 minutes. Remove, quickly turn rabbit over, and turn the potatoes and carrots. Immediately return pan to the oven and reduce heat to 350° F. Cook for another 30 minutes or more, depending on rabbit size.

Calculate total cooking time using 18 to 20 minutes per pound (weight before stuffing).

When done, slice rabbit and serve with a bit of stuffing, the roasted vegetables, and accompany with a dollop of *allioli* (recipe follows).

•—•

Traditional Catalan Garlic Sauce (Allioli)

THIS SIMPLE SAUCE WAS CONCEIVED in ancient Rome and adopted in Spain when it was ruled by the Romans. The Catalonian name *all-i-oli* is from the literal translation of "garlic and oil." In Latin, *allium* is the word for garlic, and *oleum* is oil. In other parts of Spain this same sauce is known as *ajoaceite*. By any name, in Spain this is the basic garlic sauce used as a foundation for more complex sauces or used as is, slathered on grilled meats, bread, vegetables, seafood, stews, or almost anything that doesn't fall into the dessert category.

The ingredients must be at room temperature to combine properly. If garlic is beginning to form green centers and tops, try to remove as much of these green portions from each clove. Place garlic in a mortar with salt. Using even motions, mash ingredients together with pestle, forming a paste. Gradually begin adding olive oil, a few drops at a time, while continuing to mix. Continue adding oil until the mixture has emulsified and resembles mayonnaise. At this point your sauce is done. Do not add any remaining olive oil you may have pre-measured for this recipe, as it may upset the balance of the emulsion, causing your sauce to separate.

6 cloves garlic, minced

1/2 teaspoon salt

1 cup extra-virgin (preferably Spanish) olive oil

MAKES I TO I 1/2 CUPS

Alternatively, this tedious process can be done in modern kitchens with a blender or (small) food processor. Blend/process the garlic and salt into a paste. Add olive oil a little at a time or in a very thin stream while processing, until the oil begins to take a pudding-like consistency.

The *allioli* of southwest France, where it is known as *aïoli*, is made with eggs and is more like a garlic mayonnaise. In this Catalonian recipe, try to use Spanish olive oil, which has a relatively high acidity that helps stabilize the creamy consistency of the emulsified sauce.

Modern Catalan Garlic Sauce (Allioli/Aliolio/Aïoli)

THE FOLLOWING VERSION, containing lemon juice and eggs, is a more modern and common way to make *allioli* or *alioli*, in both Spain and southwest France.

6 cloves garlic, minced

¹/₂ teaspoon salt

1 egg yolk*

1 teaspoon lemon juice

1 cup extra-virgin (preferably
   Spanish) olive oil

MAKES I TO I¹/₂ CUPS

Place garlic in a mortar with salt. Mash ingredients together with pestle forming a paste.** Mix in egg yolk, followed by lemon juice. When the yolk and juice are blended in, add olive oil, a few drops at a time until all the oil is blended into a custard-like sauce.

* There have been occasional reports of intestinal illness resulting from food containing raw eggs contaminated with salmonella bacteria. Some estimate that I egg in 10,000 may be contaminated with salmonella. If this is a concern to you, you may wish to omit the raw egg yolk, which serves as an emulsifying and stabilizing agent. The emulsified sauce may be a bit more difficult to achieve and more apt to separate without the yolk.

**Once the paste is made, it can be transferred to a food processor and mixed with the remaining ingredients, in the same order. The olive oil can be added in a slow, very thin, stream, rather than in drops, as you continue to blend towards an emulsified sauce, the consistency of mayonnaise.

If you prefer a change from the garlicky *allioli* sauce, which is common with roasted rabbit in northern Spain, the following will provide a more finished sauce in the French style.

OVER HIGH HEAT, pour chicken stock into a pan. Add shallots and wine. Let reduce by half. Whisk in butter and add salt and pepper to taste. Pour sauce over the rabbit.

Alternative sauce:

$^1/_2$ cup chicken stock

2 to 3 shallots, chopped fine

$^1/_2$ cup white wine

2 tablespoons butter

Salt and pepper

Aragón Lamb Roasted with White Wine and Herbs

(Ternasco Asado)

IN ARAGÓN, *TERNASCO* IS HIGHLY PRIZED tender meat from selected young lambs. In 1989, *Ternasco de Aragón* received its own set of tightly regulated Denomination of Origin guidelines, guaranteeing the quality of any meat allowed this label. Lambs allowed under the *Ternasco de Aragón* denomination must belong to one of the following native breeds: *Rasa Aragónese, Ojinegra, Roya Bilbilitana,* or *Castellana.* Each must be suckled for at least 50 days on the milk of a mother grazed on herbs in the mountain pastures of Aragón.

Ternasco de Aragón lambs cannot be over 90 days old, most falling between 70 and 90 days. The lambs typically weigh between 40 and 52 pounds, with approximately half that weight in actual cuts of meat. The best meat will be light pink and extremely tender, with a smooth layer of fat over the surface. Various parts of the lamb will be stamped with an identification number and the *Ternasco de Aragón* symbol, in indelible red ink.

The following recipe is a delicious way to cook any leg of lamb. However, if you are lucky enough to purchase a true leg of *Ternasco de Aragón,* you may wish to prepare it in the most traditional way, as described in the end comments for this dish.

CUT EXCESS FAT FROM THE SURFACE of the leg, leaving a few patches or a thin sheath of fat on the side that will be on top during most of the roasting.

Prepare the marinade by mixing together garlic, rosemary, thyme, bay leaf, wine, and a pinch of salt and pepper. Place lamb in a pan just large enough to hold the leg. Pour marinade over meat and cover, turning meat every 8 to 12 hours. (If the leg will fit into a large, self-sealing, plastic bag, place all these same ingredients in the bag, instead of a bowl. Squeeze out as much of the air as possible and seal the bag. The marinade will cover the meat more evenly in the bag.) Refrigerate overnight or up to 2 days.

Preheat oven to 350° F.

When ready to cook, remove the meat from the marinade. Remove the thyme and rosemary sprigs from the marinade and discard, reserving the liquid. Season the leg with salt and pepper. Then smear duck fat or olive oil over the meat and over the roasting pan surface. Place leg on a rack over a roasting pan.

Calculate cooking time based on 20 to 25 minutes per pound. Place the roasting pan in the oven. Pour about one-third of the marinade over the lamb. After 20 minutes pour another third over the meat. Repeat, again in 20 minutes. One hour before the lamb is done arrange potatoes and scallions in the roasting pan around the lamb. Finish cooking the lamb.

When done, place leg on a large platter. Transfer potatoes to the platter, around the lamb. Cover with foil to keep warm while the meat rests for 10 minutes before serving.

1 leg of lamb, 5 or more pounds with bone

6 cloves garlic, sliced

2 sprigs fresh rosemary

3 sprigs fresh thyme

1 bay leaf

$1^{1}/_{2}$ to 2 cups white wine

Salt and pepper

$^{1}/_{4}$ cup duck fat or olive oil

6 medium potatoes, cut into 1- to $1^{1}/_{2}$-inch pieces

4 to 6 scallions, cut into 2-inch sections

MAKES 6 OR MORE SERVINGS

Remove scallions from the pan, squeezing any liquid out of them and then discard the pieces. Skim off excess fat or oil from the pan drippings. If needed, add water, ¼ cup at a time, to the bottom of the pan to dissolve or add to the pan juices. Stir to gather up all the browned flavor into the juices. Add salt and pepper, if needed. Pour into a small pitcher.

Slice lamb and serve with the potatoes and pan juices.

In the classic method of preparing *Ternasco Asado,* all ingredients are rubbed onto or poured over the meat just prior to roasting. Traditionally, the leg is not first marinated overnight. Adding the herbs, wine, and other flavoring just before roasting allows one to taste more of the pure flavor of the lamb meat. Since I feel the taste of the lamb is enhanced by allowing all flavors to permeate the meat, I allow the ingredients to season together for a day.

Marinated Leg of Lamb with Anchovies and Garlic

(Gascony, southwest France)

SHEEP HAVE BEEN HERDED in the Pyrenean region since the dawn of history. When the Romans arrived they found tracks in pastureland along which nomadic herdsmen had already been driving sheep for thousands of years. In Spain, the Goths called the common grazing land the *mesta* and held regular meetings to palaver about sheep rearing. Sheep were the cornerstone of the Castilian economy during the Middle Ages, and Alfonso the Wise established the position of Honorable Councilor of *la Mesta* in 1273. He sanctioned a vast network of drovers' tracks as *cañadas reales* (royal tracks), which expanded when victories over the Moors freed up more land. For centuries the taxes on livestock were a major source of funds to the crown. Eventually this way of life faded in importance, and the Councilor for Grazing Land was abolished in 1836. Even today central Spain is so renowned for its roast lamb, suckling pig, and kid that the area has been christened the *Zona de los Asados*. This recipe comes from Gascony, where excellent lambs are reared and are a major component of the diet.

The marinade is similar to a classic French marinade for pork, which introduces new flavor to the meat, but tends to mask the natural taste of the pork. I find the stronger flavor of lamb a better match for the red wine marinade, which adds a complexity that enhances rather than overpowers the meat.

CUT EXCESS FAT FROM THE SURFACE of the leg, leaving a few patches or a thin sheath of fat on the side that will be on top during most of the roasting. Mash or finely mince the anchovies and smear over the exposed meat. If inserting additional garlic slices into the meat, do so before coating the leg with anchovy paste.

Prepare the marinade by mixing together the garlic, red wine, onion, thyme, bay leaf, and peppercorns. Place lamb in a pan just large enough to hold the leg. Pour marinade over meat. Cover and refrigerate for 24 hours or more, turning every 8 to 12 hours.

To cook, preheat oven to 450° F. Remove leg from marinade, reserving the liquid. Smear olive oil or duck fat all over the meat. Place leg, fat side down, on a rack over a roasting pan. Roast for 20 minutes. Reduce heat to 325° F and flip the leg over, placing fat side on top. Add a cup of water into the bottom of the pan. Continue roasting the leg for 1 hour more. A 5-pound leg will have a well cooked exterior and some rare meat at the center. For larger legs, calculate total cooking time based on 15 minutes per pound.

Strain and discard solids from the marinade, reserving the liquid. After roasting the leg for 30 minutes at 325° F, pour half of the marinade over the roast, placing the rest in a saucepan.

Remove the leg, place on a large platter and cover with foil to keep warm while it rests, and you make the sauce.

Remove any excess fat or oil that may be in the pan drippings. Pour the drippings and cooked marinade from the roasting pan into the saucepan with the remaining reserved marinade. Over medium heat, bring to a simmer and reduce by one-third. Stir in currant jelly and squeeze in the juice from the ½ lemon. At this point the sauce is ready. For a thicker sauce: before heating the reserved marinade, set aside ¼ cup of marinade that is room temperature or chilled. Mix in the cornstarch or flour. Stir this into the simmering liquid at the end, blending well to thicken.

Slice lamb and serve with the sauce.

1 leg of lamb, 3 to 4 pounds, boneless; 5 or more pounds with bone
1 tin (2 ounces) anchovies, mashed; or anchovy paste equivalent to 12 to 15 mashed fillets
4 cloves garlic, crushed
3 cups red wine
1 small to medium onion, thinly sliced
4 sprigs fresh thyme
1 bay leaf, crumbled
8 to 12 black peppercorns
¼ cup olive oil or duck fat
1 tablespoon red currant jelly
½ lemon
Salt and pepper
1 tablespoon cornstarch or flour (optional)

MAKES 8 OR MORE SERVINGS

Garlic lovers can introduce more garlic flavor into the lamb by inserting slices of garlic directly into the meat before placing it in the marinade. Slice 4 more cloves of garlic. Cut I-inch-deep slits into various parts of the meat, inserting a garlic slice into each one. Marinate the leg.

In place of smearing the leg with anchovy, a bit of anchovy fillet or paste can be inserted into the meat with each garlic slice. When a lamb leg is not marinated, a bit of anchovy and garlic are commonly inserted into the meat just prior to roasting.

The anchovy adds salt to the meat and its fishy flavor will not be discernible in the finished product. However, it can be omitted, and the surface of the meat rubbed with salt instead.

A bit of fresh thyme or rosemary can also be inserted into the meat with each garlic slice.

Isard Saddle or Haunch, Sauce Richardin
(Râble ou cuissot d'isard, sauce Richardin)

THE ISARD IS THE NATIVE PYRENEAN CHAMOIS, an antelope with short chestnut color fur and a somewhat goat-like appearance. It is the only common wild herbivore found in the mountains. Large herds can be seen in the high mountain meadows of the French and Spanish Pyrenees in summer and in lower elevation forests in winter. Isards feed primarily at dawn and dusk.

Although isard meat is rarely found in restaurants, as their flesh is considered tough and strong-smelling, hunters of the region have developed methods of overcoming these shortcomings and preparing delicious dishes from the isard.

Evidence of this is found in Edmond Richardin's book on French cooking, *L'Art du Bien Manger* (1913), in which a large proportion of the recipes are game dishes. He includes several recipes for preparing different cuts of isard. To provide you with a bit of the true flavor of wild game from the Pyrenees countryside, I include this translation of Mr. Richardin's comments and instruction for preparing a saddle and/or haunch of isard, served with a sauce of his own concoction.

"During my yearly excursions in the mountains of the Aspe and Ossau valleys and in the neighboring Spanish region, I sometimes encountered herds of ten to twelve isards. Their allure is their wariness: the slightest warning sees them leap and disappear.

For a few days, the kitchen of Lées-Athas was converted into a genuine gastronomic laboratory, in which the most fantastic culinary experiences took place. Among all the sauces we enjoyed, the one served with the saddle and the haunch received unanimous acclaims. It is presented here, in its complete procession of pots, terrines, and seasonings:

Prepare a marinade as follows: 10 carrots, 12 onions, 15 shallots, and 6 garlic cloves, all minced. Five cloves, peppercorns and juniper berries (for five centimes of each), 6 sprigs of thyme, 3 bay leaves, sage, wild thyme, 2 pimentos, salt, and a profusion of parsley. Lightly brown these ingredients in butter. Moisten with half a liter of vinegar and a liter of consommé. Bring to a boil two or three times on high heat. Let cool.

Then place the saddle or the haunch in a terrine and pour over it the marinade with all its ingredients. Marinate the meat for five or six days, depending on the season, moistening it and turning it frequently.

Remove and drain your haunch. Stud it with streaky bacon (or lardoons), tie it with string and grill it on a rotisserie.

Prepare a dark roux with three spoonfuls of flour and a good amount of the strained marinade. Add 100 grams of the game stock, a deciliter of excellent champagne, salt, and pepper. Let it reduce for 20 minutes. In the meantime, bring 4 minced shallots to a boil in a Madeira glass (2 tablespoons) of vinegar. Let it reduce, strain, and add to the sauce.

When ready to serve, pour and mix the juice of the haunch from the drip pan to your sauce.

Garnish and serve, sauce on the side.

You can use this cooking method for the haunch and leg of the roebuck and deer."

Veal Chops with Mushrooms

(Basque, Catalonia, southwest France)

VEAL IS PARTICULARLY FAVORED in Catalan cuisine. In mountain areas, dishes combining veal and mushrooms are familiar to nearly every Basque and Catalan kitchen. While rich in dairy cows, the Spanish Pyrenees region is extremely low on beef. Farmers are unable to afford the costs to raise beef cows to maturity on the precious little pasture acreage available. Calves for veal, however, require very little, if any, grazing. Hearty, simple fare often braises a haunch of veal for several hours in wine and tomatoes. In contrast, Americans consider veal as a delicate meat to be eaten in small quantities.

This recipe for veal chops is abridged from a dish created by Chef Oumar Sy of Petits Plats, in Washington, D.C. Chef Sy recommends that the red wine sauce, which is essentially a demi-glace, be made a day ahead, due to the number of steps and the time required to reduce the sauce. His creation allows you to taste the pure clean flavors of the veal and fresh earthy mushrooms, united by a rich, dark, red wine sauce packed full of concentrated mushroom.

A local mushroom species much prized by the Basque, *perretxiku* (*Tricholoma georgii*), appears in the spring. Also called *seta de Orduña* or *seta de San Jorge*, it is known for its distinctive cornmeal scent. The Basque often prepare it very simply, broiled or in scrambled eggs. For the American cook where this particular species is unavailable, the shiitake is a good substitute.

Recipe and ingredients on following page

Red wine sauce:

1 tablespoon veal fat, duck fat, or
   butter
1 small onion, chopped
4 ounces portobello mushrooms,
   coarsely chopped
4 ounces shiitake mushrooms,
   coarsely chopped
1 bottle or 3 cups red wine
2 cups veal stock,
   preferably homemade
1 bay leaf
3 stalks fresh marjoram
2 sprigs fresh thyme
Pinch of salt and pepper

Veal chops:

4 veal chops, each 1-inch thick,
   and untrimmed
Salt and pepper
1 tablespoon duck fat or butter
4 sprigs fresh thyme, leaves only, or
   1 teaspoon dried thyme (sage or
   rosemary can also be substituted)
6 cloves garlic, sliced or chopped
   small
2 to 3 tablespoons olive oil
12 ounces shiitake mushrooms
12 ounces portobello mushrooms

MAKES 4 SERVINGS

SAUCE:

Place some of the fat taken from the
chops, duck fat, or butter in a skillet
over medium heat. Add the onions.
Sauté several minutes, until onions are
slightly browned. Add mushrooms and
continue to cook until liquid has evaporated. Remove onions and mushrooms
and set aside.

Pour wine into the hot skillet, stirring
the bottom well to capture remaining
onion and mushroom flavor and particles from the pan. Transfer the wine and
deglazed bits into a large saucepan, and
pour in veal stock. Add to the saucepan
the onions, mushrooms, bay leaf, 2
stalks marjoram, and 1 sprig thyme. Boil
or simmer to reduce liquid by two-
thirds; 20 minutes or longer. Season
with salt and pepper.

Strain the liquid through a sieve to
remove the solids. Retain the mushroom
and onion pieces, and set aside. Discard
cooked herbs. Place onion and mushroom pieces into a food processor to
form a purée. Set aside. Sauce activities
up to this point can be done a day
ahead.

Preheat oven to 500° F. Sprinkle veal chops with salt and pepper.

Place an ovenproof skillet over medium-high heat, add duck fat. Toss in thyme and 4 cloves sliced/chopped garlic, sauté for a minute. Remove garlic and thyme, and set aside. Add chops to the pan to quickly sear and brown both sides. Pat the sautéed garlic and thyme onto surface of the chops. Place in oven for 10 minutes for medium-rare center. Alter the time, depending on thickness of chops. Remove meat, place on a plate and cover with foil to keep warm and let rest for 10 minutes.

Pour reduced wine sauce into skillet in which the chops were browned and cooked. Stir over medium-low heat to melt the browned scrapings into the sauce. Add the remaining 1 sprig marjoram and 1 sprig thyme into the sauce. Stir puréed onion and mushroom back into the reduced wine sauce to thicken. Add salt and pepper to taste. Sauce is done when it begins to simmer.

For mushrooms: place olive oil in a pan over medium-high heat. Sauté the remaining 2 cloves of garlic, shiitake and portobello mushrooms. Add salt and pepper to taste.

To serve, spoon sauce onto individual plates, place a serving of meat over sauce, and top with the sautéed mushrooms.

This dish requires a bit of time and dedication, but the end result is worth the effort.

Do not add more than a pinch of salt and pepper to the ingredients for the sauce before it is reduced. As the liquid reduces and flavors become more concentrated, the salt will also become more pronounced.

Ideally, for the sauce to extract all the mushroom and onion flavors, it should be reduced over very low heat for several hours.

Since most of us are unable to lend the time needed to reduce a sauce for 4 hours, I recommend reducing the liquid through more rapid simmering. Then purée the solids and stir them back into the sauce to thicken it and enrich the flavor.

Oxtail Stew

(Rabo de Toro al Estilo)

·—·

(Basque, Navarra, southwest France)

THROUGHOUT THE BASQUE COUNTRY, northern Spain, and southwest France, the recipes for oxtail stew are almost as numerous as the number of cooks. In southwest France this dish is called *Daube de queue de boeuf*. Although the basic Basque version of this dish does not include tomato or cèpes, the inclusion of these ingredients by modern Basque and southwest French cooks adds a richness similar to beef bourguignon. In Pamplona, the tails of slain fighting bulls are often used. Pamplona is the location of the eight-day Fiesta de San Fermín each July which was made famous by Ernest Hemingway's novel *The Sun Also Rises*. Tourists and locals who are foolish enough or drunk enough to test their daring against the horns can "run with the bulls" in the *encierro* each morning from a corral near the Plaza Santo Domingo to the bull ring. The fiesta has become an international fair, and this grateful ancient city has renamed the area in front of the bull ring Paseo de Hemingway.

SALT OXTAILS AND DREDGE IN FLOUR to coat all sides. Heat oil in a large pot or casserole over medium-high heat. Brown oxtails on all sides. Add onions, carrots, tomatoes, leeks, and garlic. Sauté ingredients until onions soften and begin to brown, 7 to 10 minutes. Pour in red wine and 2 cups water, add thyme, marjoram or oregano, bay leaves, and *piment de l'Espelette*. Reduce heat and simmer for $2\frac{1}{2}$ to 3 hours, until meat on oxtails pulls away easily.

Place oxtails in a serving dish, remove bay leaves, and spoon sauce and vegetables over meat. Alternatively, remove vegetable pieces from pot and blend in a food processor until smooth. Mix purée back into pot to thicken the sauce. Spoon thickened sauce over oxtails and serve.

Serve with boiled or roasted potatoes or fresh bread.

Placing the vegetables in the pot alongside the oxtails for the full cooking time will add flavor to the meat and sauce. When cooked this way, they should be puréed as a thickener for the sauce.

However, if you intend to eat the vegetables alongside the meat, I recommend doubling the carrots and onion needed and cooking the first half with the oxtails as described. Remove them with a slotted spoon after the first 1½ to 2 hours, and set aside to purée at the end for the sauce.

Replace with fresh onions, carrots, and any other vegetable you wish to eat. Continue to cook the stew for about another hour. The fresh vegetables will be cooked, but retain their own identity when eaten.

4 pounds oxtails, cut into 2-inch sections

Salt

¼ to ½ cup flour for dredging

½ cup olive oil

1 large onion, chopped

4 medium carrots, chopped

4 medium tomatoes, diced

2 leeks, chopped

4 cloves garlic, chopped and crushed

1 bottle (750 ml.) or 3 cups red wine

4 sprigs fresh thyme or 1½ teaspoons dried

4 sprigs fresh marjoram or oregano

2 bay leaves

¼ teaspoon *piment d'Espelette* or cayenne

MAKES 4 SERVINGS

Sweet Peppers Stuffed with Oxtail

(Pimientos Rellenos de Rabo)

(Basque, Navarra)

NEW WORLD PEPPERS WERE THE MOST IMPORTANT spice encountered by Columbus at a time when the spice trade was a dominant force in Europe. Early Spanish chroniclers of the New World devote a good deal of space to describing these plants. Bell peppers, paprika (a blend of several highly colored, mild red peppers), cayenne, jalapeño, and serrano peppers are all varieties of the same species (*Capsicum annuum*). Diego Alvarez Chanca first described them in 1494 following the second voyage of Columbus. The early writings emphasize observations that when grown in the Caribbean these peppers are apparently hotter than those grown in Europe. Sweet red peppers grown on the terraced hills of the Côte Vermeille in Roussillon are highly regarded today, as they have been since the Middle Ages. This recipe using oxtails is a classic example of the use of the New World's gift to the Pyrenean region.

This is a delicious preparation essentially condensing the ingredients for oxtail soup into the meat stuffing and sauce.

PLACE OXTAILS, TOMATO, CARROT, pimiento, leek, garlic, and salt in a large pot. Add enough water to cover all well, about 6 cups. Bring to a boil. Reduce heat, cover, and simmer for 2½ to 3½ hours, until the meat on oxtails pulls easily away from the bone. When cooled, separate the meat from oxtails and strain solids from the cooking broth. Reserve broth for making the sauce. Process the soft vegetables into a purée, by pushing them through a sieve, or in a blender or food processor. Mix the vegetable purée with the separated meat.

If using fresh peppers, broil or grill them to blister the skin on all sides. Immediately place them in a large bowl or container and cover for 10 to 15 minutes. Peel and slice open peppers to remove seeds and any stringy veins.

To stuff, lay peppers flat and open on a plate. Place meat over half of each, dividing the stuffing evenly among the peppers. Fold the uncovered half over the meat to enclose it. All these steps can be done a day ahead, and the stuffed peppers refrigerated until needed.

SAUCE:
Heat oil in a large skillet or pot over medium heat. Add garlic, scallions, and mushrooms, sautéing until cooked. Do not allow garlic to brown. Stir in flour; then gradually mix in tomato purée and about 1½ cups of cooking broth from oxtails. Bring to a simmer while mixing sauce to a smooth consistency. Allow ingredients to cook together for 5 to 10 minutes. Taste and season with salt and pepper, if needed.

Slide stuffed peppers into the sauce, which should almost cover them. Cook over low heat for 10 minutes. Remove and serve peppers with sauce spooned over each or lay each over a small puddle of sauce.

Oxtails are much more flavorful than the traditional cuts of beef. To extract the full flavor from the bones and cartilage, and soften the muscle tendons, they require several hours of slow cooking.

4 pounds oxtails, cut into 2-inch sections
1 tomato, cut in large pieces
1 carrot, chopped into sections
1 pimiento or red bell pepper, cut into pieces
1 leek, chopped in large pieces
2 cloves garlic, crushed
1 to 1½ teaspoons salt
6 pimientos or small red bell peppers, or 4 large bell peppers

Sauce:
2 tablespoons olive oil
2 cloves garlic
2 scallions
3 ounces mushrooms, chopped
1 tablespoon flour
½ cup tomato purée
Salt and pepper (optional)

MAKES 6 TO 8 APPETIZER
OR 4 ENTRÉE SERVINGS

Braised Pork Loin with Prunes and Pears

(Lomo de Cerdo con Ciruelas y Peras)

(Catalonia, Spain)

PIGS DATE BACK **40** MILLION YEARS in fossil history and wild pig-like animals roamed the forests and swamps in Europe and Asia for millions of years. Modern swine (*Sus scrofa*) are descendents of matings from at least two separate varieties of wild hog: the East Indian pig and the European wild boar. The earliest known records of domestication appear to be with the East Indian pig in southeast Asia around 9,000 B.C. A domesticated variety of this species was taken to China sometime around 5,000 B.C. Chinese derivatives were later introduced into Europe where they were crossed with domesticated wild boar, thus creating the genetic foundation for modern domestic swine in about 1,500 B.C. The penchant in Catalonia for flavor combinations that contrast savories such as meats with sweet ingredients such as fruits is attributed to the Moors. This recipe, of course, would not have been prepared or eaten by Moors because of the Islamic prohibition against eating pork.

The following is a wonderful melding of the savory meat and sweet fruit flavors. This dish is based on a recipe from Penelope Casas, whose collection of wonderful Spanish recipes is encyclopedic.

PEARS:

Peel and halve or quarter pears, core. Pour wine into a saucepan, add sugar and cinnamon. Bring to a simmer, add pears and cover. Depending on firmness of the pears, simmer for 7 to 10 minutes. Insert a sharp knife into a pear to test. The fruit should be soft enough for the knife to slide in easily, but the pear pieces should not fall apart or seem mushy. Set aside and let pears steep in wine at least 30 minutes or until they are needed.

Pears:

2 medium ripe, firm pears

1 cup red wine

¹/₄ cup sugar

1 stick cinnamon or

¹/₂ teaspoon ground cinnamon

PORK:

Rub surface of the meat with a bit of salt and pepper. Heat 2 tablespoons olive oil in a large pot, and brown meat on all sides. Move meat to the side, adding the chopped onion. Sauté onions until soft or translucent. Pour in red wine, stirring to incorporate the browned juices and caramelized onion, while reducing liquid by half. Add ½ cup chicken broth and bay leaf. Cover and let simmer for 30 minutes.

Heat remaining 2 tablespoons olive oil in a medium to small pan, over moderate heat. Add blanched almonds, to toast them slightly, followed by garlic. Sauté for a minute or two, but do not let garlic brown. Add thyme and oregano, and sauté for a minute more before pouring in the remaining 1 cup chicken broth. Reduce heat to low, cover, and simmer for 15 minutes. Purée this mixture in a blender or food processor. Add mixture to simmering pot.

Pork:

1½ to 2 pound boneless pork loin

Salt and pepper

4 tablespoons olive oil

1 medium onion, finely chopped

1½ to 2 cups red wine

1½ cups chicken broth

1 bay leaf

½ cup blanched almonds

4 cloves garlic, minced

½ teaspoon dried thyme
  (or 2 teaspoons fresh)

½ teaspoon dried oregano
  (or 2 teaspoons fresh)

12 pitted prunes

¼ pound mushrooms, chopped in
  large pieces

MAKE 4 TO 6 SERVINGS

Place prunes in the pot, cover, and cook for 20 minutes more. Then, add mushrooms and continue cooking for another 10 minutes. Salt and pepper sauce to taste.

Remove pork loin from the pot. Slice meat and serve with sauce, prunes, and accompany each serving with sections of warm poached pears.

Roasted Pork Stuffed with Dried Fruit

(Catalonia, southwest France)

CATALAN CUISINE WAS THE SUBJECT of one of the earliest cookbooks in Europe, the anonymous fourteenth-century *Libre de Sent Soví*. In the Middle Ages, Catalonia resembled a huge caldron that mixed a wide variety of ethnic ingredients—Roman, Germanic, Gallic, and Arabic along with Spanish cuisine as influenced by the Moors. Foreign spices gave local specialty dishes an exotic flair. This was a golden age for Catalonia economically, and this region's political influence reached from Barcelona and Perpignan to the Balearic Islands, Naples, Sardinia, and Sicily. Some of the recipes from the Catalan cookbook were reproduced a century later in the Italian *Libro di Arte Coquinaria*, which described Catalan chefs as the best in the world. Italian-born Catherine de Medici's arrival in France in 1533 is thought by many to be pivotal in the development of France's culinary arts, and many of the delicacies that she introduced were rooted in Catalan cuisine. This recipe exemplifies one aspect of Catalonia's admixture of influences—a taste for combinations of sweet and savory flavors, using fruit with meat.

PLACE DRIED FRUIT AND WINE together in a small bowl. Cover and soak for 3 hours or overnight.

Butterfly or cut lengthwise through the center of the pork loin, to form a pocket which will eventually hold the fruit stuffing. Mix together the garlic, thyme, ground bay leaf, and salt. Rub this mixture over all sides of the pork loin, including the butterflied/cut sides, and let it marinate, refrigerated, anywhere from 3 hours to a full day.

Preheat oven to 450° F.

The dried fruit should be softened from soaking in wine for several hours. In a saucepan, simmer the fruit and wine mixture, covered, for about 20 minutes. Allow fruit to cool enough to handle. Stuff rehydrated fruit into the pocket or center of the loin and tie the log-shaped roast together with string. Reserve the fruit poaching wine.

OPTIONAL: rub the bottom of the roasting pan with 2 tablespoons olive oil. Place potatoes, carrots, and leeks in the pan and toss to lightly coat all sides with oil. If needed, drizzle 1 tablespoon more of oil over vegetables. Sprinkle with salt and pepper.

Moving vegetables aside, place roast on a rack in the roasting pan. Pour 1 cup of the fruit marinating wine over the meat, and place roast in the oven. Immediately reduce the oven heat to 350° F. Cook for 1 to 1½ hours, depending on the size of the roast. Allow approximately 25 minutes per pound.

If cooking the roast without vegetables in the pan, make sure the liquid at the bottom of the pan does not completely dry out. Check occasionally and add a cup of water to the pan, if needed.

When done, remove roast, placing it on a platter. Spoon roasted vegetables around the roast and cover the platter with foil to keep warm.

Pour remaining 1 cup of wine, in which the fruit was soaked, into the hot pan, stirring well to deglaze it. Once all the pan drippings have joined with the wine, you may wish to pour the entire roasting pan contents into a saucepan. Bring the sauce to a simmer and stir in the red currant jelly. As the sauce simmers, add ¼ cup of cream, or more as needed to achieve desired thickness, and continue to stir as sauce bubbles and thickens.

Slice meat and serve with sauce and roasted vegetables.

1 cup packed, dried pitted fruit (prunes, apricots, cherries, etc.)

2 cups white wine or sherry

2 to 3-pound boneless pork loin

3 cloves garlic, minced

1 teaspoon dried thyme

1 bay leaf, ground fine or crumbled

1 teaspoon salt

Optional:

2 to 3 tablespoons olive oil

2 to 3 medium potatoes, chopped in 1½-inch chunks

3 medium carrots, chopped in 1-inch sections

2 leeks, white parts only, chopped in 1-inch sections

Salt and pepper

1 tablespoon red currant jelly (apple or cherry can be substituted)

¼ to ½ cup heavy cream

MAKES 6 OR MORE SERVINGS

Young Wild Boar Marinated in Red Wine (Marcassin au vin rouge)

(southwest France)

EDMOND RICHARDIN'S COOKBOOK, *L'Art du Bien Manger* (1913), which contains recipes dating back to the fourteenth century, includes a recipe for preparing young wild boar, *marcassin*. His short discussion introducing the recipe illustrates a good deal about the mystique and art of eating boar:

"An ignorant cook asserted that wild boar is banned from respectable tables. This myth must be eradicated!

During mild winters in the Pyrenees, when the snow does not reach the woods, herds of wild boars feed there on acorns and beech nuts dropped in autumn under the cover of the majestic trees. The flesh of a wild boar killed at that time, when prepared with skill, is not without delicacy.

My friend Jacques Estagnasié, a regular companion on my hikes in the mountains of the Aspe valley, recently brought to my kitchen the haunch of a young wild boar, which provided me the occasion of demonstrating to an entire gathering of gourmets the taste of this large game dish."

Mr. Richardin's culinary instruction of that dish provides insight into French cooking traditions. I offer the following recipe, adapted for twenty-first-century taste preferences and cooks from Mr. Richardin's recipe and instructions.

PREPARE THE MARINADE by placing in a saucepan the garlic, red wine, vinegar, carrots, onion, shallots, thyme, parsley, bay leaves, peppercorns, juniper berries, and salt. Simmer for 5 minutes, and let cool. Place boar meat, with the sheath and much of the surface fat removed, in a pan just large enough to contain it. Pour marinade over meat. Cover and refrigerate for 24 hours or several days, turning it once or twice a day.

Preheat oven to 325° F. Remove meat from marinade and pat dry with paper towels.

Heat a large casserole pan or skillet, add olive oil or pork fat, and brown the meat on all sides. Place marinade in a saucepan, add stock, and bring to a boil. To remove solids, pour through a sieve, into the casserole or braising pan in which the roast will cook. Add the meat to the pan, cover tightly, and place in the oven. Cook for 2½ hours.

Remove the leg, place on a large platter, and cover with foil to keep warm while it rests and you make the sauce.

Pour or spoon off any surface oil from the sauce. Pour the rest of the cooking liquid into a saucepan. Over medium heat, stir in currant jelly, until melted into the sauce. Season with salt and pepper to taste.

If you desire a thicker sauce, place ¼ cup of cold or room temperature water in a bowl with flour. Stir or whisk until smooth. Stir flour mixture into the simmering sauce at the end, stirring well to thicken. Pour sauce into a small pitcher or gravy boat.

Slice meat and serve with sauce and accompany with a purée of chestnuts.

3 cloves garlic, crushed

2 to 3 cups red wine

4 tablespoons vinegar

2 medium carrots, sliced

1 small to medium onion, thinly sliced

2 to 3 shallots, thinly sliced (optional)

4 sprigs fresh thyme or 1 teaspoon dried

6 stalks fresh parsley, chopped

1 to 2 bay leaves, crumbled

12 black peppercorns

6 juniper berries

½ teaspoon salt

1 (5- to 6-pound) leg of boar, or 1 (3- to 4-pound) loin

4 tablespoons olive oil

2 cups pork or veal stock

1 tablespoon red currant jelly

Pepper

1 tablespoon flour (optional)

MAKES 6 OR MORE SERVINGS

For wild boar, this marinade will create a succulent, flavorful roast. It will also infuse an exotic wild boar flavor into your non-game pork roast.

For the curious, the main abbreviations I made to Mr. Richardin's treatment of wild boar were omitting the threading of lardoons or ropes of lard throughout the meat prior to cooking, and I do not splash a "glass of aged cognac" over the meat halfway through the cooking process. I also curtailed the maceration time for the meat from four days to one or more days.

To highlight the flavor of the herbs, insert a bit of fresh thyme or rosemary into the meat with each garlic slice.

VEGETABLES
AND SIDE DISHES

Vegetables and Side Dishes

Salad with Salt Cod
(Esqueixada de Bacalao)

THIS SIMPLE, REFRESHING AND VERY CLASSIC Catalan salad is especially popular during the warm summer months. It features salt-cured cod, and will be found in simple meals at home as well as fine dining restaurants. *Esqueixada* is similar to ceviche in that it is made with "raw" cod, although in this case, previously cured and then desalted. It is milder than its Peruvian counterpart, with milder seasonings. The fish is transformed from a dry slab to an almost soft consistency after the several days of soaking in water required to desalinate the flesh, and through additional tenderizing performed by the marinade. The word *esqueixada* comes from the Catalan *esqueixar*, which means tear or shred. Most everyone agrees that the salt cod or *bacalao* is always shredded and never chopped or sliced. Beyond that, there are many different recipes, some calling for many more ingredients than this one. The traditional dish always includes salt cod, oil, vinegar, tomatoes, onions, and salt.

To refresh our palates in between visits to cava producers in Sant Sadurní d'Anoia, we lunched on an excellent *esqueixada* at the very fine Mirador de les Caves restaurant. The following recipe is adapted from a version by chef Ferran Adrià, whose wizardry at El Bulli, on the Costa Brava of Spain, consistently sets new culinary standards for kitchens around the world.

Recipe and ingredients on following page

½ pound salt cod, desalted*

12 oil- or brine-cured black olives,
    pitted and chopped

¼ cup olive oil

2 medium tomatoes, peeled,
    seeded, and finely diced

1 small sweet (red or Vidalia)
    onion, finely diced

1 small red bell pepper, seeded and
    finely diced

3 tablespoons red wine or sherry
    vinegar

4 to 5 sprigs parsley, chopped

MAKES 4 SERVINGS

REMOVE ANY BONES from desalted cod. Pull apart or shred meat with fingers or using two forks. Place shredded cod onto serving plate.

Mash olives through a sieve, into a bowl. Mix olive oil in with the sieved olives. Spoon or drizzle one or two tablespoons of olive dressing over the cod. Distribute the diced tomato, onions, and red bell pepper over the cod. Sprinkle vinegar and the remainder of the olive and oil dressing over the salad. Top with chopped parsley and serve.

* Remove salt from cod by soaking for at least 2 days, changing the water about 3 times a day.

Spinach with Raisins and Pine Nuts (Espinacs amb Panses i Pinyons)

THIS TRADITIONAL CATALAN DISH is very popular in Mallorca and the other Balearic Islands, which were once part of Catalonia. Swiss chard is sometimes substituted for spinach. Clifford A. Wright in *A Mediterranean Feast* notes that this dish reappears identically all over the Mediterranean, including Languedoc, Provence, Rome (*spinaci alla romana*), Genoa (*spinaci alla genovese*), and Greece. It is truly a popular dish with many areas claiming it as their own. There has been a strong Catalonia-Italy culinary connection since the fourteenth century. The Catalan cooking manual *Libre de Sent Soví* (1324) was influential throughout Europe, and many of its recipes appear in the Italian *Libro di Arte Coquinaria* written a hundred years later. The Italian cookbook describes Catalan chefs as the world's best. The combination of pine nuts and raisins implies the influence of Arabs. Pine nuts are small and white and come from the umbrella pine (*Pinus pinea*). Like most nuts, they should be well sealed and stored in the freezer.

We enjoyed a delicious interpretation of this dish at the restaurant Mas Pau, while staying at the inn of the same name, refurbished from an old stone farmhouse and out buildings, located a few miles inland from the Costa Brava. Their version used fresh grapes in place of raisins, added sautéed leeks, omitted the anchovies, and instead drizzled a cabernet sauvignon and vinegar reduction over all.

Recipe and ingredients on following page

1/4 cup raisins

1/4 cup pine nuts

2 tablespoons butter or olive oil

3 cloves garlic, minced or crushed

1 pound fresh spinach, washed, drained, and stemmed

4 anchovy fillets, finely chopped

Salt and pepper

MAKES 4 SERVINGS

PLUMP RAISINS BY PLACING them in a cup with enough hot water to cover, for 15 to 20 minutes.

Place pine nuts in a skillet over medium heat. Shake the pan to turn them and lightly toast on several sides. Remove and set them aside.

Heat butter or oil in the same hot skillet and add the garlic. Quickly sauté garlic until it becomes straw color. Do not brown. Add the spinach. Increase the heat while turning the spinach to heat and wilt all leaves. When all leaves are dark green and wilted, mix in pine nuts, raisins, and anchovies.

Sauté and cook on high heat for a few more minutes, to remove some of the excess liquid from the spinach. Season salt and pepper to taste. Serve hot.

We have ordered this dish in Spanish and Italian restaurants in the United States, which usually don't include anchovies. The anchovies add salt and an extra pungency to contrast the sweetness of the pine nuts in this combination, but the dish will not suffer if they are omitted and, instead, a bit of balsamic vinegar or lemon juice is added.

Layered Vegetable Gratin

A GRATIN IS ANY DISH topped with a layer of cheese or bread crumbs and baked. This particular dish is based on a vegetable gratin we enjoyed in Roussillon. The layers of cooked vegetables in a loaf pan create an attractive presentation as a side dish or first course. If you are able to cook your vegetables over a wood fire or hot coals, the light smoke will lend an outdoor or Old World quality to the dish.

PREHEAT OVEN TO 400° F.

Beat egg, pour into a wide bowl with ¼ to ½ cup water. Place bread crumbs in a shallow dish. Dip eggplant slices in egg and then in bread crumbs to coat both sides with crumbs. Brush or rub a baking sheet with 1 to 1½ tablespoons olive oil. Place eggplant slices on oiled sheet and bake for 15 to 20 minutes, check and turn slices over halfway through. Remove when slices are softened through and crumbs are slightly browned. Reduce heat to 350° F.

Over medium heat, add 2 tablespoons olive oil to a skillet. Sauté 2 onions until soft and translucent. Add garlic, and sauté for another 1 to 2 minutes. Remove and set aside.

Continued

---

1 egg

1½ cups bread crumbs

1 large or 2 medium eggplants, cut lengthwise in ¼-inch slices

4 tablespoons olive oil

3 medium to large onions, thinly sliced

3 cloves garlic, minced

Salt and pepper

4 medium tomatoes, peeled, seeded, and chopped

12 to 16 black brined or oil-cured olives, pitted and chopped

2 red bell peppers, roasted, peeled, seeded, and sliced

¾ to 1 cup grated sheep cheese, such as Idiazabal or Brebis

MAKES 6 SERVINGS

With the remaining ½ to 1 tablespoon oil, coat the inside of a baking dish. Reserve about 1 to 2 teaspoons oil, and mix in with remaining ½ cup bread crumbs. You may not need all the oil.

Sauté tomatoes and remaining 1 onion on medium low heat, until onion is wilted and tomatoes are thick and mushy. Should resemble a thick coarse sauce. Set aside.

Begin layering ingredients, starting with tomato-onion mixture, then add eggplant, olives, onions, pepper slices, ending with an even layer of cheese. Repeat this process, ending with cheese. Top with oiled bread crumbs. Bake for 30 minutes, until bread crumbs are browned. Let cool for 10 minutes before serving. Serve hot or cold.

•—•

Do not add too much salt to this, as the salt in cheese and olives will infuse into the vegetables.

You can also embellish this preparation by sprinkling in bacon, herbs, or anchovies.

This is also excellent when eaten cold, the next day.

Asparagus and Capers Gratin

(Gratin d'asperges)

(southwest France)

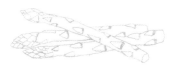

ASPARAGUS (*ASPARAGUS OFFICINALIS*) IS A PERENNIAL member of the lily family, which also includes onions, leeks and garlic. It grows wild in much of eastern Europe and Asia and was likely gathered as a food source in prehistory. The ancient Greeks cultivated it, and its name is from the Greek word meaning "sprout" or "shoot." After the fall of the Roman Empire, asparagus fell out of favor, but was repopularized by the Arab Ziryab, the ninth-century arbiter of taste. In Europe during the Middle Ages, the only active consumption of asparagus was in monasteries, where monks used it in remedies to cure rheumatism, as well as heart and skin problems. In France, Louis the XIV had his gardeners grow asparagus in greenhouses so that he could enjoy it year-round. The wild, strong-flavored asparagus that grows in the wheat fields of Spain is called *trigueros*. The succulent white asparagus cultivated in Navarra is world renowned for its more refined flavor, and the Basque food writer Teresa Barrenechea prefers the Navarran canned product to the fresh asparagus available in North America.

This recipe is a variation on the Rousillon and Mediterranean preparation styles we have tasted. When asparagus is out of season, this is also an excellent way to prepare green beans.

IN A LARGE SKILLET OVER MEDIUM HEAT, add 2 to 3 tablespoons oil, reserving 1 teaspoon, and sauté shallots until they become translucent. Add asparagus. If all the asparagus does not fit in the pan in 1 to 2 layers, place them in a large baking pan or dish and toss them with the shallots and oil and cook in a 400° F oven. Gently turn them once or twice until asparagus are heated through

2 to 3 tablespoons olive oil

2 to 3 shallots, finely chopped

2 pounds asparagus, rinsed and trimmed

1 tablespoon capers

Juice of ½ medium lemon

Pinch of salt and pepper (optional)

¼ cup bread crumbs

1 teaspoon chopped fresh herbs, such as parsley or dill

MAKES 4 SERVINGS

to a bright green color, approximately 10 minutes. Add capers and lemon juice. Toss gently. Taste, and season with a pinch of salt and pepper, if needed.

Place asparagus mixture into a baking dish or heat-proof platter large enough to hold it in 2 layers. Mix 1 teaspoon olive oil into bread crumbs. When evenly mixed, add fresh herbs to bread crumbs. Sprinkle mixture over the asparagus. Place dish under a broiler, 3 to 4 inches away from heating element, if possible. Broil for 2 to 3 minutes, or until the topping browns. Watch closely to make sure it doesn't burn. Remove and serve.

This recipe creates a thin sprinkling of browned topping. For a thicker layer of bread crumbs, double the ingredients for the gratin topping.

To add a more savory flavor to the top crust, grate and mix into the bread crumbs about a tablespoon of any relatively hard cheese made from sheep milk, such as an Idiazabal or Brebis.

Eggplant Roasted with Bacon and Garlic, with Samfaina

(Aubergines en gigot)

CATALAN AND FRENCH COOKING, one and the same in some areas of southwest France, are renown for their generous use of garlic. This interesting recipe for roasted eggplant is based on a description written by Elizabeth David of a preparation hailing from the Catalan coast. I have augmented the recipe by adding Catalan *samfaina* sauce to the dish.

Samfaina, or *xamfaina*, sauce is a more complex version of the ancient Catalan *sofregit*, a slow-cooked onion-based sauce, which seems to be the foundation of nearly all other Catalan sauces and stews. It is most often served as a sauce for fish, poultry, and other meats. *Samfaina*, as noted by Coleman Andrews, "is, for all practical purposes, virtually identical to the ratatouille of the Côte d'Azur." Given that the Catalans embraced New World vegetables, such as tomatoes and peppers, into their cuisine long before the French even considered these items for human consumption, it is most likely that the Catalan *samfaina* predated French dishes containing these ingredients.

PREHEAT OVEN TO 400° F.

Create 2 rows of 1-inch lateral incisions down the length of each whole or halved eggplant. Place incisions in approximately ¾-inch intervals. Bake eggplants for 10 minutes. This should be just enough to soften the exterior of the eggplants to make stuffing easier. Reduce heat to 325° F.

Place salt, pepper, and finely chopped basil in separate small dishes. Roll each garlic piece in a bit of olive oil, followed by rolling in salt, and pepper. Place a

---

4 small eggplants, whole, or
   2 medium cut in half

2 teaspoons or more salt

2 teaspoons or more ground black
   pepper

2 tablespoons finely chopped fresh
   basil (or marjoram)

12 to 15 cloves garlic, halved

2 tablespoons olive oil or butter

4 slices bacon, cut in ½-inch
   pieces

INGREDIENTS CONTINUED

CONTINUED FROM PREVIOUS PAGE

Samfaina sauce:

3 to 4 tablespoons olive oil

1 large onion, thinly sliced or chopped

$1/2$ medium eggplant, chopped in cubes

1 medium zucchini, about $1/2$ pound, chopped in cubes

2 cloves garlic, minced

1 to 2 red bell peppers (or green), roasted and peeled

3 to 4 medium tomatoes, peeled, seeded, and chopped

Salt and pepper

MAKES 4 SERVINGS

pinch of basil at mouth of the incision. Insert half a garlic clove, using it to push the basil into the opening. Repeat this for every other incision.

Roll a bacon piece in pepper and place a bit of basil on it. Using a butter knife, push the bacon and basil into the opening. Repeat this process for all remaining openings.

Place eggplants in a baking dish, and drizzle them with olive oil. Cover, and bake for about 1 hour.

SAMFAINA SAUCE:
Place a large deep skillet or pot over low or medium-low heat, adding olive oil. When hot, add onion, eggplant, zucchini, and garlic. Cook, stirring occasionally, until liquid from eggplant and zucchini have cooked away. Mix in peppers and tomatoes and simmer on low heat, stirring occasionally, until peppers and onions are limp and tomatoes, eggplant, and zucchini have become the consistency of a purée. Add salt and pepper to taste.

Serve eggplants with *samfaina* or a tomato sauce.

•—•

This should be served as a separate course; and as stated by Ms. David, it is "also very good cold, split open, salted, and with a little fresh (olive) oil poured over."

Since the *samfaina* sauce takes a bit of time to cook down to the proper consistency, it can be made a day or two ahead, reheated and spooned over the roasted eggplants.

Green Beans with Roquefort and Walnuts (Haricots verts au Roquefort)

(southwest France)

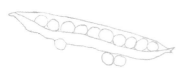

ROQUEFORT CHEESE, ONE OF THE MOST FAMOUS cheeses in the world, has been prized and protected throughout its 2000-year history. Since its beginning, Roquefort has been ripened in limestone caves along the cliffs of Cambalou above the Soulzon River. In 79 A.D., Caesar wrote of his appreciation of Roquefort cheese, which by that time had been making regular appearances in Roman markets for many years. Charlemagne, returning from battles in Spain in 778, rested and supped at the *Abbaye de Vabre* very near where Roquefort is produced. As it was Lent, the meal consisted mainly of cheese. Not fully appreciating the fine delicacy he had been served, Charlemagne began to meticulously remove the mold, until the Abbey explained that the mold was the best part of the cheese. Charlemagne was so impressed by its flavor that he requested that the Abbey send a block of Roquefort to him on a regular basis.

The cheese is traditionally made from the milk of the Lacaune, a thin-wooled variety of sheep. The cheese is inoculated with *Penicillium Roqueforti* mold, which is specially cultured on loaves of rye bread. Beginning in the nineteenth century, sheep cheeses from the *Hors Rayon* or outer region, including French Basque areas of the Pyrenees and Béarn, were allowed to ripen in the Cambalou caves to become true Roquefort cheese. This was the first cheese ever provided with an *Appellation d'Origine Controlée (AOC)* status by the French government, strictly delineating what could be named Roquefort.

As with most other cheeses, and wines, a young Roquefort is somewhat sharp. The flavor softens and becomes sweeter as it matures.

Recipe and ingredients on following page

1 pound green beans or
  haricots verts
1 tablespoon olive oil
2 shallots, finely chopped
¹/₃ cup chopped smoked or garlic
  sausage
4 ounces Roquefort cheese, crumbled (¹/₂ cup)
¹/₂ cup toasted coarsely chopped
  walnuts
Salt and pepper (optional)

MAKES 4 SERVINGS

BOIL OR STEAM GREEN BEANS for 3 to 4 minutes. They should be bright green and retain some crunch. Drain beans and place into a large bowl of cold water to stop the cooking process. Drain beans and set aside.

In a large skillet over medium heat, add oil and sauté shallots and sausage pieces, until shallots become translucent. Remove and set aside.

Add green beans to the hot skillet, cooking for several minutes to heat through. When beans are hot, sprinkle with half the Roquefort. Continue stirring to mix in cheese, allowing it to melt and coat the beans. Return sausage pieces and shallots to pan, add walnuts, and combine thoroughly. Remove from heat and toss in, or top dish with, remaining crumbled Roquefort cheese. Add salt and pepper, if desired.

Serve alongside a roasted meat and red wine.

•—•

Bacon or Bayonne ham can be substituted for sausage.

Mushroom and Shallot Tart
(Tarte aux champignons et échalotes)

(southwest France)

MUSHROOMS ARE ONE OF THE FAVORITE FOODS of the Catalans and Basque. The Catalans have retained a strong tradition as hunter gatherers, and are master *boletaires* or mushroom hunters. Families take great pride in their "hunting" abilities, and pass their skills and knowledge on to subsequent generations. In the Spanish foothills of the Pyrenees, Catalan *boletaires* have listed over 50 varieties of wild mushrooms as either "exceptional" or "very good," and over 40 more are listed as merely "edible." Freshly cut mushrooms are usually prepared very simply, by broiling, frying, or cooking in a scrambled egg omelet or *tortilla*. One of the best eating types is a species of *rovelló* (*níscalo* in Spanish), or milk cap mushrooms, called the *pinetell* (*Lactarius deliciosus*), which appears in pine forests in the fall. Other prized prey are the *cep* or *boleto* (cèpe), the *orellana* or *seta de cardo* (oyster cap), and the *rossinyol* or *rebozuelo* (chanterelle).

PIE CRUST:

Mix flour and salt together. The next steps are best done by hand, but a food processor can be used instead. Cut or crumble butter into flour, combining until flour takes on the consistency of cornmeal. Mix in drops of ice water until dough comes together to form a solid mass. Place on a sheet of plastic wrap and, with your hands, slightly flatten before wrapping it in plastic. This will make it easier to roll out later. Refrigerate for about 30 minutes, but not more than 1 hour.

When dough is ready to roll, preheat oven to 375° F.

Between 2 sheets of plastic wrap, quickly roll dough to ¼-inch thickness. Peel plastic away when ready to place crust in tart or pie pan. Place parchment paper over

> Tart/Pie crust:
> 1½ cups flour
> ½ teaspoon salt
> 8 tablespoons (1 stick) butter
> 2 or more tablespoons ice water
>
> INGREDIENTS CONTINUED

CONTINUED FROM PREVIOUS PAGE

Mushroom filling:

1 cup dried cèpes or porcini
  mushrooms

¼ cup pine nuts

2 tablespoons butter or olive oil

3 shallots, minced

1 leek, white parts only, chopped
  small

8 to 12 ounces fresh button mushrooms or similar type

2 tablespoons Armagnac or brandy

2 teaspoons to 1 tablespoon fresh
  thyme, leaves only

1 teaspoon chopped fresh tarragon
  leaves (optional)

1 tablespoon chopped fresh parsley

Salt and pepper

2 eggs

³⁄₄ to 1 cup heavy cream or half-
  and-half

½ cup crumbled or grated strong
  cheese (such as Roquefort,
  Gruyère, Idiazabal)

Makes 6 servings

surface of the dough and pour in a cup
or more of dried beans of any type over
the parchment. This will keep the dough
from bubbling up as it bakes. Bake for
15 minutes. Remove beans and parchment, and set partially baked crust aside.

Mushroom Filling:

While dried cèpes or porcinis are crisp,
break them into smaller pieces, then
rehydrate them by placing in a cup or
bowl and add boiling water. Cover, and
let steep for at least 20 minutes.

Lower oven heat to 350° F.

Place pine nuts in a skillet over medium-
low heat. Shake the pan to turn them
and lightly toast on several sides.
Remove and set them aside.

Heat butter or oil in a skillet over medium heat. Add the shallots and leek. Sauté
until they begin to turn translucent. Add
fresh mushrooms, and continue to sauté.
Saving the liquid, drain the cèpes/porci-
nis and add them to the skillet. Continue
cooking until fresh mushrooms are well
cooked, about 10 minutes. Pour in
Armagnac and cèpes/porcini liquid.
Sauté until the liquid is nearly evaporated. Stir in the herbs and pine nuts. Add
salt and pepper to taste, and set aside.

Mix eggs and cream, beating to combine well.

Place cheese evenly over the bottom of the tart crust. Fill with mushroom mixture, and pour egg mixture evenly over all. Bake for 30 minutes, or until the egg no longer jiggles. Check after 15 minutes and if crust edges are browning quickly, wrap edges in foil for the remainder of baking time.

When done, rest for 10 to 20 minutes before serving. Serve warm.

If the idea of making pie crust is daunting, a store-bought crust will work just as well.

Alternatively, you may choose to omit the crust, and bake this as a flan in a buttered baking dish. The custard dish should be placed in a water bath when baked. See baking instructions for Chestnut Flan, page 246.

For a more refined flan, purée the mushroom filling and pour into individual custard cups. Add whole toasted pine nuts on top before serving.

Chestnut Purée

(Purée de marrons)

CHESTNUTS (*CASTANEA SATIVA*) HAVE A LONG TRADITION in the Pyrenees region as a staple food, especially for rural peasants in the mountains. They were being cultivated at least 3,000 years ago. Chestnut trees are in the same family as oaks and beech and grow to 100 feet. The nuts are encased in spiny and sharp burrs, which eventually ripen and split to drop their contents onto the ground.

Chestnuts are such a nutritious food that in the sixteenth century some highlanders lived almost exclusively on them for half of the year. They can be ground into flour to make bread or pancakes. Chestnuts also used to make sweets such as jam, vanilla-chestnut cream, and candies. When dried, they can also be eaten raw, but are usually ground into flour or made into a porridge, soup, or mashed and mixed with vegetables, meat, and lard. The nutritional importance of chestnuts has declined throughout Europe since the mid-nineteenth century.

This is a basic and versatile side dish, usually served as an accompaniment to a meat course.

TO REMOVE THE SHELLS AND PEELS, chestnuts can be either roasted or boiled. In both cases start by scoring the top of the round side of each chestnut. To roast, place chestnuts on a baking sheet, and bake in a 325° F. oven for 20 minutes. If boiling, place them in boiling water for 10 minutes. Remove a few at a time from oven or hot water and peel when hot. As they cool, the inner skins will become more difficult to remove.

1 pound raw chestnuts

Milk, to cover chestnuts

2 tablespoons butter

Salt

2 to 3 tablespoons chicken or veal stock (optional)

MAKES 4 SERVINGS

Place peeled chestnuts in a saucepan and pour in enough milk to cover. Simmer on lowest setting, uncovered, for 30 to 45 minutes, or until extremely tender and the liquid has been reduced by at least half.

Place hot chestnuts and reduced milk in a blender, add butter, and purée until the consistency of thick mashed potatoes. Alternatively, push chestnuts through a fairly fine sieve before mixing in milk and butter. If too thick, add some light stock, such as chicken or veal, a tablespoon at a time to loosen to your desired consistency. Season lightly with salt to taste. Serve hot.

Serve with roasted or braised meats.

If your purée cools and/or becomes dry before serving, heat over lowest setting or a double boiler, stirring constantly, and if needed, add a bit of stock, milk, butter, or cream.

You can save a step by using peeled dried chestnuts found in some ethnic grocery stores. They rehydrate, as good as new, after 15 to 20 minutes of simmering, with the added bonus of a faintly smoky taste from the roasting process used to remove their skins.

Potato and Cabbage Cake

(Trinxat)

POTATOES ARE A NEW WORLD TUBER that was domesticated in Peru as long ago as 3,000 B.C. In 1532, the *conquistator* Francisco Pizzaro sought his fortune in Peru, and soon after his conquest in 1536 the Spanish realized that potatoes were a cheap source of food for sailors. They had reached Spain by 1539 and were common in Seville by 1573. The families of Basque sailors along the Bay of Biscay were the first Europeans to grow potatoes in their gardens, and Basques fishing for cod introduced them to the Irish by the mid-seventeenth century.

Called *papas* by the Incas, potatoes were an ideal crop above 11,000 feet on the high altiplano where corn would not grow. A short time after its introduction to Spain, around 1530, Pyrenean cooks began using this hardy tuber as one of the chief ingredients in many, now traditional, basic dishes of the region. *Trinxat* is a good example of such a dish, commonly prepared in remote areas of the Pyrenees mountains.

BOIL POTATOES IN A LARGE POT of water. When soft, remove from heat, drain and place into a large bowl. Partially mash or crush potato pieces and set aside.

Place cabbage and leeks in a pot with just enough water to simmer the vegetables, about 1 cup. Cover and simmer for about 30 minutes. When cooked, drain well, pressing out as much water as possible. Add to the bowl containing the potatoes.

Fry bacon pieces until crisp. Remove and set aside.

---

4 medium potatoes, cut in pieces

4 cups chopped cabbage

2 leeks (white and light green parts only), cut into ½-inch sections

8 to 10 slices bacon, chopped in pieces

1 shallot, finely chopped

3 to 4 cloves garlic, finely chopped

2 tablespoons white wine or broth

Salt and pepper

4 or more tablespoons olive oil

MAKES 6 SERVINGS

Pour out excess bacon grease and, over medium-low heat, add the shallot, sautéing until softened and edges turn light brown. Add garlic and sauté for 2 to 3 minutes more. While continuing to stir, pour in wine or broth to dissolve browned scrapings from the bottom of the pan.

Add the shallot and garlic mixture into the potato and cabbage bowl. Stir well to combine. Add salt and pepper to taste. The bacon can be mixed in at this point or saved to be added later, just prior to serving. Create individual potato cabbage cakes ¼ to ½-inch thick.

Place at least 2 tablespoons olive oil into a hot skillet over medium-high heat. Add cakes, in batches if the pan is not big enough, frying the first side for several minutes, until brown. Add more oil, and turn cakes over, frying second side until brown.

If bacon was not included in cake mixture, serve cakes with bacon pieces on top.

In its most elemental form this recipe consists of cabbage and potato, flavored with a bit of garlic, served with slices of fried salt pork on top.

This version of the dish provides additional layers of flavor by using bacon, and mixing it into the cake, adding a shallot, a leek, more garlic, and a drop of wine.

Baked Pumpkin with Chestnuts

(Gratin de citrouille aux marrons)

SQUASHES AND PUMPKINS, which are part of a vast gourd family known as Cucurbitaceae, are native to the Americas. Unknown in the Old World until the sixteenth century, the first definite record of pumpkins in Europe occurred in 1591. The squashes and pumpkins we know today date back to 6,000 to 4,000 B.C. Because several species of pumpkins are cultivated, there is some confusion as to their origin. At least one species may have arisen from a wild pumpkin that occurs on the plains of northern Argentina near the Andes, while others seem to have originated in North America. Pumpkins were widely eaten by native Americans from Canada to northern South America for centuries before Columbus arrived.

Europeans consume pumpkins primarily in savory dishes, unlike Americans, who tend to include them in dessert items (e.g. pumpkin pie and pumpkin bread). My first savory side dish of pumpkin was a marvelous and thick purée, in southern Spain. This particular recipe is based on pumpkin *gratin* preparations in the Gascony and Perigord areas of southwest France, to which I have added chestnuts, another regional flavor of autumn.

MASH HALF OF THE CHESTNUTS with a potato masher, or in a food processor, and set aside. Chop the remaining half into ¼-inch pieces and place in a saucepan with milk, and simmer, uncovered, for about 15 minutes. This is to soften chestnuts and reduce milk by about half to two-thirds. Set aside until needed.

16 chestnuts, roasted or boiled, and peeled (see page 218 for details)

1 cup whole milk

1½ to 2 pounds of pumpkin, peeled and cut in chunks

2 cloves garlic, minced or crushed

2 tablespoons olive oil or butter

Salt and pepper

1 egg

¼ cup grated Gruyère, cheese

MAKES 6 SERVINGS

In a saucepan, bring about ¼ inch of water to a boil. Reduce to a simmer, add pumpkin and cook for 20 minutes, covered. Pumpkin should be very soft. Using a potato masher, mash pumpkin. Add garlic, and 1 tablespoon olive oil. Continue to simmer, uncovered, for 15 to 20 minutes, to evaporate most of the liquid. Stir occasionally. When most of the free liquid has gone, and pumpkin mash has thickened, stir in the mashed chestnuts, and chestnuts in milk. Season with salt and pepper to taste. Beat the egg and incorporate it into the mash.

Preheat oven to 325° F.

Oil or butter a shallow baking dish with remaining 1 tablespoon oil. Pour in pumpkin mixture and sprinkle the top evenly with cheese. Bake for 30 minutes. Remove and serve.

Although I use milk in this recipe, in France ½ cup of cream and 2 to 4 egg yolks would be used instead. I mention this to allow you the option of a richer dish, if you wish.

Cornmeal Cakes

(Taloa/Millas/Miques de maïs)

THROUGHOUT THE PYRENEES AND SOUTHWEST FRANCE these porridge-based cornmeal cakes, similar to Italy's polenta, are often served as the starch alongside meaty stews. Corn cakes in Europe likely date back somewhere between Columbus and Cortez. Columbus mentions maize in his journals in 1492, and returned with some kernels. The Tainos in the West Indies called it *mahiz*, meaning "that which sustains life." At that time, 200 to 300 varieties of maize were cultivated, most of which had a modern appearance. When Cortéz reached Mexico in 1519, the people gave his soldiers "maize cakes" or tortillas to eat. Maize spread quickly wherever Spaniards traveled in the fifteenth and sixteenth centuries, largely because of its broad adaptability and high productivity. In Europe, the first crops were planted by poor illiterate farmers who were slow to experiment and left few records. Thus the spread of this crop went unrecorded.

The Basque name for this basic corn cake is *talo* or *taloa*. The Basque often stuff *taloa* with some leftover meat, vegetables, or cheese, to be carried in a pack and eaten while tending animals or hunting. While the generic name of *millas* is applied to a savory corn cake in most of southwest France, this simple item has several names. In Béarn these cakes are also referred to as *broye*, while in Landes they are *millas* or *cruchade*. Further east, in Gascony and Languedoc, these same porridge cakes are known as *Miques de maïs* (*armottes*, when made with semolina instead of corn), and *rimotes* or *milhas*, respectively. To add to the confusion, in Gascony or Languedoc, *millas* may appear as a sweet pudding or custard for dessert (see page 261).

Boil 2¼ cups water with duck fat or butter and salt. Gradually sprinkle in cornmeal while stirring to prevent lumps from forming. Reduce heat and simmer on low for 20 to 30 minutes, stirring frequently. Remove from heat when mixture is thick and comes cleanly away from the pan upon stirring.

Pour porridge into a rectangular pan and spread evenly. Refrigerate to allow to solidify. When cold, cut into serving-size squares and lightly coat with flour.

¼ cup rendered duck fat (alternatively, use butter or heavy cream)

¼ teaspoon salt

1 cup cornmeal

Flour for dusting (about 3 tablespoons)

2 to 3 tablespoons oil for frying

MAKES 4 SERVINGS

In a skillet, heat the oil on high. When oil is hot, fry floured cornmeal pieces until each side is brown and crisp; about 2 to 3 minutes on each side. Remove and place on paper towels to absorb excess oil.

Serve as an accompaniment to stews, garbures, or hearty soups.

Placing some parchment paper on the bottom of the pan before pouring in the corn mush will make removal from the pan easier.

Some modern versions may add some eggs or cheese to further enrich the flavor, or a bit of leavening to the porridge to lighten the texture.

Roasted "Fried" Potatoes

POTATOES ARRIVED IN FRANCE BY 1540, but *pommes de terre* were regarded as mere ornamental plants. The French eventually began to use them as animal fodder, but rarely ate them until the mid-eighteenth century. Potatoes gained full acceptance after several recipes were included in Antoine Viard's *Le Cuisinier Impérial* (1806) and Antoine Beauvilliers' *L'Art du Cuisinier* (1814).

While crispy edged, browned, potato wedges, slices, or chunks are by no means exclusive to the areas around the Pyrenees, this region, as with so many others, appreciates good fried and roasted potatoes. This simple side dish is a versatile complement to almost any savory dish in this collection. I have attributed this particular recipe to the Gascony and Perigord regions, since it calls for one of the most important ingredients in southwest France, duck fat.

ON THE STOVE OR IN AN OVEN, melt duck fat in a shallow pan or baking dish that will accommodate the potatoes in two layers. Remove from heat.

Preheat oven to 375° F.

Add potato slices to the pan, tossing, to coat each slice with fat. Arrange bottom layer of potatoes and sprinkle with minced garlic, salt and pepper. Add remaining potatoes in a top layer. Salt and pepper the top.

---

¹/₄ cup duck fat (or olive oil)

4 large potatoes, cut in ¹/₄-inch slices

2 cloves garlic, minced

Salt and pepper

MAKES 4 SERVINGS

Place the pan in the oven. After 25 to 30 minutes, turn potatoes, and return them to the oven for approximately 25 minutes more. Remove and serve when the overall appearance is golden and the edges become crispy.

⋅•⋅

Although frying is the more traditional method of achieving these potatoes, oven roasting also produces essentially the same finished product with less effort.

Replacing duck fat with olive oil will lend a more Spanish character to the taste.

DESSERTS

Desserts

Sparkling Wine Ice
(Granizado de Cava)

GENEROUS AMOUNTS OF SPARKLING WHITE WINE or *cava* are downed in the northeast of Spain every day. Unlike Americans, who reserve a touch of the bubbly for special occasions, in the shadows of the Spanish Pyrenees it is a favorite aperitif before lunch or dinner. This beverage is produced by essentially the same method as French champagne, and sells for a small fraction of the price. Driving through towns in the Penedès area, one will find producers of excellent cava on virtually every block. When you can drink *cava* for almost the same price as a soft drink, it's no mystery why *cava* flows freely in this region.

After experiencing a dazzling meal and the gracious hospitality of Martín Berasategui, one of the top Basque chefs, at the restaurant that bears his name in Lasarte-Oria, he gave us a final taste of his talent in a wonderfully refreshing *granizado de cava*. The following concoction I devised is very nearly the same, and surprisingly simple.

COMBINE THE SUGAR and 1 cup water in a saucepan. Bring to a boil and stir until sugar is dissolved. Remove from heat and let cool. Refrigerate if possible.

Using the finest grater you have, lightly scrape the skin of 1 lemon, removing only the top surface of the peel. Squeeze the juice and remove the seeds from both lemons.

1 cup sugar

2 lemons

1 bottle (750 ml.) champagne or other sparkling white wine, refrigerated

MAKES 10 TO 12 SERVINGS

Continued

Open the champagne or sparkling wine, and pour it into a 9 x 12 x 2-inch pan, or a container of equivalent volume. Mix in sugar water, lemon juice, and grated zest. Place mixture into the freezer. Check after 30 minutes. Using a wooden spoon, break up any ice formed on the sides and stir into the rest of the liquid. Continue to freeze and repeat this procedure every hour for at least 3 hours. The mixture will begin to take on a slushy consistency and eventually form into a sorbet or *granizado* of small ice crystals. Before serving, fluff the *granizado* by "chopping" up any clumps with the spoon or gently whisking the frozen mixture. Spoon into small glasses or cups and serve.

Although this can be made in an ice-cream maker, one is not needed to make this wine-based ice. The alcohol in the sparkling wine acts as an antifreeze that prevents the liquid from freezing solid. A few stirs every hour is sufficient to obtain the fine ice crystal consistency.

If you prefer a more lemony flavor, add grated zest from both lemons, instead of one.

Fruit in Red Wine

(Frutas al Vino Tinto)

(Basque regions, Catalonia)

PREPARING FRUIT IN RED WINE FOR DESSERT is common throughout the Pyrenean region, although the fruits change with availability and the preferences of the cook. In *Delicioso! The Regional Cooking of Spain*, Penelope Casas recounts the following adage from Aragón, which is known for the excellence of its peaches:

> *The housewife in her house*
> *Priests in their pulpit*
> *Soldiers in war*
> *And the peach in wine.*

The peaches used for this dish in Aragón have usually been preserved in sugar syrup, although fresh peaches are preferable if they are available. Many different fruits can be poached or immersed in wine, including figs, melons, apricots, and plums. They can be dried (prunes), fresh, or canned. In addition, some recipes call for the fruits to be baked in wine.

A majority of recipes for fruit macerated in red wine tend to involve only one fruit, usually peaches or pears. This particular adaptation, based on both French and Spanish recipes, includes several types of fresh fruit to provide variety in flavors, texture, and visual appeal. A very refreshing and healthful dessert, this is simple to prepare and is always a hit with our families and guests.

Recipe and ingredients on following page

2 to 3 cups red wine (or enough to cover fruit)

½ to ¾ cup sugar (¼ cup sugar for each cup of wine)

10 black peppercorns

1 (1- to 1½-inch) stick cinnamon

2 medium pears, peeled, cored, and quartered

2 medium peaches, peeled, pitted, and quartered

4 to 6 ounces raspberries

4 to 6 ounces strawberries

MAKES 4 TO 6 SERVINGS

POUR WINE, SUGAR, PEPPERCORNS, and cinnamon in a saucepan over medium heat. When sugar is melted and wine comes to a boil, add pears. Reduce heat and simmer pears for 4 minutes. Remove saucepan from heat and immediately add peaches to hot liquid. Cover and let sit for 5 to 10 minutes.

When the liquid is no longer scalding, but still very warm, add raspberries and strawberries. Replace cover and let cool. Allow fruit and wine mixture to sit at least 2 to 3 hours before serving. Chill before serving.

Spoon fruit and liquid into serving dishes or goblets.

The cooking times given are for ripe or almost ripe pears and peaches, that are cut into quarters. Add a few extra minutes of simmering time if fruit is not yet ripe and a bit hard. When just soft enough to be easily pierced by a sharp knife tip, but not mushy, consider them done.

Also, if you choose to halve, rather than quarter the pears, allow them to poach for 7 to 10 minutes depending on firmness of the raw pears. Double the time if poaching them whole.

In addition to the peppercorns and cinnamon, orange and/or lemon peel are also commonly added to flavor the wine syrup.

Christmas Fruit Compote

(Compota or Kompota)

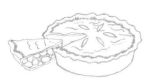

IT IS TRADITIONAL IN THE BASQUE COUNTRY to serve this compote after the big meal on Christmas Eve. It may be served warm or cold, and the combination of fruits is often varied to individual tastes or the availability of ingredients. Unlike most of Europe and the Americas, Christmas Eve in the Basque Country is not the night during which small children cannot sleep out of anticipation for Santa's gifts. The eve of the Epiphany is the traditional night during which Basque and Spanish families prepare for special holiday celebration and gift giving. January 6 is known as The Twelfth Night or the Epiphany, which marks the end of the Christmas holiday period in Spain. January 5, the eve of the Epiphany, is the night when they celebrate the event of the Three Wise Men (Kings) or the Magi bringing gifts to the baby Jesus. That night, before retiring, families will leave out food and drink for the Three Wise Men, usually glasses of brandy or sweet wine, and cakes or others sweets. Their camels are not forgotten and sustenance is provided for them as well, sometimes in the form of a jug of water, pieces of fruit, or a few handfuls of hay. Children will set out their freshly polished shoes, either on the doorstep or at the center of the common room the Wise Men are expected to visit, to awake the next morning and find them brimming with small gifts and treats.

Recipe and ingredients on following page

2 cups red wine

1¼ cups sugar

1 stick cinnamon

½ cup dried peaches

½ cup dried apricots

½ cup prunes

6 to 8 dried figs

½ cup raisins

2 apples, peeled, cored, and sliced
   into 6 to 8 wedges

2 pears, peeled, cored, and sliced
   into 6 to 8 wedges

MAKES 6 TO 8 SERVINGS

COMBINE I QUART OF WATER, the red wine, sugar, and cinnamon stick in a large saucepan or cooking pot. Stir over medium heat to melt sugar. Add dried peaches and apricots, adjusting the heat to simmer for 15 minutes. Add prunes, figs, and raisins, and continue to cook for 15 minutes more. Finally, add the apples and pears to the pot and cook for 15 to 20 additional minutes, or until apple and pear wedges are tender, but not mushy. Remove, cover, and let it cool a bit.

Serve the fruit compote either warm or chilled. To serve chilled, prepare at least three hours before serving.

The dried fruit does not need to be this exact combination. Your compote can be prepared with the most available, or preferred, fresh or dried fruit.

Reduce the cooking time for the softer, more delicate fresh fruit, such as peaches and cherries. If including fresh berries, add them at the last minute or they will become mush.

Lemon peel is often added to the simmering liquid.

Prunes in Armagnac

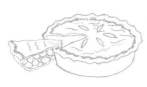

PRUNES ARE ADORED BY THE FRENCH. After California, France is the greatest producer of prunes, with 2.9 million plum trees contributing to this industry. The finest are the Agen prunes from the Garonne in southwest France. The *Pruneaux d'Agen* are essentially the same as California prunes, and were first brought to Europe by men returning from Syria during the Crusades.

Armagnac was the original *eau de vie* or brandy invented in France, the home of two other great brandies, cognac and Calvados. Armagnac is often compared and confused with cognac. However, upon comparing their areas of origin, grape varieties used, growing conditions, and distillation and aging techniques, one will find vast differences between the two. Armagnac is a blend of the juices distilled from several grapes, each contributing a unique character and quality to the final product. The best known grapes for Armagnac are the Folle Blanche or Picpoul, Baco A22 hybrid grape, and the Ugni Blanc or St. Emilion. The final product will have matured in barrels for a period of 20 to 30 years, and usually contains an alcohol level between 40 percent and 50 percent.

During our visits to southwest France, we were consistently served delightful creations prepared with prunes: homemade preserves, tarts, pastries, in cream fillings, sauces, and stuffings for meats, among other comestibles. Prunes in Armagnac is a classic combination of two beloved ingredients of southwest France, and is the basis for many a French dessert.

PLACE PRUNES IN A SMALL BOWL with tea. Cover and let sit 8 hours or overnight to allow prunes to absorb the liquid. Time can be reduced to 2 to 3 hours, if prunes are placed in freshly brewed hot tea and set aside to steep at room temperature. Remove prunes and place over paper towels to absorb excess liquid. Place prunes in a jar or other vessel that just holds the

Method 1:

12 or more prunes

1 to 1½ cups black tea

2 teaspoons to 1 tablespoon sugar (optional)

¼ to ½ cup Armagnac or brandy

MAKES 3 TO 4 SERVINGS FOR THOSE WHO ARE NOT DRIVING

fruit and can be tightly closed. If using additional sugar, combine with $1\frac{1}{2}$ to 2 times as much water (e.g. 3 or 4 teaspoons water to 2 teaspoons sugar) and heat to dissolve sugar grains. Pour into jar with prunes. Finish by adding enough Armagnac, cognac, or brandy over to fully cover the fruit. Cover tightly. Let prunes cure for at least a week in the refrigerator before using.

Method 2:

This version omits the step of first plumping the prunes with tea.

12 or more prunes

$\frac{1}{4}$ to $\frac{1}{2}$ cup Armagnac or brandy

PLACE PRUNES DIRECTLY IN A JAR, leaving a bit of space to allow the fruit to swell. Pour in enough Armagnac, cognac, or brandy to cover and reach about $\frac{1}{4}$ inch above the top of the prunes. Cover tightly and let sit for at least 4 to 6 hours at room temperature. The fruit may rise above the liquid as they swell. If not used immediately, check occasionally to make sure liquid fully covers the fruit, as they will continue to swell for a few days. Add more spirits if needed to cover all the fruit.

In method I, plumping prunes with black tea enhances their flavor. Use a strong black tea, such as an English Breakfast blend. If using loose tea leaves, brew using I teaspoon of tea per 8 ounce cup of boiling water. Do not steep the tea leaves for longer than 3 or 4 minutes or the tea will become slightly bitter.

I find that the prunes contain enough natural sugar to allow for the small amount lost in the (method I) tea and Armagnac during soaking. The prunes will remain sweet, but not powerfully so. However, for those with a strong sweet tooth, the addition of the optional sugar will replace any sweetness lost.

If placed in a jar and tightly covered, prunes plumped and completely covered in Armagnac will keep indefinitely, until needed for a last minute dessert.

Prunes in Armagnac are delicious mixed into or atop vanilla ice cream; or purée the prunes and fold into or use alongside whipped cream, to enhance a cake or other dessert. They will also add a robust flavor to Catalan Custard (page 241), if spooned into the individual cups before pouring in the custard.

Catalan Custard

(Crema Catalana)

THE CUSTARD DISHES THAT ARE SO CHARACTERISTIC of the Pyrenean region were developed by nuns in convents throughout the wine-growing areas. The wine makers in the monasteries used egg whites to clarify wines, leaving vast amounts of excess egg yolks. Custards became a means of ensuring that this ingredient was not wasted. *Crema catalana* is a custard dish that is frequently served as a dessert in Catalonia and Roussillon. It has caramelized sugar on the top, which originally was created using the central iron circles in wood stoves in homes. The old-style stoves had iron tops made in concentric circles so that the cook could use a handle to remove as many circles as needed to fit any pan. The central circle was about three inches in diameter and was an ideal size to caramelize the sugar by barely singing its surface. We enjoyed a wonderful version of this classical dish, which is apparently the progenitor of *crème brûlée*, at the lovely Mirador de les Caves in Sant Sadurní d'Anoia in the heart of sparkling wine or *cava* country, west of Barcelona.

IN A SAUCEPAN HEAT CREAM, lemon peel, and cinnamon stick over medium heat until it begins to boil. Remove from heat, discard lemon peel and cinnamon stick, and set aside to cool.

In a saucepan beat yolks together with ⅓ cup sugar until well combined and thick. Gradually whisk the cooled cream into the egg mixture. Place egg and cream mixture over extremely low heat, stirring constantly until it begins to thicken. When it is thick enough to coat the back of a spoon, pour mixture into individual custard cups, nearly to the rim. Let cool and refrigerate to set.

> 1 pint half-and-half
>
> Peel of ½ lemon
>
> ½ stick cinnamon
>
> 4 egg yolks
>
> ⅔ cup sugar
>
> MAKES 4 SERVINGS

Continued

When set, sprinkle an even layer of the remaining ⅓ cup sugar over the custard in each cup. To form the sugar crust,* place cups 1 to 2 inches from the heat source in your broiler. Watch them and remove as soon as they begin to bubble and caramelize. Let cool to allow the sugar crust to harden.

* If you have a small kitchen-size blow torch, use it to rapidly melt and caramelize the sugar. This is the best way to create the sugar crust without inadvertently re-cooking and possibly curdling any of the custard.

The lemon and cinnamon combination is very popular and traditional in Spain. However, if you are seeking more familiar comfort food, substitute vanilla in place of the lemon. Use ½ a vanilla bean, cut in half, lengthwise. Scrape the seeds into the half-and-half, adding the pod as well to get all the flavor into the liquid. Remove the bean husk before mixing with egg yolks.

If you don't have a vanilla bean, mix a teaspoon of vanilla extract to the egg and cream mixture after it has thickened, just before pouring it into individual cups.

For a truly special dessert, chop 4 to 8 Prunes in Armagnac (page 239) into pieces and stir into the hot mixture before chilling.

Cherry Custard Pudding

(Clafoutis)

CLAFOUTIS IS A CLASSIC COUNTRY DESSERT that is similar to crepe batter oven-baked in a mold and garnished with fruit. Called *millards* in some parts of France, clafoutis can be prepared with many different fruits including apricots, prunes, plums, berries, or grapes. This recipe using cherries is the most traditional and most popular in French homes and restaurants. While fresh black cherries are best, fresh plums are also an excellent partner. Depending on the cook, clafoutis can come in a variety of densities and textures. Ideally it should be a tender custard surrounded by a crepe-like crust.

PREHEAT OVEN TO 350° F.

Combine eggs, sugar, and a pinch of salt together in a large bowl. Gradually whisk in flour. Slowly pour in milk while continuing to mix or whisk. Mix in cognac/Armagnac and vanilla.

Cut cherries, or other pitted fruit, in half and remove pits. If using larger fruit, slice into wedges. Butter an 8- or 10-inch baking dish or pan. The sides should be high enough to allow the batter to rise slightly without spilling over. Arrange fruit evenly in the dish or pan and pour in milk batter. Bake for 45 to 55 minutes, until the center is jiggles slightly but is no longer liquid and the edges begin to brown. It should be the consistency of a custard. Let cool before serving.

---

4 eggs

1/2 cup sugar

Salt

2/3 cup flour

2 cups milk

2 tablespoons Armagnac or brandy

1 teaspoon vanilla extract

1 pound cherries (or other fruit:
   berries, plums, apricots, etc.)

MAKES 6 SERVINGS

While this is a classic version, innumerable clafoutis recipes exist with wide variation in these ingredients and their proportions. Variations include almond extract instead of cognac, or adding a bit of lemon zest or cinnamon to the batter.

Juraçon Custard with Peaches
(Flan de pêches au Juraçon)

THIS LIGHT DESSERT USES SWEET JURANÇON, a white wine made from Petit Manseng grapes, that has been made for over a thousand years near Pau in the Pyrénées Atlantiques. The vineyards are picturesque. Situated in steep, hilly terrain, they are planted in terraces that resemble amphitheaters. This area stays warm into the autumn largely because of south winds. This allows the *viticulteurs* to let the grapes remain a bit longer on the vines to permit a late harvest. Called *le passerillage* this overripening concentrates the sugar. These golden wines are full-bodied and emanate spicy aromas of citrus fruits and pineapples. If you don't use all of the Jurançon in this dish, it will serve as a wonderful dessert wine. Jurançon also produces a dry or sec wine, which is not appropriate for this recipe.

This dessert is surprisingly easy, and a light way to end a meal with something sweet.

PREHEAT OVEN TO 300° F.

In a large bowl mix wine and sugar together, stirring to dissolve most of the sugar. Add eggs and beat mixture until well combined and sugar is completely dissolved.

Place peaches into a large (approximately 9 x 13-inch) baking dish and pour egg mixture over them.

Place in water bath or *bain marie*. Water should come about halfway up the side of the dish. Bake for 40 to 45 minutes, top with nuts and bake 5 minutes more.

---

1 cup sweet **Jurançon** or other semisweet white wine

$1/4$ to $1/3$ cup sugar

5 eggs

5 medium peaches, peeled, halved or quartered

3 tablespoons pine nuts or almond slivers

MAKES 4 TO 6 SERVINGS

Baking this and other egg custard dishes in a *bain marie* or water bath is essential to prevent the eggs from cooking too quickly and separating into a curdled mass. Make sure the water in the *bain marie* is hot when you place the baking dish with the egg mixture into it.

To avoid spilling scalding water, it is safest to place the baking dish into the *bain marie* or outer pan, before adding the hot water. Place the two pans onto the oven rack and then pour boiling water into the outer pan.

Chestnut Flan

(Flan de Castañas con Leche)

THE SPANISH CALL CHESTNUTS *CASTAÑAS*, but the French have two words. The ordinary chestnut is called *châtaigne*, and tends to be eaten by rural people and animals such as pigs. The best and sweetest chestnut is a *marron*, which in English is called the Spanish chestnut (*Castanea sativa*). The difference lies in size and form. In a *marron* the kernel is whole and there is no dividing skin in the husk. By contrast, several *châtaignes* may be found in a husk divided by partitions so they are much smaller. *Marrons* are used for commercial candied chestnuts.

This dessert combines the richness of Spanish flan with the flavors of a sweet *castañas con leche* soup, traditional to the Basque and in Navarra. Prepared in Basque regions of both Spain and France, this dessert is similar to rice pudding, with chestnuts cooked in milk, cinnamon, and sugar.

CARAMEL SYRUP:
Mix sugar, corn syrup, and lemon juice into a pan with ⅓ cup of water. Bring to a simmer over medium-high heat, without stirring. Cook for approximately 10 minutes, swirling the pan occasionally to ensure even cooking. At this point, the bubbling syrup will begin to show some color. Continue to slowly swirl the pan as the syrup gets darker. When it becomes a dark golden color and the

---

Caramel syrup:

1 cup sugar

2 tablespoons corn syrup

¼ teaspoon lemon juice

Chestnut flan:

½ pound chestnuts, canned, roasted, or boiled

½ cup sugar

3 eggs

1 cup cream or half-and-half

1½ cups milk

1 teaspoon ground cinnamon

2 teaspoons vanilla extract

1 tablespoon Armagnac, cognac, or rum (optional)

MAKES 6 TO 8 SERVINGS

---

syrup thickens, as indicated by the slower bubbling, remove from heat. Quickly spoon or pour equal portions of the caramelized syrup into each custard cup. Turn cups to evenly coat the bottom and some of the sides.

CHESTNUT FLAN:
Preheat oven to 350° F.

In a processor, blend chestnuts and sugar to a fine consistency. Add eggs and continue to process or mix for approximately 1 minute. Add cream, milk, cinnamon, vanilla, and Armagnac. Mix for 2 more minutes.

Strain purée through a sieve to remove any pebbles of chestnut that remain. Spoon the chestnut mixture into caramel-coated custard cups. Place cups in hot water bath or *bain marie*. Water should be about halfway up sides of the cups. Bake for 30 minutes or until middle is slightly puffed.

Remove and let cool. Chill before serving. To serve individual cups, run the side of a knife blade along the inside edge of each cup, separating the custard from the cup. Place a plate on top and quickly invert the cup over the plate.

＊・＊・・＊・＊・・＊・＊・・＊・＊・・＊・＊・・＊・＊・・＊・＊・・＊・＊・・＊・＊・・＊・＊・・＊・＊・・＊・＊・・＊・＊・・＊・＊・・＊・＊・・＊・＊・

If you prefer to create one large flan in a single baking dish, rather than preparing individual cups, bake for 45 minutes instead of 30.

Although not exactly traditional, when pressed for time, instead of caramelizing my own syrup, I will spoon a bit of maple syrup into the bottom of my custard cups. Use real maple syrup.

Rice Pudding with Lemon and Cinnamon
(Arroz con Leche)

RICE PUDDING IS A POPULAR DESSERT in Spain, where some say it originated. Asturians claim to make the best in the Spain, and include a layer of toasted sugar on top. Interestingly Asturias, the only remnant of Visigothic Spain, was the focus of the Christian reconquest against the Moors. Spanish tradition says the Moors were stopped at the Covadonga National Park in the Picos de Europa (considered by some geologists to be the westernmost Pyrenees). While the Moors never conquered Asturias, this dish shows that their foods have done so. Both rice and lemons were brought to Spain by the Moors in the eighth century, and among the material legacies of Moorish Spain are intensive plantations of rice and citrus trees. The Moors introduced the farming of rice to this region, after establishing elaborate irrigation systems to regulate the flows of two major river systems, the Turia and Júcar, in The Levant (southeast Spain).

The other major ingredient of this dish—cinnamon—is the bark of the cassia tree that is grown in Malaysia and Indonesia. One of the primary articles in the spice trade, cinnamon arrived in the Roman Empire from Egypt in the first century A.D. and probably came to Spain and Gaul (France) with the Romans.

PLACE MILK, CREAM, CINNAMON STICKS or ½ teaspoon ground cinnamon, and lemon zest into a large saucepan and bring to a simmer. Stir in rice, cover, and reduce heat to let simmer on lowest setting. Stir occasionally to prevent bottom from sticking and scorching. Continue cooking, covered, until the liquid is thick

7 cups milk

1 cup cream

2 sticks cinnamon or 1 teaspoon ground

zest of 1 lemon

³/₄ cup uncooked medium- or short-grain rice, washed and drained

²/₃ cup sugar

1 tablespoon anis liqueur, such as Anis de La Asturianas (optional)

Ground cinnamon to garnish

8 to 10 tablespoons sugar (optional)

MAKES 8 OR MORE SERVINGS

and creamy, about I hour. Mix in sugar and cook, uncovered, for another I5 to 30 minutes, depending on liquidity of the pudding. It will thicken as it cools. Remove from heat

Remove cinnamon sticks and lemon zest. If using ground cinnamon, stir in remaining ½ teaspoon, and if using anis liqueur, add at this time. Spoon pudding into individual bowls or custard cups. Sprinkle ground cinnamon over the top of each and refrigerate before serving.

OPTIONAL BURNT SUGAR CRUST: Just before serving, place an even layer of sugar, about I tablespoon, over the custard surface of each bowl or cup. Place under a broiler on high. Watch carefully and remove when sugar melts and begins to brown, in about a minute. Alternatively, use a small kitchen blow torch to melt and brown the sugar into a crust. Return cups to refrigerator for up to a half hour or serve immediately.

·•·

Although ancient recipes for this dessert do not include cream or butter, these days, cooks will frequently add a bit of either one to enrich their version of this dish.

I included cream in this recipe to make up for the butterfat difference between the rich whole milk used in Europe and the low-fat milk used in the large majority of American households.

Some of Spain's finest chefs pay homage to this homespun, everyday dessert, by turning it into a divine extravagance, with the addition of heavy cream and half a dozen egg yolks.

Apple Tart

(Tarta de Manzana/Tarte aux pommes)

(Aragon, Basque, southwest France)

APPLES (*MALUS DOMESTICA*) DO NOT EXIST in the wild, being an inter-specific hybrid crop essentially invented by human cultivation. They apparently originated in Asia Minor at least 3,000 years ago and dwarf apples were brought to Greece by Alexander the Great in 300 B.C. Many different fruits were called "apples" during the Middle Ages, including dates ("finger apples"), pomegranates ("apples of Carthage") and potatoes (*pommes de terre* or "apples of the earth"). Food historian James Trager suggests that the fruit of the Tree of Knowledge in the Garden of Eden—depicted as an apple—was more probably an apricot. An apple tart is the original fruit tart, especially in France. Over the course of many centuries additional ingredients have been added to many recipes, including almonds and dark rum. The fanciest variation is the classic *tarte tatin*, in which the finished product must be flipped upside down and served with the apples neatly arranged at the top and the golden pastry on the bottom. Although about 2,000 kinds of apples are now cultivated, the Golden Delicious is by far the most common throughout France. In Spain, apples are primarily grown in the northern regions. The most famous variety being *La Reineta de Aragón*, known for its fine perfume, delicate acidity, and firm flesh for cooking.

PASTRY DOUGH:

Combine flour, sugar, and salt. Cut in cold butter, and using a knife, work it into the dry ingredients until the mixture resembles cornmeal. Add the yolks and work it into the mixture until all dry ingredients are moistened and will hold together in a solid mass. Form a ball and cover in plastic wrap and chill.

FILLING:

Beat eggs and half-and-half together in a bowl, mix in sugar and vanilla, and optional Calvados. Set aside.

TOPPING:

Toss sliced apples in lemon juice. In a skillet, over medium-high heat, melt butter. Add apples and cook for 3 to 4 minutes. Reduce heat to medium or medium-low and add granulated sugar and cinnamon. Fold or toss apples to cook both sides and coat evenly with the other ingredients, while cooking for 10 or more minutes. Apples should be slightly cooked, but not completely soft.

ASSEMBLY:
Preheat oven to 400°F. Roll out pastry dough and place in a tart dish, pie tin, or on a baking sheet. Arrange apples evenly over dough. If on a baking sheet, do not place apples on the last ½ to 1 inch of the dough. Crimp or fold some of the pastry edge rustically over apple area. Pour the egg mixture over the apples, and sprinkle brown sugar evenly over fruit.

Bake for 25 to 30 minutes, until crust becomes a light golden. Remove and let cool. Optional: Melt apricot or apple jelly and brush apples with the jelly glaze before serving.

This recipe uses Calvados, an aromatic spirit distilled from apple cider. It is a product of the Normandy area of northern France, and made from a combination of several varieties of sweet, sour, and bitter apples.

Pastry dough:
1 cup unbleached flour
3 tablespoons sugar
Pinch of salt
½ cup (1 stick) unsalted butter
2 egg yolks

Filling:
3 eggs
1 cup half-and-half (or ½ cup milk and ½ cup cream)
5 tablespoons sugar
1½ teaspoons vanilla extract
1 tablespoon Calvados brandy (optional)

Apple Topping:
4 medium apples, cut in ¼-inch slices
1 tablespoon lemon juice
3 tablespoons butter
¼ cup granulated sugar
½ to 1 teaspoon ground cinnamon
¼ cup brown sugar
2 to 3 tablespoons apricot or apple jelly (optional)

MAKES 4 TO 6 SERVINGS

Basque Tart

(Gâteau basque)

ALTHOUGH EXACTLY WHEN AND HOW the famous *gâteau basque* came into being is not clearly known, cooks have been baking them since the eighteenth century. Rather than the jam or custard-filled cake of today, historians believe it began as a bread, known as *bistochak*. When *bistochak* was transformed into the first *gâteau basque*, the filling was cherry preserves. For this reason, it is believed that the change from bread into a cake occurred in the Nivelle River valley, around the Basque town of Itxassou, which is well known for a local variety of black cherries, the *xapata*. These plentiful fruit ripen during just a few weeks in June, flooding the market with cherries, creating an abundance that is made into preserves. Today most places, in both France and Spain, offer mainly custard-filled cakes, which customers seem to prefer over the cherry-filled ones. However, as one approaches Itxassou and the Nivelle River valley, one is more likely to find his or her *gâteau* filled with cherry preserves.

The following recipe is very rich and includes both the custard and cherry fillings.

GATEAU DOUGH:

In a medium bowl combine flour, baking soda, salt, and almonds. In a separate large bowl cream together butter and sugar. When the butter and sugar are well blended, add the eggs one at a time. Completely incorporate the first egg into the butter mixture before adding the second. Stir in lemon zest and vanilla.

Add the flour mixture, stirring in about one-quarter at a time until fully blended. The dough will be a little gooey. Use a spatula to pat it into a tight ball. Dust the top with flour and place a large sheet

Dough:

1³/₄ cup unbleached flour

1 teaspoon baking soda

Pinch of salt

¹/₂ cup ground almonds

³/₄ cup (1¹/₂ sticks or 12 tablespoons) butter

³/₄ cup sugar

2 eggs

2 teaspoon grated lemon zest (approximately 1 lemon)

1 teaspoon vanilla extract or 1 tablespoon rum

of plastic wrap over it. Use spatula to loosen the bottom from the bowl and flip the dough into the plastic wrap. Dust the surface before wrapping plastic over the top. Refrigerate for about 1 hour.

CUSTARD FILLING:
Beat together the egg yolks and sugar until well blended and a creamy yellow. Add flour, mixing until smooth.

Place milk into a saucepan. Slit open vanilla bean lengthwise, scraping the insides into the milk. Add vanilla pod to milk as well. Bring milk to a boil. Remove from heat and discard vanilla pod.

Pour a small amount of the hot milk into the egg mixture, while quickly whisking. Continue to stir and gradually add the milk, until all the milk is well combined with the egg and flour mixture. Pour it all back into the saucepan over low heat. Stir or whisk constantly to prevent lumps from forming as the liquid thickens. When it becomes thick as it reaches the bubbling point, remove from heat. Add spirits while continuing to whisk.

ASSEMBLY:
Preheat oven to 350° F.

Use an 8- or 9-inch cake pan. It's best to use one in which the side band is removable. Grease the pan with butter and dust with flour.

Divide the dough into two balls. Roll out the first to a diameter 1½ inches wider than the bottom of the pan (10 or 11 inches), and about ¼-inch thick. Place the dough into the cake pan, lining the side as well as the bottom. Spread cherry preserves evenly over the bottom of the dough. Top preserves with an even layer of custard. Roll out

---

Custard Filling:

3 egg yolks

¼ cup sugar

¼ cup flour

1¼ cups milk

½ vanilla bean, or 1 teaspoon vanilla extract

1 tablespoon aromatic spirits (Armagnac, cognac, anise, rum, etc.)

1 to 1½ cups black cherry preserves or jam

1 egg white

MAKES 6 TO 8 SERVINGS

---

the top crust and lay it over the custard. If dough at the sides is higher than top crust, cut away excess. Pinch the edges of the top and bottom crust together. Brush the top with egg white.

Bake for 40 to 45 minutes or until the top has browned. Remove from oven and let cool for about 1 hour before removing from the pie tin.

• •

At room temperature, the amount of butter in this dough causes it to soften and become sticky very quickly. For this reason, I roll out my dough between two sheets of plastic wrap atop a baking sheet. As the dough softens, place the entire sheet into the refrigerator or freezer for several minutes, until it stiffens. The plastic will peel away cleanly from the pastry when you are ready to place it into the cake tin.

An alternative, is to place the gooey batter in a piping bag and pipe it, in a tight spiral, over the bottom of the pan. Spread the custard evenly over the layer, except for the ½ inch around the edges. Then pipe the rest of the cake dough around the custard, starting with the sides, working inward, until the custard is tightly covered. Brush the top with egg white before baking.

Ground almonds are not always found in a *gâteau basque*, but they add texture and flavor. A teaspoon of almond extract, though not part of a classic recipe, amplifies the presence of the ground almonds, and is a good substitute for the aromatic spirits often mixed into the dough.

Lemon Tart

(Tarte au citron)

LEMON TARTS ARE EXTREMELY POPULAR, especially in the areas along the Mediterranean where the weather is more temperate and lemons are available through much of the year. The following recipe is a luxurious lemon custard tart based on the one served at Petits Plats, a restaurant specializing in southern French cuisine, in the Woodley Park area of Washington, D.C. Two of its three owners are Frederic and Cecile Darricarrere, brother and sister, who bring French Basque influences from Biarritz to their restaurant. Third owner and chef, Oumar Sy, generously schooled me in the finer points of his creamy rich lemon tart. Chef Sy trained for six years with Jean-Louis Palladin at the famous Jean-Louis restaurant, located in the Watergate complex, and spent several more years cooking with Yannick Cam at Provence, in the heart of Washington, D.C.

PASTRY DOUGH:

Preheat oven to 400° F.

Combine flour, sugar, and salt. Cut in butter, and using a fork or spoon, work it into the dry ingredients until the mixture resembles cornmeal. Add the yolks and work it into the mixture until all dry ingredients are moistened and will hold together in a solid mass. Form a ball and cover in plastic wrap and chill.

> **Pastry dough:**
> 1 1/2 cups flour
> 3 tablespoons sugar
> Pinch of salt
> 3/4 cup (1 1/2 sticks) unsalted butter
> 3 egg yolks
>
> INGREDIENTS CONTINUED

Roll out the dough to 1/4-inch thickness, and place in a 10-inch tart pan or 4 (or more, depending on size) small individual tart pans. Partially cook crust by baking for 10 minutes. Reduce heat to 350° F.

Continued

CONTINUED FROM PREVIOUS PAGE

Filling:

3/4 cup sugar

Grated zest of 2 lemons

1 pint half-and-half

1 cup heavy cream

1 vanilla bean, cut open lengthwise, or 1 teaspoon vanilla extract

1 whole egg

3 egg yolks

2 tablespoon lemon juice

MAKES 6 SERVINGS

FILLING:

Boil 1/4 cup of water and 1 teaspoon of sugar in a small saucepan, add grated lemon zest and boil for 2 to 3 minutes. Remove and set aside.

Place half-and-half and cream into a saucepan. If using a vanilla bean, scrape insides of the bean into the cream, adding the vanilla pod into the saucepan as well. Bring to a simmer over medium heat and cook for 2 minutes.

In a large bowl whisk egg, yolks, and remaining sugar together until well combined. Remove cream mixture from the heat, and while quickly whisking the egg mixture, pour about a 1/2 cup of the hot cream into the egg mixture, and blend. Continue whisking the egg mixture, and slowly pour in the remaining hot cream. Stir in grated lemon zest, lemon juice, and vanilla extract, if not using a vanilla bean.

Pour lemon cream filling into the partially baked tarts, and bake for 25 to 30 minutes or until crust is light brown and middle is almost set, but still jiggles slightly. Remove and let cool; refrigerate for at least 3 hours before serving.

Walnut Tart

(Tarte aux noix)

WALNUTS AND WALNUT TARTS are made throughout south-west France and the Pyrenees region. While many species of walnuts are consumed, Persian or Carpathian walnuts (*Juglans regia*) are the most common in the Mediterranean. Their natural range extends from Greece and Asia Minor along the Hindu-Kush to the Himalayas, often at mid-level mountain slopes. According to Pliny, they were introduced into Italy from Persia probably during the second century B.C. and were likely brought by the Romans to the Pyrenean region. Today there are well kept walnut groves in the French departments of Lot and Dordogne, not far from the Pyrenees. Southwest France, and particularly Perigord, is famous for its abundance of walnuts and walnut products. They are crushed and pressed in autumn to produce walnut oil or *huile de noix*, which has an exceptionally fine flavor and is used in stews, sauces, salads, and other preparations. Walnut flour is also used in many baked goods.

One of the best nut tarts I have tasted was at Le Bistro, in Petaluma, California. A tiny local treasure specializing in fine French Mediterranean cuisine, it does not seat groups larger than four and is always full. The chef and owner, Corey Basso, generously shared his simple and foolproof recipe, which he adapted for the American kitchen. One American touch is his use of equal parts pecans and walnuts for a rich nut flavor. I have adapted Chef Basso's recipe into a walnut tart, and offer a slightly sweet pastry crust, rather than a regular pie crust.

Recipe and ingredients on following page

Sweet pastry dough:

1 cup unbleached flour

3 tablespoons sugar

Pinch of salt

½ cup (1 stick) unsalted butter

2 egg yolks

Filling:

3 eggs

1 cup sugar

1 cup dark corn syrup

3 tablespoons brandy (cognac or
   Armagnac)

¼ cup (½ stick) butter, melted

2 cups coarsely chopped walnuts

MAKES 6 SERVINGS

PASTRY DOUGH:

Combine flour, sugar, and salt. Cut in cold butter, and using a fork or spoon, work it into the dry ingredients until the mixture resembles cornmeal. Add the yolks and work it into the mixture until all dry ingredients are moistened and will hold together in a solid mass. Form a ball and cover in plastic wrap and chill.

FILLING:

Whisk eggs and sugar together. When combined, mix in corn syrup and whisk to blend well. Stir in brandy, followed by melted butter. Mix in nuts, stirring until well combined.

ASSEMBLY:

Preheat oven to 375° F. Use a 10-inch tart pan with a bottom piece that is removable from the side ring. Alternatively, use a pie pan. Sprinkle some flour over the bottom and sides of the pan. Roll out dough to ¼-inch thickness. Place the dough into the tart pan or pie tin. Pour filling evenly over the crust to fill the pan. If using a pie pan, the filling will not reach the top; fold the extra dough at the top over itself and shape it into a thicker crust.

Bake for 35 to 45 minutes, until the filling is set and the top has browned. Remove and let cool for about 1 hour. Before serving remove tart ring by pushing the bottom of the tart up through the exterior ring.

If you prefer a more neutral, unsweetened tart crust, to contrast with the sweet nut filling, use the tart dough recipe for the Mushroom and Shallot Tart (page 215). To create Chef Basso's pecan-walnut tart, use equal parts pecans and walnuts.

Should your household lack spirits in the brandy family, substitute one teaspoon of vanilla extract.

Cake with Fruit

(Gâteau aux fruits)

AT LA MAISON SUR LA COLLINE, a homey bed and breakfast outside the walled city of Carcassonne, Madame Nicole Galinier and her daughter, Delphine, prepared for the breakfast table each morning, a fresh, moist, buttery, cake bursting with the *fruit du jour*, as well as a variety of other baked goods and homemade preserves. After obtaining their recipe, I realized that it is very similar in both ingredients and technique to an apple cake from Cantabria, Spain, near the western-most portion of the Pyrenees.

PREHEAT OVEN TO 350° F. Grease a 9-inch cake pan and dust it with flour.

In a large bowl beat eggs, sugar, and half-and-half or milk together. In a separate bowl combine flour, baking powder, baking soda, and salt.

In a wide pan or skillet, melt butter over medium heat and add fruit. If using berries or other soft fruit, gently fold fruit into butter to completely coat all pieces, and remove. If using apples or pears, allow fruit to cook in butter for 1 to 2 minutes on each side, turning fruit only enough to ensure each side is coated and exposed to the heat once. If using walnuts, also add at this time.

Continued

---

3 eggs

²/₃ cup granulated sugar

3 tablespoons half-and-half or whole milk

1¹/₄ cups flour

1 teaspoon baking powder

¹/₂ teaspoon baking soda

¹/₄ teaspoon salt

¹/₂ cup (1 stick) unsalted butter

3 cups fruit (berries, diced apples, peaches, pears, dried fruit, etc.)

1 cup coarsely chopped walnuts (optional)

1 tablespoon rum or Armagnac

1 teaspoon vanilla extract

1 tablespoon confectioners' sugar

MAKES 6 SERVINGS

Stir flour mixture in with egg mixture, add rum and vanilla and mix to blend well. Pour all the fruit and butter into the batter, folding gently to combine.

Pour batter into cake pan and bake for 30 to 40 minutes, depending on amount and type of fruit used. Let cool and dust top with confectioners sugar.

●•··•●··•

In the similar Cantabrian cake, *(tarta)* apples are the traditional fruit used. Calvados or apple brandy is used instead of rum, and a teaspoon of cinnamon is added in place of the vanilla.

In northern Spain this simple cake is finished with a top glaze of melted fruit jelly or preserves, and served with a bit of cream or *natillas* custard.

Sweet Cornmeal Cakes
(Millas)

(Gascony, Landes, southwest France)

 CORN OR MAIZE (*ZEA MAYS*) IS THE GIANT domesticated form of teosinte, a wild grass occurring naturally in Michoacan, Mexico, where it was domesticated five to six thousand years ago. Maize diffused south to the Peruvian highlands and north to the United States and Canada a thousand years before Columbus. Corn became the basic diet of Mesoamerica and is inextricably bound with the rise of their civilizations. It had an important role in their religious beliefs and festivities, and they thought that flesh and blood were made from maize. To the Mayans, the major constellation visible in the heart of the night sky was a sacred maize plant about which the universe was ordered.

Maize produces more calories per acre than wheat, but needs more water to ripen. In North America, "Indian corn" fairly quickly became a mainstay of the colonies. The Indians also taught the settlers how so make simple breads and simple porridges when it was coarsely ground and boiled. Later the settlers learned to make hush puppies—a fried cornmeal batter. In Europe, corn cakes likely date back somewhere between Columbus' return from his expedition in 1492 to Spain with kernels of corn, and the return of Cortez from his adventures in Mexico in 1519. Corn spread quickly wherever Spaniards traveled in the fifteenth and sixteenth centuries, largely due to its broad adaptability and high productivity.

While the savory cornmeal porridge cakes pair well with stews and soups, this sweet lemony pudding-like cousin is served as a dessert in the eastern parts of southwest France. This dish is similar in consistency to spoonbread of the Old South in the United States.

Recipe and ingredients on following page

2¹/₂ cups milk

1 cup cornmeal

²/₃ cup sugar

Grated zest of 1 lemon

6 eggs, separated

MAKES 4 SERVINGS

Over medium heat, pour milk and cornmeal into a saucepan. While stirring to prevent lumps from forming, add sugar and grated lemon zest. Continue to stir frequently, until mixture becomes thick and separates from the bottom of the pan when stirred. Remove from heat.

Add egg yolks, blending each into the cornmeal mixture before adding the next. Separately, in a large bowl, beat egg whites until stiff peaks form. Fold beaten whites into the cornmeal mixture in 3 increments, incorporating most of the whites before adding the next batch.

Grease or butter an 8- or 9-inch round or square baking dish/pan. Pour in the batter and bake for 30 to 35 minutes.

Serve this accompanied by ice cream or possibly fruit marinated in wine.

Pine Nut and Almond Cookies

(Piñones)

ACROSS SPAIN, NUTS ARE A POPULAR ingredient in baked goods, a legacy left by the Moors. The richly flavored small white pine nuts used in Pyrenean cooking come from the umbrella pine (*Pinus pinea*), also called the stone pine. Called *piñones* in Spain and *pignons* in France, they are especially common in Catalan cookery. Pine nuts were introduced throughout the Mediterranean from Spain. Humans have cultivated this tree for its protein-rich food for well over 6,000 years, and it is still extensively cultivated throughout the Mediterranean. Ethno-botanists believe that before humans expanded the range of this tree over the last few thousand years, it was confined to the Iberian Peninsula, since this is the only area where pine nuts are found away from ancient trade routes. Pine nuts should be stored in plastic zipper-top bags in freezers.

In Catalonia, as in southern Spain, pine nut-covered cookies and cakes are routinely displayed in bakery windows as one of their many holidays approaches. My favorite are the rich pine nut filled and exterior studded cookies from Zucitola Patiserías, a modest bakery on the Paseo Pablo Savaste in Pamplona. In an effort to re-create this Spanish treat, I developed the following recipe. These cookies with nut paste centers are very close to the real thing. To allow most of us to make these cookies without tapping into our life savings, I recommend making these with an almond filling in place of pine nuts. I also found that most of my tasters preferred the almond filling to the richer pine nut filling. However, my husband prefers the pine nut centers.

NUT PASTE FILLING:

Place nuts in a food processor with 1 teaspoon flour (2 teaspoons if using pine nuts) and mix until the consistency of sand. Pine nuts may become the consistency of coarse peanut butter due to high oil content. Place ground nuts in a bowl and mix in sugar and lemon zest. Add egg, a little at a time, blending and kneading it into the paste. If using pine nuts, you may only need to add ½ the egg to moisten to a pliable, slightly viscous paste. If the paste is too wet, knead in a little more sugar. Knead paste to an even consistency.

Continued

Nut filling:

1 cup almonds, blanched and lightly toasted or 1 cup pine nuts, lightly toasted

1 to 2 teaspoons flour

1/2 cup sugar

1 teaspoon grated lemon zest

1 egg, beaten

Outer cookie dough:

2 cups flour

1/2 teaspoon salt

1/2 cup butter, softened

1 cup sugar

1 egg

1/2 teaspoon almond extract

1/2 teaspoon vanilla extract

1 to 2 cups raw pine nuts

MAKES APPROXIMATELY **40** COOKIES

DOUGH:

Combine flour and salt. In a large bowl, cream butter and sugar. When well mixed, add egg, almond and vanilla extracts, beating until well combined. Gradually mix flour into buttery mixture. When dough is formed, wrap it in plastic and refrigerate for 1/2 to 1 hour.

ASSEMBLY:

Preheat oven to 350° F.

Using a teaspoon, spoon out a chunk of dough and quickly roll it into a ball and press to slightly flatten. Spoon a small amount of nut paste into the center of the dough and wrap the sides of the dough around the nut filling to completely envelope it. To reshape any imperfections, quickly roll it into a ball between your palms. Roll top half of cookie in pine nuts, and press them into the dough before placing on cookie sheet.

If dough becomes too soft to work with, place in refrigerator for 10 minutes or until it stiffens up again.

Bake cookies for 15 minutes. Pine nuts and bottom edges of cookie may turn slightly golden, but cookies should not brown. Remove and let cool.

Blanche the almonds by placing them in boiling water for 30 seconds. Their skins will bubble and loosen. Rinse them in cold water and drain. Squirt each almond out of its skin.

To toast almonds or pine nuts, place them in a dry pan over medium heat, tossing and stirring the nuts until lightly tanned.

Polvorones Cookies

DURING THE PERIOD IN WHICH THE MOORS occupied and moved through Spain, they introduced *polvorones, mantecados, almendradas,* and other confections to northern and southern regions alike. *Polvorones* and *mantecados* are extremely tender cookies, usually associated with the *dulces* baked by the nuns in the convents of Andalucia in the south. These cookies are also extremely popular in Navarra, and can be found in bakeries in towns throughout the region.

PREHEAT OVEN TO 400° F. Mix flour and cornstarch together in a wide pan and place in the oven for approximately 12 minutes to brown slightly. Check and toss the flour in 4-minute intervals to brown evenly and make sure flour on the bottom does not burn. When light brown or tanned, remove and let cool.

Place cooled flour mixture in a large bowl, add cinnamon, lemon zest, sugar, and (optional) ground almonds. Cut in the butter and/or lard, mixing quickly. Knead into a smooth dough. It will just barely hold together. Wrap in plastic and refrigerate approximately 1 hour.

Continued

1³/₄ cups flour

¹/₃ cup cornstarch

1 tablespoon ground cinnamon

2 teaspoons grated lemon zest

¹/₂ cup confectioners' sugar

¹/₃ cup raw almonds, blanched and finely ground (optional)

¹/₂ cup butter (or lard or ¹/₄ cup of each)

Confectioners' sugar for dusting

MAKES 24 TO 30 COOKIES

Preheat oven to 325° F. In traditional recipes, after refrigeration the dough is rolled out to ½-inch thickness and round or oval cookies are cut out. I find it quicker to roll the dough into a log, 1½ to 2 inches in diameter, after wrapping it in plastic before refrigeration; and then creating cookies by cutting the log into ½-inch slices, similar to making refrigerator cookies.

Bake cookies on a parchment-lined cookie sheet for 25 minutes. Let cookies cool completely before gently removing. Sprinkle confectioners' sugar over cooled cookies.

* * *

These velvet-textured cookies are so delicate they barely hold together. The key to achieving this texture is lightly browning the flour beforehand to remove any moisture.

Although traditional recipes call for lard, I have also made these with half butter and half lard, and all butter. Judging from my taste testers, using all butter seems to be the best.

If using all butter, be careful in choosing your butter, as some butters contain a fair amount of water. The moisture could cause the flour to cement together a bit, hardening the otherwise fine texture of these confections.

Select Bibliography

Adrià, Ferran. *Los Secretos de El Bulli.* Barcelona: Ediciones Altaya, 1997.

Aguilar, Elvira (ed.). *Cocina Tradicional: Aragon y La Rioja.* Santillana: El Pais Aguilar, 1996.

Andrews, Colman. *Catalan Cuisine.* Boston: The Harvard Common Press, 1999.

Androuët, Pierre. *Guide Du Fromage* (English Edition). London: Aidan Ellis Publishing, Ltd., 1983.

Arguiñano, Karlos and Juan Mari Arzak. *Escuela de Cocina y de la Buena Mesa: Vol. 4, Como Preparar Carnes y Caza.* Madrid: Asegarce y Editorial Debate, 1999.

Aris, Pepita. *The Spanishwoman's Kitchen.* London: Cassell, 1992.

Arzak, Juan Marí. *Las Recetas de Arzak.* Madrid: El Pais Aguilar, 1998.

Asher, Gerald. "Taste of a Legend." *Gourmet* (December 2000).

Barrenechea, Teresa. *The Basque Table.* Boston: Harvard Common Press, 1998.

Belloc, Hilaire. *The Pyrenees.* London: Metheuen, 1909.

Berasategui, Martin. *Mis Recetas de Siempre.* Gipuzkoa: Hiria Liburuak, 2000.

Casas, Penelope. *The Foods and Wines of Spain.* New York: Alfred A. Knopf, Inc., 1982.

Casas, Penelope. *¡Delicioso! The regional cooking of Spain.* New York: Alfred A. Knopf, Inc., 1996.

Crow, John A. *Spain: The Root and the Flower.* Berkeley: University of California Press, 1985.

David, Elizabeth. *French Provincial Cooking.* New York: Penguin Books, 1970.

Dominé, André (ed.). *Culinaria France.* Cologne: Könemann Verlagsgesellschaft, 1999.

Dubin, Marc. *The Pyrenees.* London: Rough Guides, 1998.

Editors of Cooks Illustrated (ed.). *The Best Recipe.* Brookline: Boston Common Press, 1999.

Erickson, Jon. *Plate Tectonics: Unraveling the Mysteries of Earth.* New York: Facts on File, 1992.

Feibleman, Peter S. *The Cooking of Spain and Portugal.* New York: Time-Life Books, Inc., 1969.

Fuentes, Carlos. *The Buried Mirror: Reflections on Spain and the New World.* London: Andre Deutsch, 1992.

Gibbon, Edward. David Womersley (ed.). *The History of the Decline and Fall of the Roman Empire,* abridged. New York: Penguin Classics, 2001.

Higham, Roger. *The Pyrenees.* London: Columbus Books, 1988.

Hirigoyen, Gerald and Cameron Hirigoyen. *The Basque Kitchen.* New York: HarperCollins, 1999.

Huxley, Anthony (ed.). *Standard Encyclopedia of the World's Mountains.* New York: G. P. Putnam's, 1962.

Jessel, Camilla. *The Taste of Spain.* New York: St. Martin's Press, 1990.

Johnson, Hugh. *World Atlas of Wine.* New York: Simon & Schuster, 1994.

Kiple, Kenneth and Kriemhild Coneè Ornelas (eds.). *The Cambridge World History of Food.* Cambridge, England: Cambridge University Press, 2000.

Koffmann, Pierre. *Memories of Gascony.* New York: Van Nostrand Reinhold, 1990.

Kurlansky, Mark. *Cod.* New York: Walker & Company, 1997.

Kurlansky, Mark. *The Basque History of the World.* New York: Walker & Company, 1999.

Lavin, Edwin (ed.). *Traditional Recipes of the Provinces of France: Selected by Curnonsky.* Garden City, New York: Doubleday & Company, Inc., 1961.

Matthews, Thomas. "Culinary Summit." *Wine Spectator* (May 15, 1995).

Manson, Per-Henrik. "The French Frontier." *Wine Spectator* (March 15, 1994).

Millon, Marc and Kim Millon. *Wine Roads of Spain.* New York: HarperCollins, 1993.

Moreau, R. E. *The Palearctic-African Bird Migration Systems.* New York and London: Academic Press, 1972

Morgenstern, Barry and Jerry Croce. *Private Stock.* Privately published, Arlington, Virginia, 1990.

Neal, Charles. *Armagnac.* San Francisco: Flame Grape Press, 1998.

Olney, Richard (ed.). *The Good Cook: Wine.* London and New York: Time-Life Books, 1983.

Olney, Richard (ed.). *The Good Cook: Terrines, Pâtés and Gallantines.* London and New York: Life-Time Books, 1982.

Rance, Patrick. *The French Cheese Book.* London: MacMillan London, Ltd., 1989.

Read, Jan. *Wines of Spain.* London: Mitchell Beazley, 1998.

Read, Jan, Maite Manjon, and Hugh Johnson. *The Wine and Food of Spain.* Boston: Little, Brown and Company, 1987.

Richardin, Edmond. *L'Art du bien manger. La cuisine française du XIVe au XXe siècle.* Paris: Éditions d'Art et de Littérature, 1913.

Roberts, Deborah and Victoire de Montal. *French Country Living: A Year in Gascony.* New York: Little Brown & Company, 1989.

Stevenson, Tom. *The New Sotheby's Wine Encyclopedia.* New York: DK Publishing, Inc., 1997.

Strang, Paul. *Wines of South-West France.* London: Kyle Catchie, 1996.

Tannahill, Reay. *Food in History.* New York: Crown Publishers, 1988.

Thomas, Gillian and John Harrison. *Languedoc and Southwest France.* Guilford, Connecticut: Pequot Press, 2000.

Torres, Marimar. *The Spanish Table.* New York: Doubleday & Company, 1986.

Toulouse-Lautrec, Henri de, and Maurice Joyant. *The Art of Cuisine.* New York: Henry Holt and Company, Inc., 1994.

Trager, James G., Jr. *Food Book.* New York: Grossman Publishers, 1970.

Trutter, Marion (ed.). *Culinaria Spain.* Cologne: Könemann Verlagsgesellschaft, 1998.

Van den Brink, F. H. *A Field Guide to the Mammals of Britain and Europe.* Boston: Houghton Mifflin Co., 1968.

Villas, James. *The French Country Kitchen.* New York: Bantam Books, 1992.

Viola, Herman J. and Carolyn Margolis (eds.). *Seeds of Change.* Washington, D.C., and London: Smithsonian Institution Press, 1991.

Voss, Roger. *The Wines of Loire, Alsace and the Rhône.* London: Mitchell Beazley, 1998.

Wagner, Philip M. *Grapes Into Wine.* New York: Alfred A. Knopf, 1987.

Walker, Ernest P. (ed.). *Mammals of the World.* 3rd ed. Baltimore and London: Johns Hopkins University Press, 1975.

Wolfert, Paula. *The Cooking of South-West France.* New York: Harper & Row, 1983.

Wright, Clifford A. *A Mediterranean Feast.* New York: William Morrow and Company, 1999.

Regional Index

BASQUE

CATALONIA

Anchovy-Olive Spread (*Garum/Anchoïade/Tapenade*), 65

Black Rice (*Arròs Negre*), 121

Braised Pork Loin with Prunes and Pears (*Lomo de Cerdo con Ciruelas y Peras*), 192

Catalan Beef Stew (*Estouffat/Estofat*), 110

Catalan Custard (*Crema Catalana*), 241

Catalan Roasted Vegetable Spread/Pâté (*Escalivada/Escalibada*), 67

Country Pâté (*Pâté de campagne*), 84

Duck with Pears (*Ànec amb Peres*), 156

Eggplant Roasted with Bacon and Garlic, with Samfaina (*Aubergines en gigot*), 211

Fresh Marinated Anchovies or Sardines (*Boquerones en Vinagreta*), 78

Fresh Tomato and Garlic Sauce, 62

Game Hens with Garlic and Lemon, 149

Lobster and Rabbit with Lemon Butter (*Mar i Muntanya*), 171

Modern Catalan Garlic Sauce (*Allioli/Alioli/Aïoli/Ajoaceite*), 176

Monkfish with Golden Garlic (*Rap Amb All Cremat*), 128

Mushrooms with Clams (*Setas con Almejas*), 130

Partridges with Chocolate Sauce (*Perdices con Salsa de Chocolate*), 160

Pheasant with Banyuls and Walnuts, 162

Roasted Pork Stuffed with Dried Fruit 194

Roasted Rabbit with Herb Stuffing and Allioli
     (*Lapin farci aux herbes/Conejo al Allioli*), 173

Salad with Salt Cod (*Esqueixada de Bacalao*), 203

Seafood Operetta (*Zarzuela*), 138

Spinach with Raisins and Pine Nuts (*Espinacs amb Panses i Pinyons*), 205

Tomato Bread (*Pa amb Tomaquet*), 61

Traditional Catalan Garlic Sauce (*Allioli*), 175

Veal Chops with Mushrooms, 185

White Beans and Sausage (*Fabada Asturiana/Botifarra amb Mongetes/
     Haricots aux saucisses*), 108

NORTHERN SPAIN

PYRENEES MOUNTAINS

Isard Saddle or Haunch, Sauce Richardin (*Râble ou cuissot d'isard, sauce Richardin*), 183

Marinated Trout with Mint and Ham (*Trucha a la Navarra*), 134

Potato and Cabbage Cake (*Trinxat*), 220

Trout with Bacon, Sherry, and Cream (*Trucha del Cincla a lo Fino*), 132

Young Wild Boar Marinated in Red Wine (*Marcassin au vin rouge*), 196

SOUTHWEST FRANCE

Anchovy-Olive Spread (*Garum/Anchoïade/Tapenade*), 65

Apple Tart (*Tarta de Manzana/Tarte aux pommes*), 250

Asparagus and Capers Gratin (*Gratin d'asperges*), 209

Baked Pumpkin with Chestnuts (*Gratin de citrouille aux marrons*), 222

Cake with Fruit (*Gâteau aux fruits*), 259

Catalan Beef Stew (*Estouffat/Estofat*), 110

Cherry Custard Pudding (*Clafoutis*), 243

Chestnut Purée (*Purée de marrons*), 218

Cornmeal Cakes (*Taloa/Millas/Miques de Maïs*), 224

Country Pâté (*Pâté de campagne*), 84

Cream of Cod (*Brandade de morue*), 121

Duck with Pears (*Ànec amb Peres*), 156

Eggplant Roasted with Bacon and Garlic, with Samfaina (*Aubergines en gigot*), 211

Game Hens with Garlic and Lemon, 149

Garbure, 91

Garlic Soup (*Sopa de Ajo/Soupe à l'ail*), 93

Green Beans with Roquefort and Walnuts (*Haricots verts au Roquefort*), 213

Isard Saddle or Haunch, Sauce Richardin (*Râble ou cuissot d'isard, sauce Richardin*), 183

Jurançon Custard with Peaches (*Flan de pêches au Jurançon*), 244

Layered Vegetable Gratin, 207

Lemon Shrimp, 117

Lemon Tart (*Tarte au citron*), 255

Index

(Page numbers in boldface refer to recipes)

B

C

Cabbage and Potato Cake, **220**
Cailles en papillotes, **151**
Cake with Fruit, **259**
Cakes, Sweet Cornmeal, **261**
Calvados, 239, 251, 260
Camino Francés, 22, 37
Camino Santiago, El, 37
Cañadas, 17, 28, 180
Cantábria, 10, 99, 259
Capercaillies, 29
Caramel Syrup, **246**
Carcassonne, 35, 50, 53, 259
Carême, Marie Antoine, 24
Carthaginians, 19, 36, 173
Casas, Penelope, 192, 235
Castell del Remei, 45
Castelmaure, Cave Cooperative
  Embres, 51
Catalan Beef Stew, 110
Catalan Custard, 241
Catalonia, 10, 20, 21, 22, 38, 194, 205;
  see also Wine Producing Regions
Caune de l'Arago, 16
Cava, 9, 39, 43-44, 233; *see also*
  Wines, Sparkling
  D.O., 42, 43
  Codorníu, 43, 44, 125
  Freixenet, 43
  Granizado de, **233**
  Montsarra, 44, 125
  Raventós I Blanc, 43
  Rovellats, 44
Cave de l'Abbé Rous, 52
Cave Paintings, 17, 30-31

Caves
  Cambalou, 213
  Prehistoric
    Altamira, 17
    Lascaux, 17
    Niaux, 17, 30-31
Celliers des Templiers, 52, 82
Cerdanya, La, 26
Chamois, Pyrenean, 26, 183; *see also* Isard
Champagne, 38, 42, 233
Chanca, Diego Alvarez, 190
Charlemagne, 21, 213
Château Bonhomme, 51
Château de Gourgazaud, 51
Château de Riell, 52
Château d'Oupia, 51
Château La Grave, 51
Château La Voulte-Gasparets, 51
Château Les Ollieux, 51
Château de Violet, 51
Cheese
  Green Beans with Roquefort and
    Walnuts, **213**
  Mushrooms with Roquefort and
    Banyuls, **82**
Cherries, 252
  Cherry Custard Pudding, 243
Chestnut(s), 218
  Baked Pumpkin with Chestnuts, **222**
  Chestnut Flan, **246**
  Chestnut Purée, **218**
Chicken
  Basque Chicken, **145**
  Basque Rice with Chicken, **147**
Chipirones, 79, 123
  Chipirones al Ajillo, **79**
Chocolate, 160
  Partridges with Chocolate Sauce, **160**

H

Hake with Clams, Asparagus, and Peas, **126**
Ham, 134
  Bayonne, 70, 91, 173
Hare, 28, 173
Haricots aux saucisses, **108**
Haricots verts au Roquefort, **213**
Hemingway, Ernest, 132, 134, 188
Hunting, 25, 26-31, 153, 160, 162,
  164, 173; *see also specific variety of game*

I

Ibarguren, Felix "Shishito," 136
Ibex, Spanish, 26, 31
Irouléguy, 145
Isard(s), 26
  Isard Saddle or Haunch, Sauce
  Richardin, **183**
Izarra, 145

J

Jamelles, Les, 53
Jean d'Estavel, 52
Jurançon, 49, 54-55, 244
  Jurançon Custard with Peaches, **244**

K

Koffmann, Pierre, 173
Kurlansky, Mark, 16

L

Lamb
  Lamb Roasted with White Wine and
  Herbs, Aragón, **178**
  Leg of Lamb with Anchovies and
  Garlic, Marinated, **180**
  Ternasco de Aragón, 178
Langostinos (Langoustines), 117
Languedoc, 104, 121, 128, 147, 156,
  158; *see also* Wine Producing Regions
Languedoc-Roussillon, 39, 40, 82; *see
  also* Wine Producing Regions
Lapin, 28, 173; *see also* Rabbit
  Lapin farci aux herbes, **173**
Leek(s), 95
  Leek and Cod Soup, **97**
Lemon(s), 234
  Game Hens with Garlic and Lemon,
  149
  Lemon Shrimp, **117**
  Lemon Tart, **255**
  Lobster and Rabbit with Lemon
  Butter, **171**
  Rice Pudding with Lemon and
  Cinnamon, **248**
Libre de Sent Sovi, 22, 79, 126, 138,
  194, 205
Libre del Coch, 22, 126
Libro di Arte Coquinaria, 22, 194, 205
Liebre/Lièvre, 29, 173; *see also* Hare
Liqueur, Basque, 145
Liver, 84
Lobster and Rabbit with Lemon, **171**
Lomo de Cerdo con Ciruelas y Peras, **192**
Lynx, Iberian (Spanish), 28

M

Magret, 158
Magret of Duck with Walnut Garlic
Sauce, **158**
Maison Sur la Colline, La, 5, 35, 259
Maison Vergennes, 53
Maize, 23, 224, 261; *see also* Corn
Mammals
large, 25-28
small, 28
Mantecados, 265
Map, Regional, 2
Mar i Muntanya, **171**
Marcassin(s), 27, 196
Marcassin au vin rouge, **196**
Marinade for
Anchovies or Sardines, **78**
Isard Saddle or Haunch, Sauce
Richardin, **183**
Lamb Roasted with White Wine and
Herbs, Aragón, **178**
Leg of Lamb with Anchovies and
Garlic, **180**
Lemon Shrimp, **117**
Lobster and Rabbit with Lemon, **171**
Pork Loin, **194**
Trout with Mint and Ham, **134**
Wood Pigeons and Artichokes, **164**
Young Wild Boar Marinated in Red
Wine, **196**
Marmitako, **99**
Marmots, Alpine, 28
Marqués de Murrieta, 39
Marqués de Riscal, 39, 48
Marrons, 246
Flan, **246**
Purée de, **218**

Martel, Charles, 21
Mas Martinet, 44
Mas Pau, Restaurant, 45, 205
Masia del Cadet, 174
Matthews, Thomas, 153
Meats, 169-1985; *see also specific varieties of
meats*
Medici, Catherine de, 23, 194
Medieval Era (Middle Ages), 21-22, 23,
95, 138, 160, 180, 190, 209, 250
Mejillones, 104; *see also* Mussels
Menon, 24
Merluza a la Koskera, **126**
Midi, the, 39, 41, 49-53; *see also*
Languedoc-Roussillon
Migration, Southern Bird, 29; *see also*
Birds
Millas, **224, 261**
Minervois, 20; *see also* Wine Producing
Regions
Miques de Maïs, **224**
Mirador de les Caves, 203, 241
Mole Poblano, 160
Monasteries, 22, 29
Benedictine, 37, 38
Carthusian, 38, 71
Cistercian, 37
Scala Dei, 38, 44
culinary contributions, 37, 93, 209,
213, 241, 265
Poblet, Monasterio de, 38, 174
Monkfish, 128
Monkfish with Golden Garlic, **128**
Monte Perdido National Park, 15, 45
Montiño, Francisco Martínez, 71
Moors, 38
foods introduced, 21, 63, 147, 192,
248, 263, 265
invasions, 21-22, 23